The
Implications
of
Conditionality

The International Monetary Fund and Africa

Fredoline O. Anunobi

Professor and Chairman
Division of Business Administration
and Social Sciences
Selma University

UNIVERSITY
PRESS OF
AMERICA

Lanham • New York • London

Copyright © 1992 by
University Press of America®, Inc.
4720 Boston Way
Lanham, Maryland 20706

3 Henrietta Street
London WC2E 8LU England

Library of Congress Cataloging-in-Publication Data

Anunobi, Fredoline O.
The implications of conditionality : the International Monetary Fund
and Africa / Fredoline O. Anunobi.
p.   cm.
Includes bibliographical references and index.
1. Nigeria—Economic policy.   2. International Monetary Fund—
Nigeria.   3. Africa—Economic policy.   4. International Monetary
Fund—Africa.   I. Title.
HC1055.A7   1992   338.9669—dc20   92–24477 CIP

ISBN 0–8191–8794–1 (cloth : alk. paper)
ISBN 0–8191–8795–X (pbk. : alk. paper)

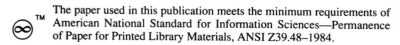

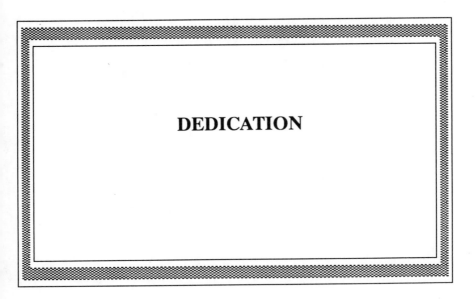

DEDICATION

To My Sweet Daughter
Ijeoma C. Anunobi

ACKNOWLEDGEMENTS

It is a great pleasure to acknowledge my indebtedness to those who have helped me shape my ideas, on the Implication of the International Monetary Fund Programs in Africa.

At this point, acknowledgements are in order. First and foremost, credit must go to my close and treasured academic advisor, Hashim Gibrill, Clark-Atlanta University. He was my prime consultant on each chapter of this research as the manuscript slowly grew. In addition, I am grateful to Larry Noble, of Clark-Atlanta University, Isola Kokumo of California Polytechnic State University, Ronald Staughter, of Alabama A & M University, Richard Ajayi, of Wayne State University, Christopher Ngassam, of University of Delaware, Marcel I. Anunobi, of Howard University, Samuel Ubbaonu, of Clark-Atlanta University, Caleb Obiegbu, of Alabama A & M University, Robert G. Sherman, of American Graduate School of International Management, Marlene Ahimaz, of University of Chicago, Paul Asabere, of temple University, Rex Harawa, of State University of New York, Ayogu Melvin, of James Madison University, Smille Dube, of California State University, Green Joshua, International Monetary Fund, Janice White, of Selma University, and Mersah Sam, of University of Michigan for carefully reading the entire chapters and offering a number of helpful criticisms, corrections and suggestions.

Furthermore, I would like to extend special thanks and deep appreciation to Kelvin Ikedum, Fred Mmaduaku, George Ikedum, Donatus Anunobi, Samuel Obinyereokwu, James Udeweke, A.O. Okeke, L.N. Ahize, Anthony Anunobi, M.A. Ozodinobi, Alphus Onyejiaku, Micah Obiegbu, Ernest Okeke, Ralph Egbuawa, Chukwuemeka O. Ojukwu, and my parents for their instrumental, financial, moral and emotional supports, during those much talked about time when researchers really need such support.

I sincerely owe my special thanks to my colleagues, students and friends at Selma University for their scholarly contributions and useful criticisms of this research. Although I cannot mention everyone who in one way or another has contributed to my academic success by name, I wish in particular to thank B. W. Dawson, President, Bettaiya Rajanna, Vice-President for Academic Affairs, C. S. Chetty, Mubinur Choudhury, S.R Anugu, Mrs. Sharada Rajanna, V. Babu, Mrs. Rama Anugu, Debra Holmes, Andre' King, Annie Cooper, and Terricina "Connie" Stewart all from Selma University for their moral advice and encouragement. To all these I dedicate and confess my complete indebtedness and eternal gratitude, for without them this study and many of my academic endeavors would not have seen the light of the day. I would also like to thank Omega T. Major for his invaluable help in editing and typing of this work. His overall special assistance in this research is highly appreciated.

My greatest debt; however, in this as in all my endeavors is to my wife, Eucharia Uchechukwu and my daughter Cynthia Ijeoma. I owe all to their love and encouragement. As I continue to look to the future with hope, I dedicate this, the most recent of my collaborative effort sustained by bonds of determination, to my sweet daughter, Ijeoma. My intellectual debt is beyond payments; shortcomings and errors in understanding, interpretation, and presentation are entirely my own.

Fredoline O. Anunobi, Ph.D.

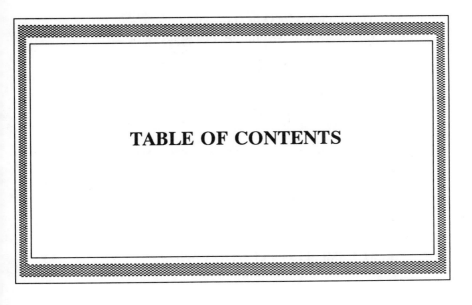

TABLE OF CONTENTS

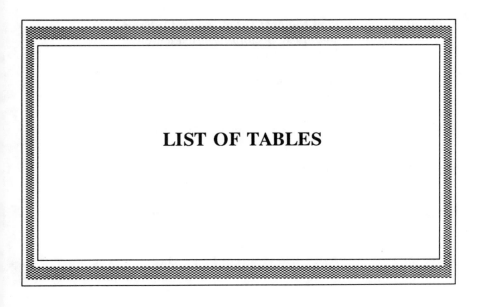

LIST OF TABLES

LIST OF FIGURES

LIST OF ABBREVIATIONS

AG	Action Group
AID	Agency for International Development
CFF	Compensatory Financing Facility
EDI	Economic Development Institute
EFF	Extended Fund Facility
EPZ	Export Processing Zone
FEC	Federal Election Commission
FER	Foreign Exchange Rate
FEM	Foreign Exchange Market
FRN	Federal Republic of Nigeria
FTZ	Free Trade Zone
GATT	General Agreement on Tariffs and Trade
GDP	Gross Domestic Product
GNP	Gross National Product
GNPP	Great Nigherian Peoples' Party
IBRD	International Bank for Reconstruction and Development
ICI	Imperial Chemical Industries
IEA	International Energy Agency
IMF	International Monetary Fund
LDC	Less Developed Country

LLDCs	Least Less Developed Countries
MNCs	Multinational Corporations
NCNC	National Council of Nigerian Citizens
NDC	National Development Corporation
NIC	Newly Industrializing Country
NNA	Nigerian National Alliance
NNDP	Nigerian National Democratic Party
NPC	Northern People's Congress
NPN	National Party of Nigeria
NPP	Nigerian Peoples's Party
OECD	Organization of Economic Cooperation and Development
PRP	People's Redemption Party
SAL	Structural Adjustment Loan
SAP	Structural Adjustment Plan
SDR	Special Drawing Right
SFEM	Second-Tier Foreign Exchange Market
SFF	Supplementary Financing Facility
TF	Trust Fund
UAC	United African Company
UPN	Unity Party of Nigeria
WAI	War Against Indiscipline

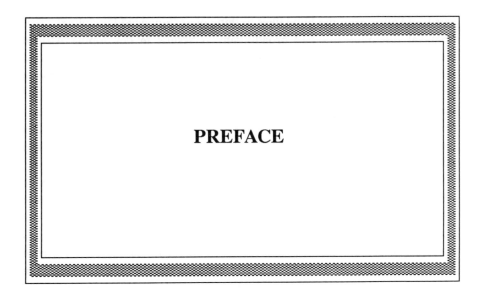

PREFACE

We have endeavored in this book to show the financial and economic predicaments of Nigeria and other African economies during the last few years and the approach adopted by the various governments in Africa to address these problems. By the mid-1980s, more than twenty-five African countries had requested for the IMF's financial and economic assistance and because of their unavoidable circumstances accepted conditions of which they did not agree. Nigeria, which is one of the major countries in Africa currently resisting IMF-imposed policies, by 1986 started to adopt the Fund's stabilization programs without the loan.

The IMF was established for the purpose of providing loans to its members states suffering balance of payments disequilibrium. However, as we have seen many African nations have always relied upon the Fund, but they feel that the Fund programs normally ignore economic and political realities and place unwarranted burden upon their economies. Hence, they rely upon the Fund only as a last resort.

Our research indicate that many African countries have had many aspects of their economic policies fundamentally altered as a result of Fund direction. All of these countries under study have been faced with repeated demands for substantial devaluation or flotation of the exchange rate, cuts and/or privatization of the parastateal sector, the abolition of subsidies, and labor retrenchment policies. They have been obliged to implement in the

POLITICAL MAP OF AFRICA

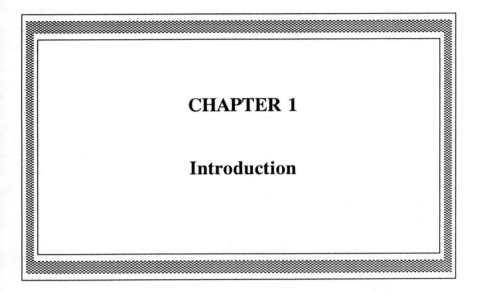

CHAPTER 1

Introduction

In the first place, the IMF usually views a Third World country to be encountering a debt crisis when its debt service ratio is consistently more than 20 percent of its foreign exchange or export earning.[1]

There are a number of prescriptions the debtor nations must have before qualifying for the IMF loans. Among a host of measures, the IMF prefers three main macro-economic prescriptions for almost all Third World borrowers. They are: (1) a reduction of government budget deficits, (2) limits to money supply growth in order to bring inflation down, (3) a policy of currency devaluation, in an attempt to boost exports and restrain imports.[2]

The Fund prefers the use of deflation as well as devaluation, in lieu of direct controls over trade as a means of limiting imports. This is based essentially on the premise that growth will take place where governments give private enterprise the freedom to make profitable investments. At present, our position is that Africa would not progress toward national economic recovery and self-reliant development if its government accepted IMF conditionality.

---

[1]Latin American Bureau, The Poverty Brokers: The IMF and Latin America (London: Latin American Bureau, Research and Action, Ltd., 1983), p. 65.

[2]"Economist," April 1983 as quoted in The Poverty Brokers, p. 15.

Over the years, there was continuing debate about whether or not IMF conditionalities would accelerate national economic recovery and assure self-reliant development desired by many Third World leaders. Some orthodox economists such as Burke Dillon, Maxwell Watts, Russell Kincaid, Peter Quirk, to mention a few, have identified IMF policies as a model for Third World economic development.   According to these western trained economists, the IMF policies if well implemented will solve the Third World economic and debt problems - because they will replace inappropriate domestic economic policies of the developing nations, which according to them, were responsible for the Third World economic underdevelopment.

These economists, particularly Peter Quirk and Burke Dillon, have more often than not concentrated their efforts on analyzing the Fund policies as effective fiscal and monetary instruments designed to achieve economic and self-reliant development of the Third World countries, ignoring those structural imbalances which the Third World leaders do not have control over and the socio economic and political implications of these policies for the lives of the people, especially the poor.

The purpose of the formation of the International Monetary Fund (IMF) in 1944 at Bretton Woods, New Hampshire was to stabilize the economies of member nations.   At its inception, its membership was composed primarily of European and North and South American countries. In the last twenty years, the membership has increased and the developing countries of Africa, Asia and Latin America are now the majority.[3] The less developed countries have become increasingly disenchanted with the operation of the IMF because their economic condition since the 1960s has grown steadily worse under the IMF policies.[4]

Article one which established the IMF states the objectives of the Fund as follows: To facilitate the expansion and balanced growth of international trade, increase employment, and real income, establish monetary cooperation, maintain exchange rate stability, encourage multilateral payments, and use its

---

[3]Michael Boddie, "Africa, The IMF and the World Bank," New Nigeria, March-April, 1983, p. 10.

[4]Ibid.

influence and resources to correct balance of payment disequilibria between members.[5]

A further objective is to give confidence to members by making the general resources of the Fund temporarily available to them under adequate safeguards, thus providing them with an opportunity to correct maladjustments in their balance of payments without resorting to measures destructive of national or international prosperity (See Appendix 12.)[6]

To achieve the objectives of Article I, the IMF lends money for short periods, usually a year or eighteen months, to members having balance of payments problems and interprets its responsibilities on banking principles, that is the need to ensure that the loan principle and interest are repaid. This has led the IMF to insist on a mix of policies which it judges will improve the balance of payments of the loan and interest. For this purpose, the Fund has pressed for programs that seek to cut government spending, remove consumer subsidies, restrict monetary expansion, reduce wages, devaluation of currency and the like.

Since 1979, the IMF began to insist on policies with a much broader objective, policies that in its opinion, would make better use of land and manpower and capital resources at the borrowing nation's disposal.[7]

> The measures now included the ending of the government's monopoly position or privatization of parastatal marketing and manufacturing enterprise; redirection of credit from the public to the private sectors; the ending of price controls and subsidies; the raising of real interest rates closer to international commercial levels; the removal of exchange and import controls; and the lowering of tariffs.[8]

These measures have serious effects on the borrowing nations. Between 1982 and 1987, twenty-five countries in Africa had taken IMF loans involving conditionality because of their debt, and the monetary and economic

---

[5]The International Monetary Fund, "The Role and Function of the IMF," No. 37, Washington, DC (1985), p. 2.

[6]Ibid., p. 3.

[7]Michael Hodd, "Africa, the IMF and the World Bank," African Affairs, volume 86. No., 344 (July 1987) p.332.

[8]Ibid.

problems of the 1980s. Nigeria, which is one of the major countries in Africa currently resisting IMF - imposed policies, by 1986 started to implement the Fund's policies without the loan. However, Nigeria, first started negotiations with the IMF for a loan of $2.4 billion in 1983 under President Shagari's administration. Before negotiations broke down the same year, the IMF had already approached Nigeria with seventeen conditions. These conditions included, as usual:

> reduction in government expenditure and the budget deficit, introduction of stricter budgetary discipline, review of on-going projects, reduction of subsidies to parastatals, restructuring of parastatals with commercial potential to make them more profit oriented, stoppage of grants to state government, rationalization of customs tariffs, an increase in interest rates and reduction of monetary expansion, phased removal of fertilizer subsides, a review of industrial incentives and policy, and export drive to broaden the export base, an upward adjustment of producer prices for agricultural commodities, strict external debt control, management and improvement in the efficiency of the revenue collection agencies, devaluation of the naira, trade liberalization, and a removal of petroleum subsidies.[9]

Among these conditions, the only three that could not be agreed upon were devaluation of the naira, trade liberalization, and a removal of petroleum subsidies.

Although President Shagari and his successor General Mohammed Buhari had indicated their intention to implement many of these policies in order to refinance Nigeria's trade debts, it was Major General Ibrahim Babangida's regime which followed Buhari's administration that actually implemented them. The monetary and economic policy proposed by President Shagari was first adopted as an interim policy by the Buhari administration, but was later confirmed as the new government's policy in the budget of May 1984. It was still the policy that was in operation until the military coup d'etat which unseated General Buhari's government took place in August 1985.

---

[9]Onyema Ugochukwu, "The Trouble with the IMF," West Africa, (26 October 1984).

The present government has cut the federal deficit drastically, established the Second-Tier Foreign Exchange Market (SFEM) that aimed to devalue the naira, the Onosode Committee was asked to review on-going projects, subventions to parastatals have been reduced and plans to privatize some of them have been announced.[10] Subsidies have been cut for fertilizer as well as education and health.

Purpose and Scope of the Study

In this study, we concern ourselves with the examination and analysis of some specific policies of the Fund implemented by African governments such as: (1) devaluation of national currency, (2) reduction of government spending, especially human services expenditures, (3) increase in interest rates in order to encourage saving, (4) control the rate of expansion of the money supply in order to dampen inflation, (5) imposition of wage control, (6) raise in taxes, (7) cut in subsides especially in agriculture, education, and petroleum, (8) reduction or dismantling of barriers to foreign private investment and to free trade in general.

Since the objective of this study is to indicate the socioeconomic and political implications of the Fund supported programs in Africa, the research will be based on the evaluation and assessment of the aforementioned policies. A critical examination of the degree of success and/or failure of these policies in addressing African economic development, will be the foundation for assessing the degree of appropriateness or inappropriateness of the IMF policies in Africa.

The above stated policies were chosen because they always reflect the IMF preference in dealing with almost every Third World country that has balance of payments disequilibria. A critical assessment of these policies will also serve as a decision guideline to many African and other Third World countries that have not entered into agreement with the Fund supported programs.

In addition, the research examines the history and evolution of the IMF, its operation and policy prescriptions, and the nature of its involvement

---

[10] Ibrahim Babangida, "Nigeria Budget Aims to Reflate Economy" West Africa, February 1987.

in Africa. To this end, the role of the IMF in Sudan, Zambia and Nigeria is dealt with along with the economic policy of the Buhari and Babangida regimes. Furthermore, the political, social and economic implications of the Fund-supported adjustment programs on the lives of the people, especially the poor, will be critically examined. At this point, however, only "standby" arrangements were included in the analysis because they were essentially the only high-conditionality Fund-supported austerity programs to be implemented throughout the period under analysis. We also analyze and evaluate critically in this text the Zambia and Sudan's economic and debt problems and the solutions offered by the International Monetary Fund to address these problems. We further examine in detail and compare the foreign exchange measures and related actions adopted by the two military governments to address Nigerian economic crisis and self-reliant development and the IMF forces that shaped these policies. In addition, we provide a concluding assessment of the Buhari's independent foreign exchange control measures and the IMF economic stabilization measures implemented by the Babangida regime. In the final analysis, we suggest alternative approaches to Fund stabilization in Africa. Such suggestions evolved from our discovery of the reasons for the failures of the Fund-supported stabilization programs in solving Zambian, Sudanese and Nigerian economic problems.

Africa was chosen for this study because this is the first time in history the majority of African States have chosen to implement the IMF policies for their economic recovery and self-reliant development.

Theoretical and Conceptual Framework

The search for economic development has been a major problem facing almost all nations in today's history. However, evidence continues to suggest that the countries in Africa and many other Third World countries are still underdeveloped. In an effort to understand the dynamic of underdevelopment of the underdeveloped nations, two major theories have emerged: The development and underdevelopment theories.

The theory of development which emerged to explain the causes of underdevelopment of the LDCs offered the following explanations and assumptions:

Foremost among these fundamental assumptions is the belief that the primary task of the underdeveloped countries is to undergo the process of modernization. Although there are variations in the definition of this concept, in general, modernization is always used as a euphemism for "Westernization" and implies the transformation of the underdeveloped nations in the image of developed countries of the western world.[11]

In light of Harris' arguments, S.N. Eisenstad provided us with an excellent definition of modernization:

Historically, modernization is the process of change towards those types of social, economic, political systems that have developed in Western Europe and North America from the seventeenth century to the nineteenth and have then spread to other European countries and in the nineteenth and twentieth centuries to the South America, Asia, and Africa continent.[12]

These orthodox economists also believe that modernization and economic development of the less developed countries are always in the best interest of both developed and underdeveloped nations; and that the developed countries have encouraged and contributed to the modernization of the LDCs. According to the proponents of the conventional wisdom, modernization and development of the underdeveloped countries have been hindered by many internal, rather than external, factors such as political instability, lack of capital, low savings, population explosion, inequities in the distribution of wealth, maldistribution of resources, low management and technological capacity. As C. E. Black put it in his book The Dynamic of Modernization:

Societies in the process of modernization must therefore be considered both as independent entities, the traditional institutions of which are being adapted to modern function, and also as societies under the influence of many outside forces. Indeed, the outside influences are so powerful that

---

[11]Richard Harris, The Political Economy of Africa (London: Halsted Press, 1975), p. 2.

[12]S. N. Eisenstadt, Modernization: Protest and change (Englewood Cliffs: Prentice-Hall, 1969), p. 1.

> modernization is sometimes thought of primarily as acculturation - the adoption of the culture traits of another society....The models adopted by modernizing leaders, except in the societies that were first to modernize, are always derived in a considerable degree from outside their own society. The problems they face, however, are domestic and in essential ways unique.[13]

Orthodox theorists identify internal factors such as traditionalism, capital scarcity, rapid population explosion, political integration, political instability, and the like as hindrances to modernization and development in general in the less developing countries.

Also, orthodox theories of political economy implicitly assume that certain institutions are not only essential but also imperative for political and economic development to take place and continue to progress. Some institutions such as civil service, military force, political parties (not a single national party system), and exchange or free market economy are said to be necessary for political and economic development to occur and prosper.

The writings of many social scientists from North America and Western Europe present typical examples of orthodox political and economic thoughts. For instance, prominent American political scientists such as James Coleman, Gabriel Almond, David Apter, Morton Kaplan, Samuel Huntington, Karl Deutsch, and many others often use efficiency, institutions, political parties, bureaucracy, law and order, and leadership as their variables for measuring the level of modernization and political development. Orthodox theorists are nothing but model-builders and are as much influenced by theory building activities traditional to the classical school of thought in the realm of the social sciences. Modern traditional theorists are merely carrying over the theories of scholars like David Ricardo, Adam Smith, Thomas Malthus and others in the classical school of thought. Their theory is based on continuity and the transformation of Western Europeans and North American institutions and models into the less developed countries. Their analysis of whether a country is developed or not is usually based upon how much such a country fits into the Western model.

---

[13]C. E. Black, The Dynamic of Modernization (New York: Harper & Tow, 1966), p. 50.

Furthermore, orthodox theorists emphasize the positive effects of foreign firms on the political and socio-economic life of the Third World nations. They argue that foreign investments facilitate political and economic developments, transfer skill and technology, create stability, increase gross national product and income, provide employment and industrialization, strengthen the balance of payments position, and improve the standard of living of the recipient nations.[14]

Further, orthodox theorists also share the belief that the diffusion of capital and technology from the developed nations to the underdeveloped countries will accelerate economic development of the LDCs.

> Even the neoclassical economic theory predicted harmony among all components of the world economy. In this theory, trade was regarded as the catalyst which would bring economic interdependence, share benefits fairly, and spread development to all nations of the world irrespective of their nature, size and structure of production.[15]

Third World countries have relied on the Western definition and explanation of development to solve their economic problems. Yet one of the major features of the present day world economic order is the unequal relationship between the developed nations and the developing countries. The developing countries have relied heavily on the principle of comparative advantage (a classical theory of international trade) often initiated by the developed countries, without favorable results. According to this theory, countries should specialize in the production of those commodities in which they have greatest comparative advantage - over the other nations. In this process, the classical theorists argue that there would be proper international division of labor and technological diffusion between nations. As it turned out, the benefits of the comparative advantage of international trade accrued disproportionately to the developed nations at the expense of the less developed countries.

---

[14]For example, see the writings of economists such N.A. Clara Martin, "Home and Foreign Investments", This Week, July 1975, J. K. Galbraith, "The Need for Foreign Investment", Foreign Policy (2 August 1975).

[15]Olayinka Sonaki, "Economic Dependence: The Problem of Definition," Journal of Asian and African Studies XIV (1979): p. 33.

In the first place, the current low profile into which many scholars and analysts are holding orthodox or traditional theories of political and economic development is attributable to the many weaknesses and failures of the traditional theories. These weaknesses and failures of the orthodox theories are manifested in the fact that for more than a century now orthodox theories of political economy have failed to lead to the growth and development in the Third World countries. Instead of helping to solve the problems of underdevelopment, traditional theories of political economy have caused increased unemployment, backwardness, poverty, inequality, and class conflict in the less developed countries.[16]

Also, the built-in weaknesses of orthodox theories to explain political economy have caused many scholars to reexamine or re-evaluate the authenticity or validity of these theoretical and conceptual frameworks. Hence, the result of re-evaluation has been the increased acceptance of the critics' viewpoint as represented in "radical" theories of political economy.

The variation evident in national postures toward international economic issues undoubtedly is also based on countries' positions in the international economic system. Rules governing international trade (like rules governing international relations) often evolve according to the wishes of the stronger players. Historically, these have been the advanced capitalist countries of Western industrialized world, notably Britain in the nineteenth century and the United States in the twentieth century. The more powerful states frequently have used military superiority and economic advantage to exercise leverage over others. As Block put it:

> This leverage is generally used to create an international order with a high degree of openness so that capitalists from the strongest economy will be able to take advantage of opportunities for profit in other countries. In short, a world order in which the flow of goods and capital is determined largely by market forces will maximize the advantage for the

---

[16]"Orthodox or Traditional Theories" here refer to scholars such as Adam Smith, David Ricardo, Alfred Marshall down to economists like John M. Keynes, Arthur Lewis, Paul Samuelson, and other capitalist-oriented economists.

country with highest level of technical development and with the most enterprising and strongest firms.[17]

Furthermore, more powerful capitalist nations prefer open systems because, capital, raw materials, and technology give them more opportunities to profit from a system that operates in accordance with the principle of comparative advantage.

In particular, the less developed countries share a profound sense of frustration with the international trade order developed after World War II. This frustration stems from a number of substantive trade practices and institutional characteristics of GATT that, in their view, combine to inhibit the development of their economies and relegate them to a secondary status in the world economy. Less developed countries are particularly sensitive to the tariff structures of most advanced industrialized states. Negotiation under GATT's auspices has reduced the average level of tariffs on dutiable manufactured and semi manufactured products to less than five percent. While the manufactured and semi manufactured products of particular export interest to less developed countries such as textiles and semi processed metal or wood products typically face tariff levels of two to four times this average, and tariffs on these items have frequently been ignored altogether in GATT negotiations. In addition, agricultural commodities face a variety of trade barriers. These include quantitative restrictions, tariff, health, and environmental regulations that are designed to protect the agricultural sector in advanced industrial states.

Less developed countries argue, further, that certain institutional characteristics of GATT contributed to the emergence of these trade practices and made it difficult for them to secure trade reforms commensurate with their needs. Their main objection to the Most Favored Nation (MFN) principle is that it inhibits rich states from granting preferential treatment to LDCs exports of manufactured goods as a spur to their development efforts. As John Evans put it in his book The General Agreement on Tariffs and Trade:

---

[17]Fred L. Block, The Origin of International Economic Disorder, (Berkeley and Los Angeles: University of California Press, 1977), p. 3.

In the past, there are no industrial products of importance that are not produced for export by some developed country. Therefore, no country can now eliminate tariffs on manufactured goods for the benefit of the developing industries or poorer countries without simultaneously opening its markets to unrestrained competition from developed countries (because of the MFN principle). It is this problem that has given rise to the demands of less developed countries that the most favored nation clause of GATT be suspended in their behalf.[18]

The inequality of international trade under the classical arrangement included the manipulation of the less developed countries through non-compliance with the provisions of General Agreement on Tariffs and Trade (GATT). Since World War II, the General Agreement on Tariffs and Trade has provided the framework of rules for the nations' management of their commercial policies. Thus GATT's most pervasive concern has been that:

trade restrictions not discriminate between supplier countries. Any advantage, favor, privilege, or immunity granted in trade with one country shall be accorded immediately and unconditionally to like trade with GATT members.[19]

Consequently, GATT structures its provisions in three areas - discriminatory trade controls, quantitative trade restrictions, and the settlement of disputes over trade policy of countries.

Third World countries have also relied on the institutions that emerged at Bretton Woods, New Hampshire in 1944, such as, the IMF, and the International Bank for Reconstruction and Development known as the World Bank to solve their monetary and economic problems. However, available data indicated that the policies prescribed by these two institutions to solve the Third World economic problems more often than not make the Third World economic problems even worse. Evidence indicates that the LDCs' problems could not be fully explained with the orthodox theories of development and this enables us to look for another alternative analytical and

---

[18]John W. Evans in the Global Partnership, R. Gardner and M. Milikan, ed. (New York Praeger, 1968), pp. 92-93.

[19]Richard E. Caves and Ronald W. Jones, in World Trade and Payments (Boston: Little, Brown and Company, 1981), p. 240.

conceptual framework. However, the theoretical and conceptual framework that will be used in writing our research will be based on the theory of development of underdevelopment as perceived by Andre Gunder Frank. Our choice of this theory is well thought out because many countries of Africa, Asia, and Latin America are still suffering from the political economy of underdevelopment since their independence. Also, as Third World scholars, we believe that we cannot fully understand or explain the causes of underdevelopment of the LDCs based on the orthodox approach. As Richard Harris indicates in his book: The Political Economy of Africa:

> The study of Africa in western academic circles has been hopelessly biased by the influence of government funding on academic research, grants from the large private foundations, the bureaucratization of knowledge by disciplines, the prevailing social and political ideologies, and the general ethnocentricism of western scholars, experts and policy makers. To correct the distortions resulting from this situation, a great deal of intellectual effort and research needs to be concentrated on the real barrier to development in Africa and the manner in which these barriers can be overcome. This means that Africa's economic dependence and subordination to foreign interests must be openly acknowledged. In addition, attention must be focused on those strategies of development and configuration of power which will lead to a political economy of 'rapid, self-sustained expansion, controlled and directed by and for the African people themselves.[20]

Also, we believe that we cannot hope to build effective or sufficient development theory and policy for the majority of the world's population who suffer from underdevelopment and dependency without first learning how their past economic and social history gave rise to their present underdevelopment. Yet most historians study only the advanced capitalist societies and pay little or no attention to the colonial and underdeveloped areas.[21]

---

[20]Harris, The Political Economy of Africa, p. 1.

[21]Andre Gunder Frank in Charles K. Wilber The Political Economy of Development and Underdevelopment (Random House, New York: 1973), p. 94.

This is true because the capitalist world-economy originated in one part of the globe and then expanded to include all parts such as Africa, Asia and Latin America. For this reason Frank strongly believed that the contemporary underdevelopment is in large part of the historical product of past and continuing economic, political, social and cultural relations between peripheral economies and the now developed economies. Frank puts it this way:

> Since the historical experience of the colonial and underdeveloped countries has demonstrably been quite different, available theory therefore fails to reflect the past of the underdeveloped part of the world entirely, and reflects the past of the world as a whole only in part. More important, our ignorance of the underdeveloped countries' history leads us to assume that their past and indeed their present resembles earlier stages of the history of the now developed nations. This ignorance and assumption lead us into serious misconceptions about contemporary underdevelopment and development. Further, most studies of development and underdevelopment fail to take account of the economic and other relations between the metropolis and its economic colonies throughout the history of the worldwide expansion and development of the mercantilism and capitalist system. consequently, most of our theory fails to explain the structure and development of the capitalist system as a whole and to account for its simultaneous generation of underdevelopment in some of its parts and of economic development in others.[22]

Radical theories seek to logically demonstrate that political and economic development have many aspects to be considered. They prove that political and economic development go beyond economic and political stability or maintenance as perceived by orthodox theories. Radical theories try to include ideas based on historical facts and characteristics of human society in its approach to analyze the contemporary underdevelopment of developing societies.

Also in contrast to orthodox theorists, radical theorists lay stress on the material aspect of society. That is, the relationship between owners of means of production and the social class relations. In order to explain political and

---

[22]Ibid.

economic development process, radical scholars lay emphasis on the existing sources of conflict within society based on historical analysis and the production relations. They seek to explain the impacts of extraneous influences such as colonialism, neocolonialism, and imperialism on production and development of developing societies. Hence, radical scholars lay emphasis on the relationship between development and underdevelopment, between the rich and the poor, between the advanced industrialized countries--the metropoles--and the less developed raw-material-producing nations--the peripheries.

Above all, radical theorists such as Gunder Frank, Paul Baran, Frantz Fanon, Paul Sweezy, Walter Rodney, and others lay bare the contradictions involved in the global domination of finance capital by advanced capitalist states and the aspirations of the poor, less developed countries for development. These scholars point out that the control of the natural resources and production relations of the underdeveloped countries by the developed countries raises the question as to whether advanced industrial societies really want the less developed countries to develop or not. The answer, radical scholars emphasize, is simply that the developed nations are not genuinely interested in the development of underdeveloped countries since the advanced capitalist states are not willing to relinquish the control of the natural resources of the developing nations. Therefore, the clue to development, as far as the radical theorists are concerned, lies with whoever in the final analysis controls the means of production of any given society.

These theorists further point out that a great deal of damage has been done to development efforts of the less developed countries by the institution-conscious of orthodox theories of political and economic development. According to them, the less developed countries of today are the same territories that have been either under direct colonial domination or suppressed under economic, military and political domination by imperial powers for a very long time.[23]

So, for these reasons, Frank convincingly argues that the bulk of this conventional wisdom is invalid when confronted with the empirical reality of

---

[23]In this analysis, the first category are the former colonial countries in Africa, Asia and Caribbean; in the second category, the territories of Latin America are typical examples. Yet up till now these countries with a long history of close contacts with developed countries still remain underdeveloped.

the underdeveloped countries; and ineffective if not detrimental as an intellectual basis upon which to develop policies aimed at promoting their development. Frank further proceeds:

> It is generally held that economic development occurs in a succession of capitalist stages and that today's underdeveloped nations are still in a stage, sometimes depicted as an original stage of history through which the now developed countries passed long ago. Yet, even a modest acquaintance with history shows that underdevelopment is not original or traditional and that neither the past nor the present of the underdeveloped countries resembles in any important respect the past of the now developed nations. The now developed countries were never underdeveloped though they may have been undeveloped.[24]

Furthermore, Frank like other radical scholars such as Immanuel Wallerstein and Walter Rodney disagree that the underdevelopment of the less developed countries is a result of their internal economic, political, social and cultural deficiencies. According to Frank, the beginnings of the Third World's systematic impoverishment were linked to imperialism, which he posits, not only brought Third World countries into the global economy but did so in a structurally unequal manner. The present pattern of international economic relations results to asymmetrical exchange. The benefits of these ties are shared unequally between core (the industrialized center of the world economy) and periphery (the underdeveloped countries of the third world). Because of the superior information, technological know-how, wealth, and market advantages at its disposal, the core remains at a decided advantage in its exchange encounters with the third world countries in the periphery. Frank strongly believes that:

> In reality, the now underdeveloped nations have long since been incorporated and integrated into the single world embracing capitalist system to whose development they contributed and still contribute with cheap labor, raw material or, in a word, with investible surplus capital. In the process - that is, in the

---

[24]A. G. Frank Capitalism and Underdevelopment in Latin America (New York: Monthly Review Press, 1969), p. 4.

process of capitalist development and of the economic development of capitalist metropolis in Europe and North America - the social physiology of Africa, Asia, and Latin America has been totally and uniformly changed into what it is today, the structure of underdevelopment which was created by and still is consolidated by the development and structure of the world capitalist system. He further argues that the structure and causes of underdevelopment in Africa, Asia, and Latin American nations are distinguished by their remarkable uniformity. In other words, Frank sees the underdevelopment of all of these countries as resulting from the same cause, their incorporation in the world capitalist system as dependent satellites of western Europe and North America.[25]

He also rejects the prevailing belief that the developed countries diffuse capital to the underdeveloped countries by demonstrating facts that indicate the reverse; that is, that there has been a diffusion of capital from the underdeveloped to the developed nations. This is very true, if one examines the role of multinational corporations in the LDCs.

The role of multinational corporations in the Third World countries has not escaped the attention of radical theorists. This is why one of the major controversial issues in contemporary national and international affairs is the question of the role and impact of multinational corporations (MNCs) especially in less developed countries now commonly referred to as the Third World. Radical theorists see multinational corporations as agents of capitalism and avenue for spreading the capitalist mode of production to the Third World. Multinational corporations, these scholars argue, carry with them explicit and implicit domination and control of their client countries. The conclusion usually drawn by radical political economy theorists is that the large investments of multinational corporations more often than not result in exploitation, dependency and underdevelopment for the recipient nation.[26]

---

[25]Ibid., p. 128.

[26]Some leaders in the developing nations see large foreign investments as a threat to real freedom and a means of forcing developing nations to compromise some of their sovereignty. For example, see Kwame Nkrumah, Neo-colonialism the Last Stage of Imperialism (New York: Modern Reader, 1971) and Julius K. Nyerere, Ujamaa, Essays on Socialism "The Arusha Declaration", the section on "What of External Aid?" (New York: Oxford University Press, 1971), pp. 21-22.

Also radical theorists and other critics of the capitalist mode of production see capitalist investments as means by which multinational corporations and banks in capitalist countries are able, as a result of finance capital, to perpetuate the capitalist system. The theorists point out that through large investments foreign investors are able to effectively determine and control the level and rate of development in developing nations simply by regulating more or less the national income, employment, prices and market through investment strategies.[27]

Frank finally offered two hypotheses which were very important to our study of the IMF policies and African economic development. His first hypothesis says that the developing countries experience their greatest economic development and particularly their most classically capitalist industrial development if and when their ties to the center nations are weakest.[28] His second hypothesis is the reverse of the first one. That is, the most underdeveloped regions are those that in the past had the closest ties to the metropole. They were the greatest exporters of primary products and a major source of capital, but they were abandoned once the business declined.[29]

> In order to understand the system of dependent reproduction and the socioeconomic institutions created by it, we must see it as part of a system of world economic relations based on monopolistic control of large-scale capital, on control of certain economic and financial centers over others, on a monopoly of a complex technology that leads to unequal and combined development at a national and international level. Attempts to analyze backwardness as a failure to assimilate more advanced models of production or to modernize are nothing more than

---

[27]See V. I. Lenin Imperialism, the Highest Stage of Capitalism (New York: International Publishers, 1970). Hary Magdoff The Age of Imperialism (New York: Monthly Review Press, 1969). J. A. Hobson, Imperialism--A Study (Paperback edition: Ann Arbor, Michigan, 1965). David S. Landes, "The Nature of Economic Imperialism" in the Journal of Economic History, (December 1961); James O. Connor in R. I. Rhodes, ed. Imperialism and Underdevelopment. Karl Marx, Critique of Political Economy, any edition; Paul M. Sweezy Monopoly Capital (New York: Monthly Review Press, 1968); Kwame Nkrumah, Neo-Colonialism, The Last Stage of Imperialism.

[28]A. G. Frank, quoted in Robert I. Rhodes, Imperialism and Underdevelopment: A Reader (New York/London: Monthly Review Press, 1970), p. 10.

[29]Ibid., p. 13.

ideology disguised as science. The same is true of the attempts to analyze this international economy in terms of relations among elements in free competition, such as the theory of comparative costs which seeks to justify the inequalities of the world economic system and to conceal the relations of exploitation on which it is based.[30]

The theory of a capitalist development of underdevelopment stimulated many writings about underdevelopment in Africa, Asia, and Latin America. Walter Rodney amassed historical detail in support of his thesis that Europe underdeveloped Africa. He perceived underdevelopment to be related to exploitation. According to him, the underdeveloped nations are products of capitalist, imperialist, and colonialist exploitation; they are underdeveloped, not developing because they are not escaping from their backward conditions.[31] Like Frank, Rodney examined metropoles and satellites and the dependent relationship between them. Other scholars whose major contributions are worthy to mention here are Arrighi, Amin, Fanon, Nkrumah and Claude Ake. Their major contributions will be seen somewhere along the line in this research.

Given the biases and inadequacies of the orthodox paradigm it becomes necessary that an alternative theoretical analysis must be utilized to examine the reality of the present structure of underdevelopment and the prospects for development in Africa, Asia, and Latin America. Frank's conceptual and analytical framework seems to provide such an alternative. According to this theoretical scheme:

any valid examination of the reality of the underdeveloped countries must be based on: (1) a holistic conception of their dependent satellite relationship to the developed capitalist metro pole; (2) their internal class and social-cultural structure (which has been determined by their past and present economic exploitation, and political domination); and (3) the prospects for their genuine liberation and development through the

---

[30]Theotonio Dos Santos, "The Structure of Dependence", in Charles K. Wilber, ed., The Political Economy of Development and Underdevelopment, (New York: Random House, 1973), p. 116.

[31]Walter Rodney, How Europe Underdeveloped Africa (Washington, D.C.: Howard University Press, 1981), p. 14.

destruction of the present external and internal structural configuration and the pursuit of an effective strategy of development.[32]

In the overall analysis dependency and underdevelopment theorists have viewed politics as a reflection of global and economic relations. Underdevelopment theory has furnished potent insights into the nature of constraints on Third World development. Its usefulness and vitality lie, first and foremost, in the importance it attributes to external factors in the explication of the Third World's present predicament. The orthodox theory of development is invalid because it does not, in our analysis identify the determinant social whole. It does not direct our attention to the relations between the underdeveloped countries and the developed ones, to the historical process and world system which have made the former underdeveloped and the latter developed.

In fact, the usefulness of this approach is even more apparent when one examines the impact of colonialism and neocolonialism which characterized Nigeria and many Third World countries. As Richard Harris put it:

> In the colonial period the traditional pattern of economic relationship in Africa were largely destroyed and in their place were created satellite economies whose primary function was to produce one or a few 'cash crops' or raw materials for export to the colonial mother country.[33]

He further stated that:

> The economic principle of colonial rule dictated government in what was believed to be the best interest of metropolitan capital, in short the operation of the colony as if it were a subsidiary company. As a result, the modern sectors of African economies are export biased in a way which distorts even short-term comparative advantage.[34]

---

[32]Frank, summarized by Harris, The Political Economy of Africa, p. 6.

[33]Ibid., p. 11.

[34]Reginald Green and Ann Seidman, Unity or Poverty? Economic of Pan Africanism (Baltimore: Penguin, 1969), p. 127.

For instance, in African economies, trading firms such as UAC, CFAO, and SCOA made fortunes from domination of the export-import trade in the colonies to which they were given privileged access.

The whole of the African economy is geared to the interests of the foreign capital that dominates it. Africa's banking institutions, like those of most other third world nations, are offshoots of the Western banking and financial houses. During the period of colonialism African businesses were dominated by Western monopolists who were anxious to make huge profits.

> [After independence,] these same firms continue to play a predominant role in the export-import trade of the now independent states which were formerly their colonial preserve. As a result of their colonial legacy, the present day economies of the Third World countries are characterized by a lop-sided dependence on the export of raw materials and the import of manufactured goods from the former colonial metropoles, with the U.S. increasingly assuming a major role in both exports and imports.[35]

The structural imbalance in these countries' economies resulting from the over dependence on the export of one or a few primary products makes these economies extremely vulnerable to external factors and seriously hinders their internal development. For this reason and other similar reasons Green and Seidman conclude:

> An economy limited to specializing in the production of a few primary products for export is, by the definition of economic independence here used, highly dependent. Loss of markets can be catastrophic and sharp falls in the price of exports only a little less so. The national rate of growth will be no higher than the rate of growth in export receipts.[36]

Colonialism's impact is perhaps most obvious in Africa because it was the last continent to gain political independence from the colonial powers. Africa also suffered more than other continents from the effects of the slave trade. Millions of Africans were shipped to European colonies to work on

---

[35]Harri, The Political Economy of Africa, p. 12.

[36]Green and Seidman, op at pp. 79-80.

plantations and in mines, as a part of the trading system the Europeans had established. After the slave trade had ended in the mid-1800s, a new form of colonialism emerged in 1884 which resulted to the scramble for and partition of Africa. Its practical effects were to divide Africa into territories and create boundaries which often ignored ethnic divisions.

Kwame Nkrumah, in his book Toward Colonial Freedom (1962), summarizes the purpose of colonial administration in Africa and elsewhere. According to Nkrumah, the aim of all colonial governments in Africa has been the struggle for raw materials and cheap labor. He explains how the African states export raw materials at low cost and in return pay a high price for the manufactured goods and services. The colonial powers saw Africa and other less developed countries of Asia and Latin America as a source of market for their over production and over saving that resulted from the exploitation of man by man. Therefore, these colonies became avenues for capital investment, not for the benefit and development of the African states, but for the benefit of the European investors.

Nkrumah finally explains how the European colonial powers had used different policies:

> (i) To make colonies non-manufacturing dependencies, (ii) to prevent the colonial subjects from acquiring the knowledge of modern means and techniques for developing their own industries, thereby making the colonial subjects the simple producers of raw materials through cheaper labor and consumer of European manufactured goods at high price. And how finally, the colonial powers had prohibited the colonies from trading with other nations except through their mother country.[37]

However, this kind of economic imperialism has benefitted the colonial masters more than the colonial subjects. In the overall analysis, the deformed development that took place under colonialism has rendered the economies of the present day states of Africa and other Third World countries highly dependent on external economic interests and made their balanced development extremely difficult.

---

[37]Kwame Nkrumah, Towards Colonial Freedom: Africa in the Struggle Against World Imperialism, (London: Panaf, 1962), p. 10.

Furthermore, most African countries gained political independence during the 1960s, yet their economies are still shaped in part by their past experience as European colonies. African economies inherited economic dependence. This dependence could be used by the imperialist forces to further their objectives. The dependence rest on two forms, a continued colonial division of labor and foreign control of key sectors of the economy. This pattern of relations resulted to unequal development.

Investment and trade are not the only form of dependence. Development aid has become an important instrument for the neocolonial policies. As a result of balance of trade deficits, the Third World countries have been forced to finance imports as well as their development programs through borrowing from foreign sources. This in turn has led to their increased dependence on foreign capital and foreign aid from western governments and their institutions.

However, a close study of the political economy of African, Asian and Latin American countries has indicated that despite huge technological and economic prosperity and development of the twentieth century, there are certainly more people living below poverty level in the world today than there were in the last four decades. This situation is a clear evidence that the "aid" granted by rich countries and huge amounts of capital that have been sent into the Third World nations by foreign businesses have not to any significant degree contributed to their development. This is so because the "aids" be it bilateral or multilateral and foreign investments by multinational corporations from the imperial Western powers are geared more at making profits and gaining political influence for the industrialized countries than for purely helping the development of the Third World.

Furthermore, developing countries possess and supply the greater percentage of the world's raw materials, but they have benefitted very little from their contribution to the world output. The advanced capitalist states and their organizations have controlled and manipulated international trade and finance through prolonged unilateral action or dictation and determination of prices of raw materials and finished products. The prices of their raw materials decline constantly while prices of manufactured goods, technology and capital equipment continue to rise. At the opening of a conference of one hundred and ten Third World countries on trade strategy at the International Congress Center near Dakar, Senegal, 1974, President

Leopold Senghor of Senegal reportedly stated that poorer countries had been exploited for too long by the capitalist states. He maintained that:

> This conference must above all define the objectives of the new international economic order and adopt methods of realizing these objectives. We in the Third World have to use our natural resources to break the traditional patterns of world trade.[38]

Other speakers in the conference reportedly remarked that the gap between the rich and poor nations had been widened by Western inflation which has caused less developed countries higher prices for manufactured imports while their primary raw materials steadily decline in value.[39]

Nigeria is no exception to the general problem facing less developed countries as discussed above. In spite of its abundant natural resources, its contact with Western civilization under British colonialism, foreign "aid" and investments and international trade, the country remains underdeveloped and the majority of its people poor.

Nkrumah had demonstrated the economic impact of development aid and foreign aid in general in his book Neo-colonialism: The Last Stage of Imperialism. According to Nkrumah, "unequal exchange" means that for the Third World the loss is often more than what is given in development aid. Nkrumah has this to say:

> In the first place, the rulers of neo-colonial states derive their authority to govern, not from the will of the people, but from the support which they obtain from their neo-colonialist masters. They have therefore little interest in developing education, strengthening the bargaining power of their workers employed by expatriate firms, or indeed for taking any step which would challenge the colonial pattern of commerce and industry, which it is the object of neo-colonialism to preserve. 'Aid', therefore, to a neo-colonial state is merely a revolving of credit, paid by the neo-colonial master, passing through the neo-colonial state and returning to the neo-colonial master in the form of increased profits. Secondly, it is in the field of 'aid'

---

[38]West Africa, 5 February 1975, p. 7.
[39]Ibid.

that the rivalry of individual developed states first manifests itself. So long as neo-colonialism persists so long will spheres of interest persist, and this makes multilateral aid - which is in fact the only effective form of aid - impossible.[40]

The natural tendency of foreign investors in Africa, as elsewhere in the underdeveloped world, has been to invest only in the high profit sectors of the African economies. The lucrative profits which they make from these sectors are immediately sent back to metropolitan banks and/or their home offices. According to Spero, this practice prevented domestic capital formation and resulted in a net outflow of capital from the Third World economies to the developed capitalist economies in the form of repatriated profits, royalties, interests and the like.[41]

In line with the argument, Arrighi also pointed out that not only did foreign investment prevent domestic capital formation in most African and other developing countries, it also resulted in a drain on valuable foreign exchange earnings. The transfer of profits and remittances to the metropolitan countries requires that the Third World countries give up for this purpose the foreign exchange earned from the sale of their exports and needed for the purchase of their essential imports.

The theoretical advantage of Frank's theory of the development of underdevelopment in the study of the IMF policies and Nigerian economic development is that it allows us to understand the role international political economy is playing in fostering economic dependence of Nigeria and many Third World nations. Contrary to the arguments of traditional development theorists, underdevelopment and dependency will continue in the world as along as the exploitation of the less developed countries by the developed ones continues.

Whether or not this situation will change largely depends on the role of Third World leaders, the dominant class, the comprador class and many others that help in the exploitation and underdevelopment of their countries because of their relations with capitalist states. It is only the decisions and

---

[40]Kwame Nkrumah, Neo-Colonialism: The Last Stage of Imperialism (New York: International Publishers, 1966), p. xv.

[41]J. E. Spero, The Politics of International Economic Relations (New York: St. Martin's Press, 1980), p. 276.

actions on the part of these groups that would shake the very foundation of capitalism and its institutions. Recently, a radical political economy paradigm has become quite popular, particularly in the developing nations, because of its series of apparent superior qualities over orthodox theories in explaining the causes of underdevelopment and dependency of LDCs; as well as its usefulness in analyzing political and economic impacts of North-South relations in the contemporary international political economy. Also, the relative utility of this approach is based on its explanation of the importance of history in understanding the dynamics of the Third World underdevelopment. This approach also enables us to know that in the Third World countries both the internal and external factors are responsible for their economic underdevelopment, and that most internal factors we see in the underdeveloped countries are caused by the external factors. Frank's analytical framework provides us with an explanation as to why many countries in Africa, Asia and Latin America with the available natural resources they have could not develop as independent political and economic entities. However, we recognize the general criticism that the development of underdevelopment thesis always blames the external factors rather than the internal factors for the economic problems of underdeveloped economies. This popularly held view was the main reason for our focusing on the development of underdevelopment; to find out which of these factors are more responsible for causing Nigeria and other Third World economic underdevelopment. For this reason, we hope that better comprehension of our hypothesis and further pursuit of the proposed historical, holistic, and structural paradigm may help the peoples of the underdeveloped world understand the causes and eradicate the reality of their development of underdevelopment and their underdevelopment of development.

Significance of the Study

The accelerated inflation and large payments imbalances that have plagued the world economy in recent years have created new challenges for economic policy. Institutions such as the International Monetary Fund and World Bank have found themselves operating in a global environment markedly different from that for which they were originally designed, and developing countries have found their aspirations threatened by large increases in their payment deficits. There have been wide disagreements about the most suitable policy responses by developing countries to these problems and about the appropriateness of the stabilization programs favored by the IMF.

Despite the increasing attention that has been focused on this controversy, remarkably little work has been performed in an attempt to determine systematically whether Fund-supported policies actually aggravate economic problems of the less developing countries or whether the relationship between the two phenomena is indeed merely coincidental. As of date, one of the studies that even remotely attempts to empirically examine this issue in a systematic manner is one written by Bienen and Gersovitz (1984). Bienen and Gersovitz present a number of case studies of Fund-induced stabilization policies and conclude that there is no reason to believe that Fund-induced adjustment policies aggravate economic problems of developing countries. In spite of the fact that their research is one of the most systematic and rigorous examinations of this issue to date, it should not be construed as being empirically conclusive. As a result, Bienen and Gersovitz cite a number of historical cases which support their a priori theoretical convictions about the relationship between Fund-supported programs and Third World economic problems. They failed to review all or most of the relevant cases. Hence, one cannot understand from their research how generalizable the relationship is beyond their relatively small sample space. While their extensive knowledge and familiarity with a number of cases are interesting their findings simply cannot be treated as instructive or generalizable in the absence of additional comparative systematic and empirical support.

Apart from the Bienen and Gersovitz (1984) research, a growing but still clearly small body of literature addresses the question of Third World economic problems and Fund-induced stabilization programs. However, few of these studies, have examined the topic as directly as Bienen and Gersovitz. Many have addressed the problem only tangentially. The few researches that have discussed the problem in a more central manner have failed to explore the issue in any systematic fashion.

In spite of the lack of focus, direction, and methodological rigor that generally characterizes these studies, the findings shown in these research must, nonetheless, be contemplated strongly. Despite the fact that, these studies do not yield a completely consensual compromise, they by and large suggest that Fund-supported adjustment programs tend to exacerbate Third World economic problems. Thus, a confusion exists between the conclusions presented by Bienen and Gersovitz (1984) and the findings shown in the bulk of the other literature in the area.

This study aims to address this confusion by examining the Fund-supported adjustment programs and the Third World's economic problems in a systematic fashion using Nigeria as a case study. This study critically examines whether or not the introduction of the Fund supported adjustment programs do significantly aggravate Third World economic problems, with particular reference to Nigeria. The inspiration for this study grows largely out of the failure of the social science scholars to address this issue in such a fashion.

In addition to the rather cursory examination of this research by the academic scholars to date, comprehensive research on this problem remains conclusively at ground zero. Our study will at this time provide a detailed examination of the Fund supported adjustment programs on Nigerian economic development.

Also, writers on the IMF and the Third World are mostly western authors. Their views, writings and theoretical concepts always reflect the interests of imperialistic capitalist countries, and as such, there is a scarcity of literature from the Third World perspective. Even the Third World scholars who have done some major works on the IMF activity in the less developing countries never addressed the IMF involvement in Nigeria. Hence, this study is the first in depth analysis done on the IMF-Nigeria relations. Thus, this study facilitates a better understanding of the nature of Fund conditionality and of the objectives and characteristics of Fund stand-by arrangements.

Organization Structure of the Study

This study is divided into twelve chapters. Chapter one contains an introduction, statement of the problem, theoretical and conceptual framework, and significance of the study. Chapter two examines the historical foundation and theoretical considerations of the International Monetary Fund from the Third World perspective. Chapter three presents the historical impact of British colonial rule in Nigeria. Chapter four addresses the post colonial economy of Nigeria and the National Development Plan.   Chapter five provides in a very systematic fashion the origin and development of Nigeria's economic crisis.   Chapter six examines the history and evolution of the International Monetary Fund, its operation and policy conditionalities. Chapter seven addresses the IMF and the Zambia's Debt problems. Chapter eight examines the role of IMF and World Bank in Sudan.   Chapter nine analyzes the African economic crisis and the nature of IMF involvement. Chapters ten and eleven assess the Buhari and Babangida's economic policies and the level of the International Monetary Fund influence. Chapter twelve provides the concluding assessment and recommendation.

CHAPTER 2

The Historical Foundation And Theoretical Considerations Of The International Monetary Fund: Third World Perspective

The next question that follows is: "What is this institution that engenders such responsibilities? What gives it so much power over the lives of the poor? Since the IMF has become the central and most powerful of the Bretton Woods institutions, it merits close examination by all committed to economic justice for the poor."[1] These are among the main issues that will be examined closely in our study. And whether the policies dictated by the Fund will enhance national economic recovery and self-reliant development without necessarily causing too much harm to the poor people is central to our study. Furthermore, we strongly believe that upon the completion of this study, our findings will indicate lines along which further study and research could fruitfully proceed.

The increase importance of developing countries as recipients of the IMF's upper tranche and extended Fund facility credit, and the expectation that this trend will continue in the 1980s, make the LDCs critical for the IMF and the IMF critical for the LDCs. This is true because the IMF was not formed with the LDCs in mind. Also, it was not the Fund's intention to finance large and persistent deficits. Much comment on the IMF is directed toward proposing reforms in its lending practices, but here we have two major

---

[1]Hunger, The International Monetary Fund and the Third World (February 1980).

theoretical concerns that guide our study: (1) what rules govern IMF actions when confronted with a set of development objectives somewhat at variance from its own? In other words, can the IMF be used for development and economic prosperity of LDCs? (2) what scope does the typical LDC (Nigeria) have for charting its own course while at the same time operating within an international capitalist framework?

The IMF is an international organization charged with managing international monetary problems. It operates under the aegis of the western capitalist system and is dominated by the Group of Ten. In a broad generalization, there are three worlds in the capitalist mold. The first consists of those countries that can attract international commercial loans mainly because of the structure and strength of their economies. The second world comprises those countries that cannot attract these loans because they are relatively underdeveloped. They have limited infrastructure and their economies are weak. Then there are those grey area countries that lie in-between the two extremes.

The present IMF policy is to treat all member countries alike:

> The Fund has always avoided dividing its members into categories and has sought to preserve the principle of uniform treatment of all members. This is attractive if it can be done without jeopardizing the interests of either group. But can it?[2]

Nowzad had summarized the philosophy of the Fund towards LDCs:

> The Fund (as is evident from the Articles) has a market-oriented, pro-free enterprises, pro-capitalist, anti-socialist philosophy, with a pronounced bias in favor of free trade, private investment, and the price mechanism. This reflects a 'vision of the world' inspired and imposed by industrial countries, in particular the United States, on debtor (implicitly developing) countries. Many economists and politicians genuinely believe that the policies implied by this philosophy are in the best interests of developing countries. It must be recalled, however, that these officials are western-trained and believe in the efficiency of the market. The imposition of this

---

[2]John Williamson, The Lending Policies of the International Monetary Fund (Washington, D.C.: Institute for International Economics, August 1982), p. 13.

philosophy is facilitated by dominant voting power of the industrial countries; in this way, the Fund serves the interests of creditor countries and helps to preserve their resources from claims by developing countries to larger resource transfers. In brief (as one head-of-state has put it), the Fund is a 'device by which the rich countries increase their power over the poor'.[3]

The IMF has two major philosophies that express the above view in its "low conditionality" and "high conditionality." The former applies to the developed countries which are characterized by relatively full employment, high industrialization and strong economies that might suffer periodic "balance of payment problems." What these countries need from the IMF are small adjustments of their currency and small loans relative to their economies to make these adjustments. High conditionality loans are large loans relative to the economy of the debtor country. These loans address major financial problems characterized by repayment of former loans and the building up of some basic infrastructure.

The main difference between low conditionality and high conditionality is the level of IMF influence. Low conditionality countries have access to commercial banks, so the percentage of the money needed to correct their balance of payments deficit from the IMF only allows for nominal IMF advice to correct the problem. High conditionality countries with a greater dependency on the IMF have to undergo more stringent IMF dictates.

> The Fund clientele has shrunk to this second group of countries, in which the commercial banks seek to avoid exposure,...low income countries, which currently receive two-thirds of the Fund's total commitments, account for a mere 7 percent of the banks' exposure in non-oil developing countries.[4]

The IMF increasingly has the responsibility of managing the LDCs' financial problems. IMF insistence on "high conditionality" causes severe shocks to the economies of the LDCs. However, the organization would

---

[3]Bahran Nowzad, The IMF and Its Critics (Princeton: Princeton University Press, 1981), p. 7.

[4]Rimmer de Vries, quoted in John Williamson, The Lending Policies of the International Monetary Fund, p. 13.

become an aid donor if there was no conditionality. The LDCs not only want loans at lower rates, but they also advocate a restructure of the IMF to reflect the present realities of its functions. It was funded to adjust world monetary policies, but today's main influence is on the economies of LDCs. The above IMF responses are generally economic solutions, but there is a political aspect to IMF conditions. Sharpey is of the opinion:

> That there is a relationship between the ability and willingness of developing countries to accept the Fund conditionality and the amount of resources the Fund is able to make available. While the Jamaican authorities had allowed the economy to deteriorate dramatically before going to the Fund, the conditions for this agreement were out of all proportion to the resources the Fund made available. Even if the agreement was seen by the Fund as a test of the government's determination to implement tough stabilization measures, the size and conditionality of the Fund resources provided little scope and encouragement for the government to adhere to this goal.[5]

The Jamaican position was not unlike Britain's situation. The British, because of their deteriorated economy, were granted an IMF "high conditionality" loan of $3.9 billion. The British complained bitterly about the stipulations, but were spared the IMF harsh terms by: (1) the increasing revenues of North Sea Oil; and (2) influencing the IMF because of her unique relationship with the United States.

> Even making due allowance for the fact that the British ministers mistakenly sought U.S. involvement in an attempt to avoid conditionality, this involvement was most unfortunate. It is the Fund's mission not that of the U.S. Treasury Secretary, or even the under secretary for monetary affairs, nor the chairman of the U.S. Federal Reserve Board to assess the outlook, drawing requirements, and necessary conditions pertaining to the applicant country. Such involvement can place pressure on the Fund's managing director, even if the advice of another government is not directly made to him, and could wrongly

---

[5]Jennifer Sharpey, in John Williamson, ed. International Monetary Fund Conditionality (Institute for International Economics, Washington, D.C., 1983), p. 260.

influence his decision. It should be strictly avoided in the future.[6]

The point to be made is that developed countries are resistant to "high conditionality," and Britain used her political influence in the IMF to avoid harsh terms. Britain was able to do this because she had the necessary and sufficient conditions of a developed economy, and was able to stabilize her economy with an increase in revenue.

The IMF has a principal role of constructing and maintaining an international economic system based upon capitalist forms of production and exchange. Constructing an economic system in which market forces operate without state restraints, and profit is accumulated by private capital is, particularly, central to this role."[7] The growth of the international economy on this basis was seen as the priority of the IMF, with the development of national economies as secondary. The IMF was originally formed to facilitate the expansion and balanced growth of world trade, and to contribute thereby to individual states' growth and development. Although the founders' orientation at that time was toward the fractured economic relations of the advanced industrial states, the same priority toward the international system and the construction of an international market system make up the IMF's role today.[8]

The construction of such an international system according to Laurence, requires the Fund to have leverage over the national economies within it, for the rules of the international system rest upon the policies and rules of national states. The IMF's ability to operate on these also rests on its role regarding member states' balance of payments. In this system, countries' external payments represent a real constraint on policy, and the IMF's role in providing balance of payments finance enables it to operate on these constraints so that they exert pressure towards the adoption of national policies which contribute to a market-based international system rather than to hinder it.

---

[6]Malcolm Crawford, in John Williamson, ed. International Monetary Fund Conditionality, p. 438.

[7]Laurence Harris quoted in World Recession and The Food Crisis in Africa ed by Peter Lawrence (London: James Currey, 1986), p. 92.

[8]Ibid.

The Prime Minister of Jamaica, Michael Manley, strongly shares the belief that: International Monetary Fund prescriptions are designed by and for developed capitalist economies and are inappropriate for developing economies of any kind; the severe suffering imposed on developing society through International Monetary Fund conditionality is endedured without any real prospect of a favorable economic outcome and without an adequate foundation of social-welfare provisions to mitigate the a hardships experienced by the peoples; and the notion that with International Monetary Fund approval, international commercial banking institutions will supplement the funds made available by the International Monetary Fund is a fallacy.[9]

The conditions attached to International Monetary Fund loans that require deflationary domestic economic policies, reduction of public expenditures (often designed to reduce income inequalities within society), and liberalization of international trade and investment policies expose the International Monetary Fund to harsh criticism from decision makers in Africa and other Third World countries. The acceptance of Fund policy prescriptions immediately limits the options of the Third World countries. In some cases, they may be required to leave socialist policies designed to reduce, if not eliminate, domestic income inequalities, or to protect local production from displacement by foreign imports or direct foreign investment, or even to sever existing links with the international capitalist system. The International Monetary Fund, according to radical political economists, imposes capitalist domestic and foreign economic policies on borrowing countries, hence ensuring the dominance of the advanced market economies over the less developed countries. The Fund's reliance upon conventional liberal economic advice, its rejection of noncapitalist policies, and its attempts to bind borrowing countries to the current political-economic system (through their vulnerability and indebtedness) are all seen as evidence that the International Monetary Fund serves the interests of the dominant capitalist states.

---

[9]Michael Manley, "The International Monetary System and the New International Order", Development Dialogue 1980-1982, p. 5.

In most Third World countries, this usually produces the opposite effect or negative outcomes, because the anticipated deflation forces many producers into bankruptcy because they will be unable to service their large foreign loans. In these nations, bankruptcies may create or in some cases have created severe liquidity crisis in that country's banking system.

In addition, Harry Magdoff charges that "the very condition which produce the necessity to borrow money in the first place are continuously reimposed by the pressure to pay back the loan and to pay the interest on these loans".[10] One radical critic of the International Monetary Fund writes that "International Monetary Fund missions descend like vultures in the wake of right-wing coups in countries such as Ghana, Indonesia, and Brazil."[11] In addition, "the financial discipline imposed by the International Monetary Fund has often eliminated the need for direct military intervention in order to preserve a climate friendly towards foreign investment."[12]

Radicals claim that it is no coincidence that President Buhari was unable to find any loans after the International Monetary Fund rejected his request for funds because of his unwillingness to accept and implement International Monetary Fund policy conditionalities. Also, they point out that in the wake of the military coup in August 1985, the International Bank for Reconstruction and Development indeed provided funds with the advice of the International Monetary Fund. What is more, this was followed by loans from other sources, both private and public.[13]

Furthermore, the International Monetary Fund is perceived by many to be the inchpin of the whole international monetary and economic order, which is designed to perpetuate capitalism, and dependency of developing

---

[10]Harry Magdoff, The Age of Imperialism (New York: Monthly Review Press, 1966), p. 98.

[11]Cheryl Payer, "The Perpetuation of Dependence: The IMF and the Third World", Monthly Review, Vol. 23, No. 4, (September 1971), p. 37.

[12]Ibid., p. 38.

[13]The same incident happened in the case of Jamaica under leftist Prime Minister Michael Manley. His refusal to accept International Monetary Fund conditions of reduced public employment, budget cuts, and higher prices for desperately needed loans during 1980 led commercial banks to refuse extension of further credits until Jamaica resumed negotiations with the International Monetary Fund. Manley's electoral defeat by Edward Seaga, a strong advocate of private enterprise, resulted in a prompt renegotiation of the Fund Loan package and the resumption of private bank credits. The same is true with President Allende of Chile who refused to accept the Fund policies because of its socio-economic and political effects. Also, see New Nigerian, 8 October 1986, p. 5.

countries to the advantaged capitalist states. Cheryl Payer argues in this way that:

> The [International loan] system can be compared point by point with peonage on an individual scale. In the peonage or debt slavery, system the worker is unable to use his nominal freedom to leave the service of his employer, because the latter supplies him with credit (for overpriced goods in the company store) necessary to supplement his meager wages. The aim of the employer-creditor-merchant is neither to collect the debt once and for all, nor to starve the employee to death, but rater to keep the laborer permanently indentured through his debt to the employer. The worker cannot run away, for other employers and the state recognize the legality of his debt; not has he any hope of earning his freedom with his low wage.
>
> Precisely the same system operates on the international level. Nominally independent countries find their debts, and their continuing inability to finance current needs out of imports [sic], keep them tied by a tight leash to their creditors. The IMF and [IBRD] orders them, in effect, to continue laboring on the plantations, while it refuses to finance their efforts to set up in business for themselves. For these reasons the term "international debt slavery" is a perfectly accurate one to describe the reality of their situation.[14]

Cheryl Payer puts the negative or adverse effects of such a prescription this way:

> The programs result, typically, in the takeover of domestically owned businesses by their foreign competitors. The stabilization program puts a squeeze on domestic capital in several ways. The depreciation which it causes cuts deeply into their sales. Devaluation raises the costs in local currency, of all imports needed for their business, and of all the unpaid debts resulting from past imports. This, a severe blow in itself, is compounded by the fact that the contraction of bank credit makes it more difficult than before to get the loans they need to carry on operations.[15]

---

[14]Cheryl Payer, "Perpetuation of Dependence: The IMF and the Third World", p. 40.

[15]Cheryl Payer, The Debt Trap: The International Monetary Fund and the Third World, (New York: Monthly Review Press, 1974), p. 41.

Payer further maintains that the liberation of imports robs these nations of the protected market they had enjoyed before, thereby making them vulnerable. The author asserts that "liberation of imports tends to benefit the foreign-owned firms, which are dependent of foreign inputs-raw materials, machinery, and spare parts-imported from another branch of the same multi-national corporation."[16]

As Payer noted above, these policies bring about untold hardships and misery to millions of people in these developing countries. Severe reductions in such programs as government spending on social services and subsidies always inevitably raise havoc with domestic markets. Robert Pollin and Eduardo Zepeda pointed out in the Monthly Review that, the "IMF was never ambiguous in its intention to cut back sharply on public enterprise, government subsidies, price controls, and deficit spending."[17] They stressed the fact that the Fund did not realize that such public sector activities provide the primary basis for effective demand in all economies of most Third World nations.[18] The authors assert that, the IMF on its part:

> Argues that domestic firms should shift to an export orientation after the public sector contracts. But this ignores what almost all economists recognize, that capturing export markets requires the time and sustained promotional effect, even after a country's products have become more competitive through devaluation.[19]

As stated by Kenneth W. Grundy, in The Atlanta Journal and Constitution, "to many in the West, the International Monetary Fund (IMF) is the financial white knight sent to save sick Third World economies from collapse. But to Third World leaders, the cure may be worse than the disease.[20] Pollin and Zepeda, writing in the Monthly Review, hit at the heart of the IMF politics. They convincingly argued that, the IMF has always

---

[16]Ibid.

[17]Robert Pollin and Eduardo Zepeda, "Latin American Debt," Monthly Review 38 (February 1987): p. 5.

[18]Ibid.

[19]Ibid.

[20]Kenneth W. Grundy, "To Some Poor Nations, IMF Cure is Worse Than the Disease," The Atlanta Journal and Constitution, 4 October 1987, p 6D.

represented the interest of the international banks and the developed countries' governments, particularly those of the United States, and has taken the initiative in organizing this group into what is in effect a coherent creditors cartel. The aim of the Fund's austerity program is therefore in full accord with the primary goal of the creditors cartel.[21] It was as a result of this factor among other that led to the Arusha Initiative of 1980, which called for the Fund's replacement by a new world monetary order. According to the Arusha Initiative: Money is power. This simple truth is valid for national and international relations. Those who wield power control money. An international monetary system is both a function and an instrument of prevailing power structures.

In the light of these policies just enumerated, the next question is: How does the Fund operate? That is, how does it get the money which it lends to its clients? We have noted earlier that, in almost all cases, the Fund will subject a debtor nation to undergo drastic changes in the way that country does business. For example: (a) reduction of state intervention in the economy and selling off some state companies: (b) more favorable tolerance of foreign investment and as pointed out in our introduction; (c) an austerity program including devaluation, price increases and spending cuts.

There are three ways in which the IMF gets funds it loans out to members. They are: (1) Quota, this is the method in which members contribute money to Fund in accordance with the members respective gross national product (GNP). This means the total worth of goods and services a country produces with respect to its volume of international trade. The wealthier a country, the more it contributes. This is where the center nations like the U.S., Japan, Britain, France and Germany have so much controlling influence in the structures of the Fund by virtue of the share of their huge contributions. It works this way: Twenty-five percent of the quota has to be paid in either Special Drawing Rights or in hard currencies, the latter being the currencies of the economically strong nations which are in demand, either to purchase that country's exports or to act as a reserve of value which, it is hoped will not be hit by devaluation. The rest can be paid in the country's

---

[21]Monthly Review, 38, (4 February 1987): p. 3.

own currency.[22] (2) the second method in which the Fund gets its resources is through the money the Fund borrows either from its members (over and above their quota contribution) or non-members, (3) the third way the Fund has its money is through Special Drawing Right (SDRs) which the Fund allocates to members from time to time. The SDR is not real money in a sense that the member nations can spend directly. Instead, they are credits in the member's account with the Fund. In essence, this can be used to buy from the Fund the hard currencies that the member nation needs to pay its foreign debts.

Moreover, beyond these policy prescriptions of the International Monetary Fund, less developed countries have sought to increase their access to Fund resources through enlargement of their quotas and implementation of a proposal to link new SDR allocations to increase development assistance for the less developed countries. However, between the 1970s and mid-1980s, IMF quotas were doubled. This has expanded the resources of the IMF to SDR 90 billion. Third World nations will be able to borrow more as their quota, like everyone else's are increased proportionately. As it turns outs, less developed countries as a group still account for only about 30 percent of total Fund quotas.[23]

The Third World nations have been far more frustrated in their efforts to link special drawing rights to their development aspirations. SDRs are created in accordance with international liquidity needs and are disbursed to member states of the Fund in proportion to their quotas. Hence, the Third World nations receive only approximately 30 percent of any new SDR allocations. For many years less developed countries have pressed for a variety of proposals that would distribute new SDR allocations primarily to nations - either directly or through such International Organizations as International Bank for Reconstruction and Development. Ronald Walter in Foreign Policy comments on this:

> Because of the less developed countries' great need for imports, the newly granted reserves would finance increased purchases from the advanced industrial societies; the purchases would in

---

[22]David H. Blake and Robert S. Walters, The Politics of Global Economic Relations (New Jersey: Prentice Hall, Inc., Englewood Cliffs, Third Edition, 1987), p. 61.

[23]Onyema Ugochukwu, "The Trouble With the IMF", New Nigeria, p. 4.

turn contribute to the development objectives of the developing countries. Greater liquidity would, but instead of SDR reserve sitting more   or less idle in rich countries with balance-of-payment surpluses, they would be working to provide needed goods and services in the poor countries-goods and services that would be obtained largely from the advanced industrial states of the West. Special Drawing Rights would, in essence, be allocated to less developed countries with the expectation that they would be recycled to the advanced industrial countries. Hence, decision makers in advance industrial sources have remained very cool to such proposals, since the SDRs are to have the possibility of emerging as the principal international reserve asset replacing existing international currency, the U.S. dollar.[24]

The complaints of the Third World nations about the International Monetary Fund extend beyond the limits upon and terms attached to their borrowing condition. They seek a more potent role of the International Monetary Fund's decision-making process. The Fund relies upon a weighted voting arrangement reflective of countries' quotas. Although less developed countries comprise three-fourth of the IMF membership, they hold only about one-third of the votes.[25] The United States alone has according to Blake and Walter 19.8 percent of the votes in the International Monetary Fund, and the five largest industrial countries of the West together account for 40 percent of the votes in the Fund. Until well into the 1960s, moreover, the most important international monetary deliberations and decisions took place in the Group of Ten - a body meeting under the auspices of the Organization for Economic Cooperation and Development in Paris that performed a kind of executive function for the entire international monetary order, including the IMF. The Group of Ten comprises only the most important advanced industrial states, and the less developed countries were seldom even consulted about deliberations conducted.

Over the years the less developed countries have fought to enhance their "voting power in the International Monetary Fund and to move international monetary decision making into forums; including International

---

[24]For a brief overview of SDR link ideas see "SDRs and Development, $10 Billion for Whom", Foreign Policy, No. 8, (Fall 1972), p. 102-128.

[25]Blake and Walter, The Politics of Global Economic Relation, pp. 61-63.

Monetary Fund, where their power could be felt. Thus, in response to these pressures, in combination with other events, the International Monetary Fund has become a more central forum for key international monetary deliberation."[26] Gruhn also indicates that:

> The most capital flows to low income African states made up mainly of concessional aid, much of it from the network of international donor agencies themselves. These flows, their targets and their management, are directly and intentionally held in the hand of international bureaucrats. In this second context, the IMF, by design, and in the previous context, by default and design, can influence the quantity and type of international capital flows to the African LDCs. But perhaps as serious as their power over funds is the increasing control over African policies -- economic, political, social -- which can be demanded as preconditions for a favorable consideration for assistance. Not only can the IMF tell a country what policy reforms it must institute but in quite a few African states the IMF and other international agency personnel can and do insist that African ministries be supervised by international officials on the ground. It is not surprising that the term recolonization comes to mind as one views such a degree and extent of external, albeit international, bureaucratic control.[27]

Nigeria, agreeing to become a patient of the International Monetary Fund, surprises some and dismays many, particularly inside Nigeria, because many people have assumed that the Nigerian economy had options and alternatives other than the IMF policy prescriptions for its economic recovery.[28] Chapter 8 argues in line with Gruhn that Nigeria actually has alternative arrangements other than the IMF macroeconomic policies in addressing its economic problem.

> Furthermore, the Brandt Commission, in its first report, argued that the conditions imposed on deficit countries had forced unnecessary and unacceptable political burdens on the poorest,

---

[26]Ibid.

[27]Gruhn, p. 38.

[28]Ibid., p. 44.

on occasions leading to IMF riots and even the downfall of governments.[29]

It has been charged that the IMF programs are not solving the structural balance of payment problems that most debtor countries confront; rather, the exorbitant costs of the IMF restructuring fall on the weak shoulders of the poorest segment of the population as was the case in Chile, Peru, and Jamaica to name a few. The draconian measures ignite social unrest in these countries.

Further still, it has been charged that many of the MNCs (multinational corporations) in the center nation use their economic power and political leverage to compel developing nations to seek Fund assistance, thereby acquiescing to the conditionality. This will, in the final analysis, benefit the center nations which use the Fund's resources as an instrument of their own foreign policy objectives as has increasingly become the case in Central and Latin America.

As noted, country after country assessments point to the fact that the IMF policies do not work in many of the cases. The prescriptions preferred by the Fund for solving the balance of payment problem of Third World countries, particularly those committed to reform rather than radical change, end in disaster. Instead, the Fund medicine exacerbates the illness of the patient not only socially but economically as well.[30] Further, it has been charged that the Fund is politically biased in its overall thrust of its policies when it encounters reform-oriented regimes. The bottom line in this case is to realign these Third World government's policies in accordance with a defined package of economic and political priorities suited to the needs of center nations.[31]

Also, President Nyerere in the North-South Conference of July 1980 on the International Monetary System and the New International Economic Order indicated that:

> There was a time when a number of people were urging that all aid to the Third World countries should be channeled through

---

[29]Latin American Bureau, Poverty Brokers: The IMF and Latin America, pp. 31-32.

[30]"The Bank, the Fund and the People of Africa," This Week, September 1987: p. 17.

[31]Ibid., p. 23.

international institutions.   They honestly believed that such institutions would be political and ideologically neutral.[32]

The Fund has an ideology of economic and social development which it is trying to impose on the poor countries irrespective of their own clearly stated policies.   And when we reject IMF conditions, we hear the threatening whisper: "without accepting our conditions you will not get our money, and you will get no other money."[33]

Teresa Hayter has documented the purpose and objective of foreign aid to the developing nations.   In her book, Aid As Imperialism, she demonstrates how the international institutions such as, the IMF, the World Bank and the United States Agency for International Development have colluded by acting only in their interests, under the guise of aid for the developing countries.   It is an open secret that aid serves the purpose of the advanced capitalist countries.

> Aid is, in general, available to countries whose internal political arrangements, foreign policy alignments, treatment of foreign private investment, debt servicing record, export policies, and so on, are considered desirable, potentially desirable, or at least acceptable, by the countries or institutions providing aid, and which do not appear to threaten their interest.[34]

On the surface, this would appear to be the necessary conditions to solicit another's help, but one has to consider the history of exploitation and the terms of trade that developed countries have had over developing ones.

Hayter further elaborated on her observation by examining the operations of these agencies in four Latin American countries: Columbia, Chile, Brazil, and Peru.   Although the circumstances were not quite similar, the underlying results were.   In dealing with those countries that have had populist governments intent on making mild reforms, such as expansion and redistribution of land, the IMF will call for devaluation of their currency and

---

[32]President Nyerere, Development Dialogue, (Hammarskjold Foundation, July 1980-1982), p. 8.

[33]Ibid., p. 9.

[34]Teresa Hayter, Aid As Imperialism (England: Penguin Books, Ltd., 1972), pp. 15-16.

cuts in government expenditures which also conflict with the national policy, therefore hindering further negotiations with the IMF. The World Bank and AID have tried to influence the political process, but because their aid was on a long term basis, it was not easy to sever relationships. The question that needs to be asked is who benefits from aid given by those international agencies?

> The critical issue is whether the present systems of economic and social organization in Latin America, based on private enterprise, a respect for property, however unequally distributed, and economic and political dependence on the United States, are capable of providing real improvements in the conditions of life of the masses of the people. The policies of the international agencies imply that they are, or that such improvement is unnecessary secondary to other considerations or simply that the United States, supported by the major financial agencies, is determined to preserve the existing situation for as long as possible...[35]

John Cavanagh also did some studies on the "Debt Crisis." In his book, From Debt to Development, he stated that, "in most Third World discussions of the impact of the debt crisis, IMF austerity or conditionality is mentioned first." The IMF lends to a financially troubled country only after that country submits to an economic program of demand management. The logic behind the program is that if a country is spending more than it takes in, demand for goods and services must be reduced, imports cut, and exports boosted.

This is traditionally done through a combination of policies: (1) making imports more expensive (via devaluation of currency), and (2) making basic goods more expensive (via the elimination of government subsidies).

The author summarized the treatment as follows:
> The IMF approaches its patient in much the same fashion as the medieval doctor. Regardless of the disorder, leeches are applied and the patient is bled. At best, the remedy supplants the original disorder with a new agony, often more lethal than original. Even for countries where the IMF remedy ups the

---

[35]Ibid., p. 163.

trade balance, the underlying debt, and development crisis go on, and the pain produced is even more severe.[36]

Hence, different segments of the Third World populations respond to the bleeding, the financial squeeze, and the export orientation in different ways.

He further noted that:

Despite the IMF's precipitous growth from forty-five original member nations to 151 today, it still remains one of the least democratic of all international organizations. Unlike most United Nations agencies, where the one-nation, one vote principle governs, the IMF assigns votes roughly according to the economic size of each nation. Hence, all black African nations together possess less power than Great Britian. The United States with 20 percent of the total voting power, exceeds the combined total of Latin American and Black Africa. Another factor enhancing U. S. and other developed country power is that the Soviet Union and several eastern European nations are not members.[37]

Cheryl Payer states the basic foundation of the IMF operations in her book, The Debt Trap: The IMF and the Third World. It is necessary to have an organization like the IMF because of growing interdependency and trading among nations. When nations trade, they have different balances because of the division of labor and capital around the world. The developed countries trade among themselves predominantly in finished goods and trade with the LDCs for raw materials. Historically, the developed countries have had the advantage in trading, because raw materials are price inelastic depending on the whim and fancy of the developed countries. As importantly, the developed countries have control of the markets, and often use the market forces to depress or accelerate the usage of developing countries' raw materials.

Over time the developed countries have had the advantage over the developing nations in trading resulting in unequal exchange rates. The

---

[36]John Cavanagh, From Debt to Development: Alternative to the International Debt Crisis (Washington, DC.: Institute for Policy Studies, 1985), p. 9.

[37]Ibid., p. 21.

fluctuation in demand for raw materials and the pricing of them by the developed countries have exacerbated the unequal exchange problem. The IMF as an international organization should be addressing the problem of equality in trading and unequal exchange rate, but its record is one of failure to address those issues, while it blames the victim, the Third World countries, for inefficiency.

The IMF, according to Payer, serves as a forerunner to all major sources of credit in the developed capitalist world whether private lenders, governments or multilateral institutions such as the World Bank. If not approved by the IMF, the particular country will find it difficult to refinance its trade deficit from its creditor nations and their agencies.

She, therefore, concludes that, in fact what occurs is:

> The IMF is not the real villain of the piece, though it is the agent of the villains. They are in multinational corporations and capitalist governments which are the natural enemies of Third World independence and can usually mobilize the resources to crush it.[38]

This adds weight to Hayter's notion, that aid was a secondary source of influence. I believe, now, that the existence of aid can be explained only in terms of an attempt to preserve the capitalist system in the Third World. Aid is not a particularly effective instrument for achievement; hence, its current decline. but, in so far as it is effective, its contribution to the well-being of the peoples of the Third World is negative, since it is not in their interest that exploitation should continue.[39]

The IMF today continues to provide short-term balance of payments financing and now oversees the loose system of floating exchange rates that has replaced the fixed exchange rates system agreed upon at Bretton Woods. More importantly, the IMF has become the institution which holds up or releases lending by both official aid agencies and private commercial banks - neither of who will lend for long to governments out of favor with the IMF. Thus, the IMF has vast power not only virtually to determine which countries

---

[38]Payer, The Debt Trap: The International Monetary Fund and the Third World, pp. xii-xiii.

[39]Hayter, Aid As Imperialism

will qualify for external loans, but also dictate national economic policies to debtor nations' governments.[40] The adoption of the IMF-backed policies has, in fact, become the quid pro quo for receipt of IMF credit - and hence loans from other private and public sources.[41]

Finally, the world has been dramatically transformed since the Bretton Woods Conference. While the formal monetary framework and the values it expresses remain unchanged. The less developed countries have insistently questioned the legitimacy and adequacy of monetary rules, laws and mechanisms in whose design the majority of them did not participate. Furthermore, there was an inherent contradiction in the international monetary system itself: between the role of the United States dollar as the main source of international liquidity and its function as a stable international store of value. The prolonged payments deficits of the U.S. led to the suspension by that country, in 1971, of the convertibility of the dollar into gold and to the termination of the system of fixed exchange parities.[42] This evolution reflected a crisis in the industrialized capitalist system. More specifically, they represented the erosion of the conceptual foundations upon which the Bretton Woods system was built and the consequent loss of legitimacy on the part of the International Monetary Fund.

---

[40]Blake and Walter, The Politics of Global Economic Relations, p. 60-61.
[41]Ibid.
[42]J.E. Spero, The Politics of International Economic Relations, p. 53-55.

Figure I

DEVELOPED AND LESS DEVELOPED NATIONS

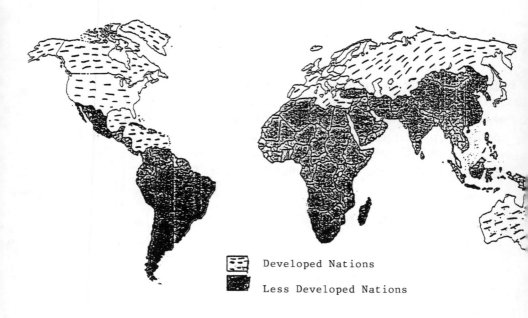

Developed Nations

Less Developed Nations

CHAPTER 3

The Historical Impact Of British Colonial Rule In Africa

This chapter will be used to discuss how Nigeria became entrenched as a dependent part of world economy, first through slave trade and later, through British colonialism. It is important to point out the essential linkage between slave trade, British colonialism, multi-national corporations and modern world imperialism in order to understand the essential nature of the discussion on the economic colonialism in Nigeria and the International Monetary Fund. Therefore, the intention here is to present in a capsulated form the historical analysis of the development of Nigerian society and polity especially before the IMF involvement. The discussion will be a review of Nigeria's emergence as a dependent less developed social formation, showing fairly broad historical features of the political and socio-economic structure and relations.

Anyone who is familiar with the history and diversities that exist in Nigeria will agree that it is not possible to generalize about the history of Nigeria even as of today, not to talk of pre-colonial days. However, attempt will be made here to mention the important features of Nigerian history. No detailed analysis will be attempted. The heterogeneity in Nigeria is so pronounced that to attempt a detailed discussion of the historical background of the country in this work will completely remove the work from its subject-matter and objective.

The main focus will be on the major events, major ethnic groups, and the major political and socio-economic structure and relations. This approach is not an attempt to despise the "minor" events and minority groups within Nigeria. It is not done out of bias for or against any group. It is simply that the nature of the discussion, particularly as essential in this work, does not permit detailed analysis and full attention to all the diverse ethnic groups, events, and politico-socio-economic structure, relation, and systems in pre-colonial (and even modern Nigeria).

The country is bounded on the west by the Republic of Benin (formerly Dahomey), on the north by the Republic of Niger, on the east by the Republic of Cameroun, and on the south by the Gulf of Guinea. Nigeria's coastline is intersected by an intricate network of creeks and rivers and by the great Niger Delta. The most important river in Nigeria is the Niger--the third longest river in Africa.

Nigeria is rich in mineral resources. The most important among these resources are petroleum oil, limestone, coal, tin, columbite, gold and silver, lead-zinc, gypsum, glass sands, clay, asbestos, graphite, iron ore, stone and zircon. While the deposits of some of these minerals have been fairly well determined, further surveys have been found to be essential in order to locate and assess the reserve of others. Nigeria is the only country in West Aftrica producing coal. It has reserves of about 245 million tons.

Nigeria is one of the world's most important producers of tropical timbers. The country is also one of the world's largest producer of cocoa. Other important products in Nigeria are rubber, groundnuts, cotton and soya bean. Over the greater part of the rain forest belt in Nigeria, yam and cassava are the main food crops. Other food crops of varying significance are plaintain, maize, coco-yam, rice fruits and vegetables,. The savannah zone of the country provides excellent grass land for cattle rearing and the bulk of the country's cattle, sheep and goats come from the area. These provide beef, milk, hides and skin mainly for local consumption.[1]

Nigeria as a political unit in the modern sense really came into being only in 1914. However, the making of the country spanned a much longer period and embraced epochs of Arab influence in the north and European influence in the South.

Although the early history of Nigeria has been largely a matter of speculation and legendary stories, it is a recorded fact that Europeans did not

---

[1]Federal Ministry of Information, Nigeria. Nigeria Handbook, 1973, Chapter 1.

explore the interior of what came to be Nigeria until the beginning of the 19th century. Also it is known that up to the beginning of that century, there existed in the area strong forest kingdoms such as the Yoruba and Benin Kingdoms which had once been the most powerful kingdoms along the Western coast of Africa spreading as far out as what is Accra in Ghana today. Also, within the frontiers of what came to be formed into Nigeria by the British, towards the north were the great kingdom of Bornu with a known history of more than 1,000 years; the Fulani Empire which had, centuries before its conquest by the British,ruled most of the savannah areas of the country and the city-states of the Niger Republic of modern Africa.[2]

The area which came to be named "Nigeria" consisted of a population made up of diverse ethnic groups. Nigeria still retains this feature today. The major ethnic groups are Hausa, Yoruba, Ibo, Fulani, Kanuri, Ibibio, Tiv, Ijaw, Edo, Annang, Nupe, Urhob, Igala, Idoma, Igbirra, Gwari, Ekoi, Mumuye, Alago, Ogini, Isoko, Higgi, Bura Efiki, Ghamba, Shaua-Arab, Kaje, Tari, Kambari, Eggon, Kobehi, Anga, Karkare, Birom and Yergam.

The population that was formed into Nigeria occupied a geographical territory much larger and different from what is now Nigeria. There were no political and geographical boundaries or demarcations in any way close to what are known in africa today.   The tribes or clans used natural demarcations such as rivers, mountains, valleys, rocks and so on to identify "boundaries" between their farmland holdings.

When the colonialists arrived, they introduced clearly marked political boundaries between the tribes and separated them arbitrarily. The story of the scramble for Africa is quite familiar and needs not be repeated here. The Berlin Conference of 1884 finalized the partition of Africa among the Western European nations. The colonialists created illusory political boundaries and

---

[2]See: J.C.O. Anene Southern Nigeria in Transition 1885-1906 (Cambridge University Press, England, 1966). Sir Alan Burns, History of Nigeria (Allen and Unwin, 7th ed., 1969); R.E. Bradbury, The Benin Kingdom and Edo Speaking People of South-western Nigeria (London: International African Institute, 1957). Samuel Johnson, History of the Yorubas, op. cit; Daryll Forde and P.M. Kabbery, West Aftican Kingdoms in the 19th Century (Published for the International African Institute by Oxford University Press, 1967) H.A.S. Johnson, The Fulani Emprie of Sokoto (London: Oxford University Press, 1967); Sir Charles Orr The Making of Northern Nigeria (Cass, 1965. Reprint of 1911 edition); E.G. Parrinder, The Story of Ketu, An Ancient Yoruba Kingdom, 2nd ed. I.A. Akinjogbin, ed., (Ibadan University Press, 1967); A. Shultze, The Sultanate of Bornu translated by P.A. Benton (Cass, 1968), J. U. Egharevba, Short History of Benin (Ibadan University Press, 1968).

destroyed the unity of the ethnic groups by scattering then in different countries under different European colonialists. For example, some parts of Yoruba land came under the British and the other parts were forced under French rule. Yoruba territory extended far beyond the borders of present-day Nigeria. The Yoruba language is still the mother-tongue of many groups in various parts of West Africa--particularly along the coast--outside Nigeria. This shows the arbitrary nature of the political and geographical boundaries set up without regard and respect for cohesion, unity and cultural ties that were in existence among the diverse ethnic groups. Parts of Yoruba land were placed in Benin Republic (formerly Dahomey), Togo and other countries along the coast of West Africa; parts of Hausa and Fulani territories were placed in French-speaking countries of Upper Volta, Chad, Niger and Central Africa Republic. In the eastern part of Nigeria, some of the Ibibios were placed in Cameroon and Gabon while the others and the many other ethnic groups were grouped together as part of Nigeria. The point being raised here is not that a nation-state should be made up solely of one ethnic group, rather it is meant to emphasize the big disregard for ethnic solidarity and continued cohesion involved in the political boundaries of African countries drawn by the colonialists.[3]

The first Europeans to visit the coast of what is modern Nigeria were the Portuguese. In the winter of 1472-73, Fernando Po and Pero de Centra first explored what was formerly the Bight of Biafra, and Bight of Benin. In 1485, Jao Affonso d'Aveiro, a Portuguese made the first journey to Benin.

The first English ships, under the command of Captain Windham, reached the Bight of Benin in 1553. After a journey of about six months, one of the ships penetrated the Benin river and some members of the crew and other British merchants landed and went to visit the Oba of Benin.

The Portuguese trade with Benin consisted at first mainly of pepper which later gave way to slaves in which all the European powers at that time participated. The arrival of Captain Windham in the Bight of Benin broke Portuguese trade monopoly on the West coast of Africa. From then on

---

[3]See Kopytoff, Jean Herskovits, A Preface to Modern Nigeria: The "Sierra-Leonians" in Yoruba, 1830-1890. (Madison: University of Wisconsin Press, 1965).

England was to establish herself not only as a leading trader on the coast, but also as one of the chief exporters of slaves.[4]

The stimulus to this colossal traffic in human beings was the discovery of the America and the realization of their mineral and agricultural potentials. Thus, in the next 500 years, the west coast of Africa became a center of European enterprise and rivalry with slaves as the prize.

When the desire to find markets for Britain's new industries became higher than the need to get slaves to work in America, Britain took active part in the movement for the abolition of the horrible trade in human beings. With the increased desire for finding markets and sources of raw materials, Britain intensified it participation in the exploration of the African coast. In West Africa, the exploration journey which started with the coast was soon extended to the interior. British explorers penetrated the hinterland of the Niger river area. With all forms of strategies including force and intrigue, the European explorers gradually gained influence and foothold around the River Niger and in the interior of West Africa.

The African chiefs and leaders were not happy about European penetration of Africa. For example, in the area that was later named Nigeria, many leaders and chiefs resisted vehemently European intrusion into their land. Even when many of the African chiefs and leaders were of Nigerian nationalists who were then organizing for political action to press for the right to self-determination for Nigerians. The circumstances of the time and the pressures of the nationalist leaders, the pioneer of whom was Herbert Macaulay, followed by Dr. Nnamdi Azikiwe, Chief Obafemi Awolowo, Chief Bode Thomas, Mbonu Ojike, Aminu Kano and others made it clear to the British,that Nigerians wanted more autonomy. Constitutional conferences on Nigeria were held in London in 1953 and in Lagos in 1954 under the chairmanship of the British Secretary of State for the Colonies at that time.

As a result of the 1953 and 1954 conferences a new constitution, which formed the basis of what was the Nigerian constitution which was suspended when the military came to power in 1966, came into force on October 1, 1954. Nigeria then became a federation consisting of five component parts: the

---

[4]Nigeria Handbook, 1973 op. cit. Chapter 2. See also: Michael Crowder, The Story of Nigeria, 2nd ed. (Faber, 1966); G.I. Jones, The Trading States of the Oil Rivers (Oxford University Press, 1963).

Northern, Eastern and Western Regions, the Federal Territory of Lagos and the quasi-Federal territory of the Southern Cameroons (now part of the United Republic of Cameroon) under United Kingdom Trusteeship. The Federal Government was given exclusive jurisdiction over such important subjects as aviation, banks, census, customs, defense, exchange control, external affairs, immigration, police, shipping, mines and minerals, posts and telegraphs, railways and trunk roads, trade and commerce between Nigeria and other countries and between the Regions. Jurisdiction was shared between the Federal and other Governments on such subjects as bankruptcy, electricity, industrial development, insurance, labor, registration of business names, scientific and industrial research, statistics and water power. Residual matters for which no provision was made in either the exclusive or the concurrent legislative list or in the Constitution Order-in-Council became the responsibility of the Regional legislatures.   In 1957 another constitutional conference on Nigeria was held in London. In that conference, arrangements were completed to enable then Eastern and the Western Regions to become self-governing later in the same year. The first Federal Prime Minister of Nigeria was appointed in August 1957. It was also decided that a second chamber--House of Chiefs--should be set up in then Eastern Region. Then the Northern and Western Regions were already having bicameral legislatures. It was decided too that after the dissolution of the House of Representatives towards the end of 1959 there should be two legislative houses at the Center for the Federation--the House of Representatives which should have 312 elected members and the Senate with 44 nominated members.

In September 1958, the Constitutional Conference resumed once again in London where it was agreed that the then Northern Region should become self-governing in March 1959. The British Government also agreed that if a resolution for independence was passed by the new Federal Parliament early in 1960, the British Government would agree to that resolution and would introduce a bill in its own Parliament to enable Nigeria to become a fully independent country on the 1st of October 1960.

Elections to the new House of Representatives were held December 1959. At the first meeting of the Federal Legislature in Lagos in January 1960, both Houses unanimously passed the resolution calling for independence. The British Government followed up with introducing a bill in its own Parliament to grant full independence to Nigeria on October 1, 1960. The Nigerian (Constitution) Order-in-Council, 1960 was passed on September 12, 1960. This Order came into effect on October 1, 1960, and Nigeria became an independent sovereign nation with effect from that date. The first Nigerian Governor-General, Dr. Nuamdi Azikiwe, took office in November of the same year--still as a representative of the British crown. The former British Cameroons, (united Nations Trust Territory administered by the British Government as part of Nigeria) opted to split into two. Northern Cameroon joined Nigeria and Southern Cameroon joined French Cameroon to form Cameroon Republic.

The Mid-Western Region was created in August 1963 following a referendum held on 13th July 1963. On October 1, 1963, Nigeria became a Republic within the commonwealth of nations.

Nigeria with a population of about one hundred million people, may yet offer an alternative to the usual Third World stereotype of underdevelopment, dependency, and political instability due to external forces beyond its control.

The structure and nature of underdevelopment and dependency in Nigeria are the product of both internal and external factors. As we mention earlier in this chapter, when the British arrived, they introduced clearly marked political boundaries between the tribes and separated them arbitrarily. It was part of a larger movement by which almost the entire African continent was placed under European administration. By 1900, the whole continent, with the exception of Liberia, Morocco, and Ethiopia, was under different European administrative managements.The colonial powers include Britain, Germany, Portugal, Italy, Belgium, France, and Spain. Figure 2 puts the whole situation in a proper perspective. They had divided the people and the land according to their trade and commercial objectives. The geographical boundaries created by the European powers had much to do with political and socio-economic realities of African states in general and Nigeria in particular. The Northern and Southern Protectorates of Nigeria and the Colony of Lagos were classic instances of what was happening throughout Africa.

Their amalgamation into one country called Nigeria in 1914 revealed the British view of Africans at that time. The British tended to regard all Nigerian societies as homogeneous. The assumption was that Yoruba urban kingdoms, the Fulani governed emirates, communities such as the Nupe and

Tiv, the village unity of the Ibos, the commercial ports of the Niger delta and the mixed societies of Lagos could all be "melted in a single pot". That assumptions showed a total lack of understanding of the complex nature of Nigerian Societies. Colonial rule was thus imposed without enough understanding of the implications and consequences.[5]

The artificiality of Nigeria's boundaries and sharp culture differences among its peoples point up the fact that Nigeria is a British creation and the concept of a Nigerian nation is the result of the British presence. This situation forces Callaway to conclude that Inherent traditional divisions within the country were underscored and reinforced by the former colonial power, Great Britain.

With the achievement of political independence in 1960, the economy of Nigeria is still shaped in part by its past experience as an European colony. Understanding colonialism's impact is important for gaining insight into the causes of Nigeria's current problems. However, this research is not going to detail any significant degree the historical foundation of colonialism and its socio-economic impact on the political economy of Nigeria. This chapter briefly examines the historical development of Nigeria. An examination of the historical development will be utilized to address the contemporary political arrangements that emerged after independence. The historical foundation of Nigeria's political and economic history will provide the framework to understand the dynamics of the economy and post-independence political developments. According to Callaway:

> The structure of the economy is related to pre-colonial cleavage, colonial exploitation and post independence political maneuvering. Divisions in Nigerian society are both horizontal and vertical. Emerging class distinctions were deeply cut by ethnic cleavages while a colonially inherited federal structure reinforced social inequalities and economic imbalances.These

---

[5]For analysis of British Colonial Administration in Nigeria, see James Coleman Nigeria: Background to Nationalism, (Berkeley: University of California Press, 1958); S.O. Okafor, Indirect Rule: The Development of Central Legislature in Nigeria, (Nigeria: Ibadan, Nelson Ltd., 1981); Uma Eleazu, Federation and National Building, (Devon: Arthur H. Stockwell, 1977).

imbalances exacerbated perceptions of political domination and unequal modernization. The result was full-scale civil war.[6]

Figure 2

EUROPEAN COLONIALIZATION IN AFRICA (1884-1900)

French
British
Portuguese
German
Italian
Spanish
Turkish
Independent

---

[6]Barbara Callaway, "The Political Economy of Nigeria" in Harris ed. Political Economy of Africa, P. 95

Callaway further explains that the emergence of the military rule had served only to reschedule the working out of more permanent solutions in the Nigerian political system.

> Nigeria is an artificial creation of European diplomacy and expansionism. Its role in the world capitalist economy was as a primary producer for the manufacturing industries of Europe on which it in turn depended for manufactured goods.In particular, the British administration's perception of the Nigerian economy came chiefly through its foreign trade in which British merchant houses played a predominant role. The economy was dominated by extra-territorial firms concerned with marketing the country's primary agricultural products. The traditional society was disrupted and social relations rearranged in accordance with the needs of colonial capitalism.Foreign concerns made huge profits, but did not use them for industrial investment within the country.The country was thus locked into a situation that virtually excluded industrialization either as a way of increasing self-reliance or of increasing the standard of living.With the rise of the oil industry, Nigeria has clearly joined the group of countries primarily exploited for their mineral rather than agricultural resources. Despite the increased revenues,capital formation for industrial development has not followed to any significant degree. Production relations remain frozen into a shape that was determined by the way in which the Nigerian economy has been forcefully fitted into the world market under the control of foreign business interests. Despite flag independence, the fundamental situation of economic dependence and underdevelopment persists.[7]

Historical Background of Nigeria

In reality,

> Nigeria is a British imperial creation and as such its fundamental history reflects British imperialistic concerns. The roots of serious divisions between peoples and cultures which bedevil any quest for Nigerian unity existed before the British

---

[7]Chibuzo N. Nwoke, "Towards Authentic Economic Nationalism in Nigeria", Africa Today, (October 15, 1987).

arrived on the scene, but British colonial policies greatly exacerbated these tensions.[8]

This chapter, therefore, covers the period from 1960-present. However, a history of pre-independence will be briefly examined. The objective is to show what type of political, economic and social structure the British colonial government developed for Nigeria during the colonial period and the impact it is still having on the political economy of Nigeria.

With a land area of 357,000 square miles and a population estimated between 90 and 100 million, Nigeria is by far the most populous country in Africa. The Northern region was the largest of all the regions, containing four-fifths of the land area and about half of the population. Following the two military coups of 1966 (January and July), the country was divided into twelve states in 1967; in 1976 seven states were created and in 1987 two more states were added on to bring the total to twenty-one states. (See Figures 3 through 6) Since our analysis will cover aspects of the First National Plan (1962-1968) and developments within the political system at this period, frequent reference will be made to regions and regional governments. This period is essential in our study because it is the first time Nigeria had implemented the First National Development Plan after her independence in 1960.

Regional government in Nigeria originated with the constitution of 1946 which established consultative bodies in the regions. These bodies were eventually to achieve legislative powers, and by 1963, the framework of the federation had virtually been consolidated.

The interesting aspect of these constitutional arrangements was that there was a built-in pattern of conflict and competition among the regions; despite this, there had to be complete agreement amongst all the regions before the federal machinery could function adequately. The initiative seemed to rest more with the regions rather than the federal authority, a situation which was not conducive to cohesiveness even assuming that the regions were composed of like peoples. The Northern region furthermore, because of its size and population, occupied a dominant position by the sheer fact that it was larger

---

[8]Billy Dudley, Instability and Political Order: Politics and Crisis in Nigeria (Ibadan, Nigeria: Ibadan University Press, 1973), P. 96.

Table I

THE 21 STATES OF NIGERIA (23rd SEPTEMBER 1987)

State	Capital
Akwalbom	Uyo
Anambra	Enugu
Bauchi	Bauchi
Benue	Makurdi
Borno	Maidurugi
Cross River	Calabar
Gongola	Yola
Imo	Owerri
Kaduna	Kaduna
Kano	Kano
Kastina	Kastina
Kwara	Ilorin
Lagos	Ikeja
Niger	Minna
Ogun	Abeokuta
Ondo	Akure
Oyo	Ibadan
Platea	Jos
Rivers	Port Harcourt
Sokoto	Sokoto

SOURCE: Provided by the Author

Figure 3

THE FOUR REGIONS (1963 through 1967)

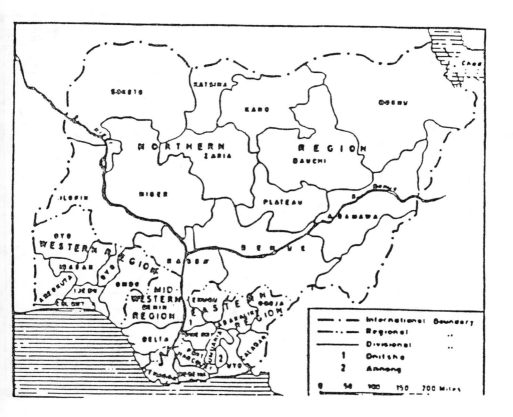

Fig. 3. Nigeria: The Four Regions (1963 through 1967).   Source: Edwin Dean, Plan Implementation in Nigeria 1962-1966.   Ibadan: Oxford University Press, 1972.

Figure 4

THE TWELVE   STATES DECLARED IN 1967.

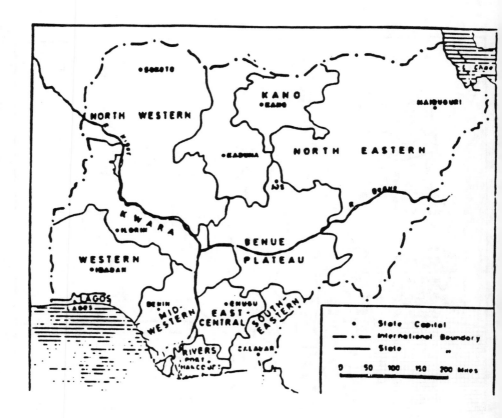

Fig 4. Nigeria: The Twelve States Declared in 1967. Source Dean, Plan Implementation in Nigeria 1962-1966.

Figure 5

THE NINETEEN STATES

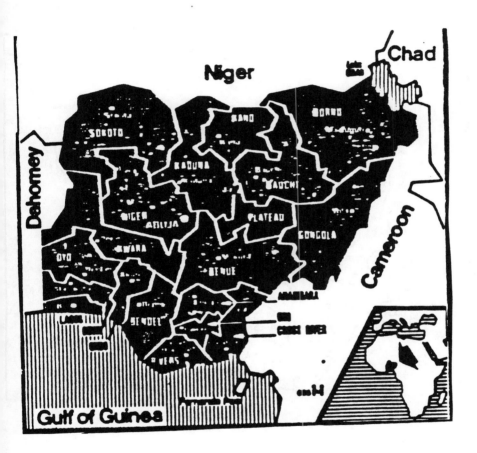

Fig. 5 Nigeria: 1976, The Nineteen States. Source: African Development, Vol. 10, No. 3, (March 1976).

Figure 6

THE CREATION OF TWO NEW STATES

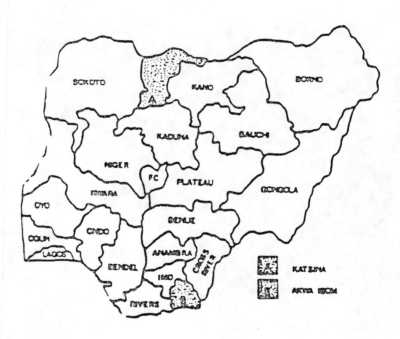

Fig. 6. The creation of the two new states: Katsina and Akwa Ibom, was announced in a Government National broadcast of 23rd September, 1987. Source: Africa Research Bulletin, October 14, 1987.

than all the other regions put together.[9]

Nigeria consists of numerous ethnic groups with over 200 languages spoken across the nation. The precariousness of the regional arrangement, however, becomes clearer when one discovers that the three major ethnic groups occupied the three regions respectively at the outset. The Northern region consisted basically of the Hausa-Fulani; the Eastern region of the Ibo, while the Western region had the Yoruba as its major ethnic group. As was mentioned previously, the North, because of its size and numerical superiority, was bound to occupy a position of dominance despite its economic and educational backwardness. The Eastern region was the most densely populated of all the regions, accounting for the substantial migration of Easterners to other parts of the federation. Not mentioned in this arrangement were numerous minority groups who were to spearhead the demand for the creation of smaller states which would recognize their existence.

Perhaps the only diversity which has served Nigeria well has been the diversity of its exports which have made the Nigerian economy a relatively strong one by African standards. Like most African countries, Nigeria is an export-oriented nation. Helleiner demonstrates that government revenues coming from the foreign trade sector accounted for over 61 percent of all government revenue in ten of the twelve years prior to 1962"[10] recent statistics indicate that the percentage continues to rise. However, unlike most other African countries, Nigeria's size accounts for an unusual diversity of agricultural products. Exports include cocoa, cotton, rubber, groundnut, palm produce, tin and crude oil. The discovery of large quantities of crude oil has made Nigeria one of the largest exporters of oil, and many Nigerians believe that by now the country should have financed substantial development. Despite the strength of the Nigerian economy in the 1960s and 1970s, the

---

[9]For informative accounts of Nigerian constitutional developments, provisions and powers at various levels, see O.I. Odumosu, The Nigerian Constitution: History and Development (London: Sweet and Maxwell, 1963); K. Ezera, Constitutional Developments in Nigeria (London: Cambridge University Press, 1960); F.A.O. Schwarz, Jr., "Nigeria's Constituion and Economic Development, " in Managing Economic Development in Africa ed. W.H. Hausman (Cambridge, Massachusetts: M.I.T. Press, 1963).

[10]Gerald K. Helleiner, Peasant Agriculture, Government, and Growth in Africa (Homewood, Illinois: Irwin, 1966).

political framework was weak and was to result in four coups, a civil war and military rule which continues till today. In order to place all the above in some kind of perspective, we have to go back and say something about British colonial administration of Nigeria.

British Colonial Administration

By 1914, the colonization of the whole of Nigeria was complete. However, the North and South of the country were treated as two separate administrative and political entities. The resulting effect of this policy was a development of standards in the two regions of the country which became impossible to compromise at the time of independence.[11]

The British employed the colonial policy of "Indirect Rule" in the administration of the North. The central aim of Indirect Rule according to Callaway is the idea that traditional authorities in the colonies should be recognized where ever possible and that the metropolitan power should seek to coopt them into the colonial administration by calling them Native Authorities and ruling through them at the local and domestic level.

In Northern Nigeria, both the Hausa and Fulani understood the working of a hierarchical system of authority. The addition of one or more tiers of authority over a many tiered structure which was based on the allegiance of the masses to traditional patrons, while dramatic was not revolutionary. Indeed, it has been argued that the superimposition of colonial authority generally was supportive of the traditional hierarchical nature of authority in Northern Nigeria.[12] Frederick Lugard, a British citizen and the first governor of Nigeria, who was largely the architect of this system, came to the conclusion that the administration of the North would be considerably enhanced by employing the services of the traditional rulers in cooperation

---

[11]S.O. Okafor, Indirect Rule: The Development of Central Legislature in Nigeria, (Nigeria, Ikeja Lagos: Thomas Nelson Nigeria, Ltd., 1981), pp. 42-50.

[12]For accurate accounts of this statement see C.S. Whitaker, Jr., Politics of Tradition: Continuity and Change in Northern Nigeria, (Princeton, New Jersey, Princeton University Press 1970), Chapter 1. See also the work of S.O. Okafor Indirect Rule: The Development of Central Legislature in Nigeria (Ikeja Lagos, Nigeria, Thomas Nelson Nigeria, Ltd., 1981); J.S. Coleman, Nigeria: Background to Nationalism (Berkely and Los Anglees, University of California Press, 1963); Sir Alan Burns, History of Nigeria (London: George Allen and Unwin 1969). Callaway, The Political Economy of Africa.

with British officials rather than attempting to administer the region directly.[13] Lugard had good reason for this choice. First, Northern Nigeria was considerably large and the British government would have had to commit great sums of money and considerable number of personnel to the territory, a course which would not have been popular with the home government at the time. Secondly, the existence of the Fulani, another imperial power who had arrived in the North almost a hundred years before the British, would have caused antagonisms which the British would rather avoid. Thus, Lugard felt that as long as certain principles of humanity and justice were observed, the Northern rulers and institutions should be preserved and "Indirect Rule" would, therefore, serve British interests better.

> However, Southern Nigeria was characterized by totally different structural systems of authority and the transfer of the Native Authority system to this area had vastly difficult results. The Southwestern portion of Nigeria is the home of the Yoruba people. The British did not understand the system of chiefly rule among the Yoruba. Here, traditional rulers, called Obas, ruled over large towns whose population worked on farms in the surrounding countryside.   While the Yoruba share a common cultural heritage and each large Yoruba town is governed by an Oba and his council, the people as a whole lacked any overall central authority.
>
> The British assumed the Obas had autocratic powers similar to that of the Emirs in Northern Nigeria. The British, failing to perceive the true nature of the system, gave the chief powers they would never have had in the traditional society and removed the traditional checks on their power, thus corrupting traditional authority.[14]

Also, in Southeastern Nigeria the Europeans were generally frustrated in their efforts to implement Indirect Rule System. Here traditional rule was essentially consensual and there was no formal administration. Further,

---

[13]For a concise but informative account of the making of Nigeria and the role of Lugard, see Obafemi Awolowo, The Peoples Republic (Ibadan: Oxford University Press, 1968); see S.O. Okafor, Indirect Rule: The Development of Central Legislature in Nigeria, (Nigeria: Lagos, Thomas Nelson, 1981), pp. 37-41.

[14]Callaway, The Political Economy of Africa, p. 97.

Eastern Nigeria's population density of about 800 per square mile is the densest in Africa.   In spite of this great density of population, the predominant tribal group here, the Ibos, live in small village groups rather than in "traditional urban centers" as do the Yoruba. Each Ibo village is a unit unto itself and owns allegiance to no higher authority.   In these acephalous villages, elders elected on the basis of age and achievement ruled by agreement.[15] According to Callaway:

> Central political authority was completely lacking. The density of population and the high degree of social fragmentation made the administration of this area particularly troublesome for the British.   A central concept of Indirect Rule was that all communities possessed indigenous leaders who wielded authority who could demand a certain degree of obedience and respect, who could be coopted into the Native Authority System! Northern Nigeria corresponded to this preconception clearly, but the situation in the East was far more complex and hence made the conditions of control much more elusive. In their frustration at not being able to "find" the traditional authorities, the British created chiefs by warrant and armed them with powers which from a traditional perspective were arbitrary and in direct conflict with accepted custom.
>
> The concentration of Nigeria's three major cultural groups in three distinct areas of the country made the British division of the country into three regions appear logical. Yet, each of the resulting three regions, North, West and East, was characterized by cultural make-up which made the three-part division less than fully logical. Although Nigeria indeed has three main cultural groups, some 250 different people live within its boundaries. Thus, in each region a preponderant majority dominated a heterogeneous group of cultural and linguistic minorities.[16]

Indirect Rule had a serious implication on subsequent development within the nation. Rather than act as a force for national unity, the aim of Indirect Rule was to preserve traditional division and keep the country

---

[15]Ibid. pp. 97-98.
[16]Ibid. 98.

divided into small distinct groups. The most conservative units within the traditional power structure gained most by Indirect Rule and hence developed an interest in preserving the status quo.[17]

The British policy in the area of religion further compounded regional differences. In line with the preservation of Northern institutions, Islam was retained as the basic cultural and religious force to the exclusion of Christian missionary influences. Magnanimous as this might seem, this policy was to result in a severe imbalance between North and South, an imbalance which still plaques Nigeria today.

The missionaries who had been active in the Southern part of the country since the mid-1840s had opened schools, and with education came intellectual scholar who could now read and write European language which the North did not enjoy. The final result of this policy was that at independence the North was basically feudal-orientated with a backward economy and lacking important social services (health, education, etc.) which the South with its head start and orientation had acquired and was in a hurry to expand. To compound the problem, the British maneuvered to give control of the Federal government to the North (in the 1959 constitution). This was justified by the claim that only in this way could stability and unity be maintained at independence, which was to come in the following year. Awolowo goes so far as to suggest that the British realized that the conservative element in the North would tend to cling to the former administration even after independence and, consequently, they felt that their interests would be served by Northern politicians rather than the "agitators of self-rule" in the South.[18] The North, realizing its own backwardness and fearing that the South was bound to take advantage of it in a strong federation, was, therefore, unwilling to take the plunge when the question of independence came up. Consequently, a basic suspicion was to arise between the regions over the years, and national politics became a sort of competition where the nation's resources were the prize; this was further compounded by ethnic particularism and patronage which became the access to the means of modernization.

With the coming of independence, the political parties prepared themselves to organize on a regional basis, since it was only through control

---

[17]Ibid.

[18]Bafemi Awolowo, The People's Republic (Ibadan: oxford University Press, 1968), p. 79.

of the regions that access to the center could be achieved. The three major parties were the Northern Peoples' Congress (N.P.C.), the National Council of Nigerian Citizens (N.C.N.C.), and the Action Group (A.G.); they were the strongest party in the Northern, Eastern and Western regions respectively. At the time of independence in 1960, the country was ruled by a coalition of the N.P.C and the N.C.N.C, while the A.G. was the leading opposition party. The North, because of its more abundant population, was always assured a dominant position in federal executive and legislative bodies, and the other parties (minor ones have not been mentioned) had either to form coalitions amongst themselves to confront the North or seek some sort of alliance with the North so as to guarantee access to the federal machinery. Meanwhile, ethnic politics was in its heyday, and the corruption, intrigue and excesses which were to occur would command a whole study in themselves.[19]

The important political features of Nigeria during 1960-1965 were the achievement of political independence in 1960 and the failure of the existing political parties to form a viable alliance, despite claiming to represent the interests of the main ethnic groups. The political history of Nigeria serves as an illustration of a federation with vast historical, social, and cultural differences among its various elements. It also demonstrates the effects on a federation where the various elements professing to be bound by common interests are actually seeking the greatest share of the "national cake" for themselves, and where there is an inequitable sharing of power between the center and the regions. Here, my position is that the military intervention of January 16, 1966, culminating in the civil war, was the result of the inter-ethnic tension suppressed in colonial Nigeria.

Brief Comment on Nigerian Civil War (1966-1970)

There is no accurate account of the first coup in Nigeria. However, it seems there was an initial attempt by some Eastern and Western Officials to rid the country of the corrupt politicians. It has been suggested that there was then a 'coup within the coup' by the Ibo officers which resulted in the escape

---

[19]Richard Sklar's book is perhaps the most illustrative accounts of the dynamics of ethnic politics in Nigeria; see Richard Sklar, Nigerian Political Parties (Princeton: Princeton University Press, 1963), p. 100

of all Ibo politicians and a resulting military government with the Ibo element in control. Luckham has demonstrated that there was indeed a correlation in terms of the conspirators' ethnic affiliations and their survival rates in both coups (January and July). With regard to the first coup, there was at first a general feeling of relief in the nation that the corrupt civilian regime had been removed. But, this gradually turned to cynicism at the coincidental survival of all the Ibo officials.[20] As the months passed, this was to result in a determined effort on the part of Northern officials to regain control.

The end effect of this state of affairs was a justifiable frustration on the part of certain Southern elements who felt that the dominant position of the North with the resulting intrigues (especially in the Western region) to find some access to the seat of power, was a hopeless situation which could not be resolved by the constitutional provisions at hand. The Ibo officers who staged the coup of January 1966, acted out of insecurity. This insecurity rose out of the fear of Northern hegemony, a situation which the Ibo officers were convinced would condemn their people to second-rate citizenship at best. Several prominent government officials were killed during this coup, and it is significant that the Prime Minister (a Northerner) and the premier of the North were amongst those murdered,[21] while Dr. Nnamdi Azikiwe, the President (an Easterner), was away on vacation In Europe at the time. Also, murdered was the premier of the West who had sought and obtained a coalition government with the Northern politicians.

The new government headed by General Aguiyi Ironsi (an Ibo) had not been in office a full six months before another coup. engineered by Northern officers, was staged. It had been motivated by a fear that the Southerners would dominate the North both economically and politically; it is interesting to note once again that it was the insecurity felt by another segment of the population which served as the primary motivating force behind the second coup.[22]

---

[20]Robin Luckham, The Nigerian Military: A sociological Analysis of Authority and Revolt 1960-1967, (Cambridge: Cambridge University Press, 1971).

[21]Joseph Okapaku, Nigeria: Dilemma of Nationhood, (New York: Third Press, 1972).

[22]An accurate account of the two coups and the underlying political motivations behind them will be seen in the book by Luckham: see Robin Luckham, The Nigerian Military: A Sociological Analysis of Authority and Revolt 1960-1967 (Cambridge: Cambridge University Press 1971).

The first military government under Ironsi proved to lack any initiative. Apart from the complete removal of the 'political class' from government, little change was made in the political process. Ironsi made attempts to revise the structure of the federation by simply replaced the top civilian administrators with military personnel. The result of Ironsi's few months in office was the creation of a fundamental insecurity on the part of Northern officials who saw their former hold on the federation slipping away.

In July of the same year, the Northern officers carried out a counter-coup accompanied by the mass slaughtering of Ibo soldiers outside the Eastern region. Lt. Colonel Gowon emerged as the head of the Federal Military Government. The resulting bitterness which was to arise in the Eastern region and amongst Ibo's all over the federation, because of the mass slaughtering of their people (especially in the North), and the insecurity which the Ibo's felt in the federation as a whole, led to the declaration of Eastern secession under Colonel Ojukwu.[23]   For reference purpose see tables 2 and 3 for January and July 1966 coups.

In fact, so strong was the fear of the Northern officers that they had actually considered carving out the Northern region from the federation. The new government headed by then Lieutenant Yakubu Gowon (chosen because of his Northern minority origins) had hardly settled down when it was confronted by the prospect of secession by the Eastern region. The Ibos, who feared that the reversal of the political situation was bound to render them impotent within the jurisdiction of a Northern controlled federation, finally declared secession under Colonel Ojukwu. The resulting civil was is well known for the immense damage to property and human life inflicted on the nation (particularly to the Ibos). The federal government emerged victorious, and the Gowon regime settled down to the business of the reconstruction and consolidation. An uneasy tranquility was to be witnessed in the nation, but as the years passed, a growing opposition to the Gowon regime came to be manifested. Complaints ranged from corruption in high places to the use of

---

[23]This is a brief summary of the causes of the war which can be viewed from various dimensions. It is, however, indisputable that the majority of Ibo's felt truly insecure and this enhanced Ojukwu's ability to rally the majority support of his people. An interesting collection of essays which examine the causes of the war from different perspectives can be found in Joseph Okapaku (ed.) Nigeria: Dilemma of Nationhood. (New York: The Third Press, 1972), pp. 117-123.   See also Robin Luckham: The Nigerian Military; A Sociological Analysis of Authority and Revolt 1960-1967, (Cambridge; Cambridge University Press, 1971).

Table 2

NUMBER OF SENIOR OFFICERS KILLED AND SURVIVING COUP OF JANUARY 1966

REGION OF ORIGIN	KILLED	ABSENT FROM NIGERIA	IN NIGERIA	TOTAL
West	2	2	2	6
North	4	0	1	5
Mid-West	1	1	1	3
East	0	0	7	7

Source: Robin Luckham, The Nigerian Military, P.43.

Table 3

ETHNIC AND REGIONAL ORIGIN OF VICTIMS OF JULY COUP 1966

REGION	DEATHS BY OFFICERS	DEATHS BY MEN	ETHNICITY	DEATH BY OFFICERS ONLY
East	31	154	Ibo	27
Mid-West	5	14	Non Ibo, Mid-West	2
West	3	3	Non Ibo, West	6
North	0	0	Yoruba	4

Source: Robin Luckham, The Nigerian Military, P. 76

government appointment to build personal fortune[24]. One noticeable difference was that the ethnic rivalries seemed to have taken second place; there was more concern for administrative and economic efficiencies on the part of the government. Though couched in radical rhetoric, the following passage taken from a radical journal, manage by a group which called it self the "Nigerian Revolutionary Communists", is not a typical of how many average Nigerians saw the Gowon regime. The reference to 1976 applies to the date at which the Gowon regime promised a return to civilian rule:

> Economic failure constitutes the fourth fundamental reason why the army is scared to death at the mention of 1976. By that year, the bourgeois young officers would have been in power for ten years, of which the Gowon regime would have the account for 90% of that period. The important question is, what can they show as symbols of their achievement apart from the few road flyovers in Lagos, a few major roads in the country (some of which were so badly constructed that they have had to be rebuilt); some office blocks which house the booming commercial businesses; some prestige but wasteful building; and then the increasing presence of ferocious monopolies.[25]

Though a greater concern for social and economic issues seems to have superseded the ethnic issue, one cannot conclude that ethnicity no longer mattered in the consideration of stability in Nigeria. The presence of the military (a coercive institution) undoubtedly accounted for the apparent calm of public debate. It might not be forgotten, however, that citizens had not had any mass participation in the political process for over ten years, and with the reactivation of the political parties in 1978 and a general election for return to civilian government in 1979, the issue was bound to appear in some form or another in the future.

It came as no surprise when the Gownon regime was over thrown in the summer of 1975 and replaced by the military regime of Murtala Mohammed. The assassination of Mohammed only served to remind most observers of the Nigerian political scene that the political crisis of the

---

[24]An excellent account of the problems besetting the Gowon regime can be found in the magazine Africa, no. 49, (September, 1975), pp. 1045-1047.

[25]African Red Family, Vol. 2, no. 3, (1975), p. 15

Nigerian society was far from being solved. However, the new government under Murtala Mohammed no sooner than it had taken over set to work in correcting the administrative disorder which had set in under the Gowon regime. The old military governors were fired and replaced by new ones. There were also mass dismissals from the civil service with tribunals established for investigation of corruption under the Gowon regime.

In spite of these changes, the return to civil rule was the prime concern of Nigerians. In his broadcast to the nation on National Day, October 1, 1975, Mohammed reiterated the military government's intention to hand power over to a democratically elected government on October 1, 1979. According to him, a five-stage program was to be implemented before the assumed date. The primary concern of the first stage was the creation of new states. On the issue of creating the new states, Mohammed stated that the final decisions would be made by April 1976. The Constitutional Drafting Committee was given twelve months to complete the work. That would enable the newly emerged states to put their governments in proper place during the second stage.

Among the five stage program advocated, Mohammed was able to implement one, that is the creation of new states. The regime, in effect, created seven more states, catering to the further demands which had been voiced since the creation of the twelve.

At this point, however, the local government system would be reorganized with elections at the local government level based on individual qualification, without political parties. A constituent Assembly would be organized, which would comprise both elected and appointed officials. According to him, that body would be considered amended, and finally approved by the draft constitution. Again, the deadline set for the completion of the second stage was October 1978, so as to facilitate the preparation for the general election, the third stage. Stages four and five involved the elections for the state legislatures and the elections at federal level respectively. These last three stages were proposed to take place one year after the second stage. These processes would enable the military to withdraw by October 1, 1979.[26]

---

[26]Nigerian Daily Times, 6 June 1977, p. 13.

The momentum slowed down temporarily when Mohammed was assassinated in an attempted military coup by a group of army officials on February 13, 1976. The revolting officers were, however, overcome and executed, and the new head of state, General Obsanjo, generally continued with the policies of his predecessor. A return to civilian rule was also scheduled for 1979 with the reorganization of political parties set for 1978. The Obasanjo regime generally promoted an increased administrative efficiency of the bureaucratic machinery and showed a genuine interest in the return to civilian rule. Since it assumed power in February 1976, a new draft constitution had been written and was under national review; election for local representatives had scheduled as part of the program towards the return to civilian government, and there was a lively national debate (encouraged by the regime) as to the course political socio-economic development in the nation should follow. However, the constitution drafted left unsolved two fundamental issues concerning economic development: the census and the appropriate formula for revenue allocation. These were left because of their political nature to the incoming civilian administration.

Obasanjo also lifted the ban on political parties so that preparation could begin for stages four and five of Mohammed's plan. The formation and approval of political parties were left in the hand of the Federal Election Commission (FEDECO). Out of 50 political parties that were formed, FEDECO was able to choose the following which reflected national character: The Unity Party of Nigeria (UPN) under the leadership of the late Obafemi Awolowo; the National Party of Nigeria (NPN) led by Alhaji Aliyi; the Nigerian People's Party (NPP) under the leadership of Dr. Nnamdi Azikiwe; and the Great Nigerian People's Party (GNPP) led by Alhaji Waziri Ibrahim. [27]

Again, the formation of political parties in the second republic reflected ethnic differences. During the election, however, all the results pointed to the NPN as the majority party, and Alhaji Shehu Shagari was announced as the president-elect of the Second Republic.

The NPN was able to gain the support of the NPP headed by Dr. Azikiwe to achieve a working majority in both the federal Senate and the federal House of Representatives; similar to that of the 1959 election. Of historical significance was the fact that the leadership of the NPN comprised

---

[27]Daily Times, 14 April 1980.

former leaders of the parties which formed Nigerian National Alliance (NNA) in 1965, notably the Northern Peoples Congress (NPC) and the Nigerian National Democratic Party (NNDP) in the West.[28]

The return of Nigeria from military rule to a democratically elected government was seen as a victory for democracy in Nigeria. However, the political victory of Nigeria between 1979 (when President Shagari took the oath of Office) and December 31, 1983 (when he was ousted in a military coup) had a significant impact in Nigerian history. There was widespread corruption in the ruling party at the center and by the various state governments. Special tribunals set-up by the military to uncover corruption and mismanagement among the overthrown politicians found almost every one guilty.[29] Hence, the end of the Shagari administration in Nigeria was welcome news to most Nigerians. Between 1983 and 1988, Nigeria was governed by two military governments, that of Buhari and Babangida regimes.

By 1984, the economy of Nigeria was in shambles. Hence military intervention was virtually assured. The Buhari regime not only inherited declining revenues based on fluctuating petroleum sales, but it was faced with mounting foreign and domestic debts. On coming to power, the Buhari government declared war on corruption and indiscipline throughout Nigeria by means of a much publicized program christened W.A.I. (War Against Indiscipline).[30] The Buhari regime recovered large sums of money from former politicians during it short tenure in office. As far as the development strategy of the Buhari regime was concerned, the fact that the regime lasted for only less than two years makes an evaluation of its policies more problematic. However, since it was the first regime to come to power because the economy of Nigeria was in shambles, an evaluation of its success in the minds of most Nigerians would be affected by the fact that unemployment increased dramatically while the regime was in power and inflation continued to rise. Given the above problems and other similar problems, another military coup which bought General Babangida to power took place in August 27, 1985.

---

[28]Shehu Othman, "Classes, Crisis and Coup: The Demise of Shagari's Regime" Business Concord, (8 April 1986), p. 44.

[29]National Concord, Lagos, 6 May 1985, p. 11

[30]Daily Times, "War Against Indiscipline" 9 April 1984, p. 11.

In conclusion Nigeria since 1960 has experienced eight changes of government, administration and numerous foiled coup d'etats. Out of eight regimes that ruled Nigeria since her political independence two were constitutionally elected civilian regimes and six have been military regimes.

Table 4

CHANGES OF GOVERNMENT IN NIGERIA FROM 1960-1988

PERIOD OF RULE	HEAD OF GOVT.	TYPE OF GOVT.	TYPE OF CHANGE
1959-1966	Sir Tafawa Balewa	Civilian Rule	Elected
1966	Gen. Ironsi	Military Rule	Coup
1966-1975	Gen. Gowon	Military Rule	Coup
1975-1976	Brig. Murtala Mohammed	Military Rule	Coup
1976-1979	Gen. Obsanjo	Military Rule	Coup
1979-1983	Shehu Shagari	Civilian Rule	Elected
1983-1985	Major Gen. Buhari	Military Rule	Coup
1985-Present	Gen. Babangida	Military Rule	Coup

Source: Provided by the author.

Based on Table 4, one finds that eight regimes have ruled Nigeria in succession over a period of twenty-eight years. However, each regime, on the average, ruled Nigeria for three years and five months. As a result of this, no meaningful economic program of any country can be accomplished within a short period of time, particularly as Nigeria is a developing country with a series of problems usually associated with the LDCs. It is even worse if the country has no continuity of development programs as a result of the abrupt successions of government that it has experienced.

CHAPTER 4

The Post-Colonial Economy Of Nigeria
And The National Development Plan

Having established this brief overview of the political history of Nigeria in Chapter 3, we now turn our attention to early attempts at development planning of the country. It has been our objective to trace the early development plans to see how they differ from the economic policies prescribed by the IMF, as well as to see the effectiveness of these development plans in addressing Nigerian economic problems. Our aim is to see whether Nigeria will still continue to rely on the orthodox model of economic development for its development plans. Chapter seven of this book must be approached with the above views in mind.

Like other African countries, the development plans drawn up in Nigeria before independence were not really development plans. The British, anxious that the economic viability of Nigeria be considerably enhanced, were aware of the fact that certain infra-structure had to be provided; hand in hand with these came certain social services which could provide for the most basic welfare needs of the Nigerian masses who would provide the labor for the exploitation of the nation's resource. Consequently, the colonial departments, at the request of the home government, drew up budgets for anticipated expenditures which in turn allowed the home government some criteria for the allocation of funds to the colony. These so-called plans, however, had no coherent development strategy, and there was simply no coordination of the various segments of the economy. Karmarck, writing on the beginning of the planning process in colonial Africa, offers us a generally descriptive account of planning at this early date:

> Africa is the continent of economic plans. Every country in Africa (except South Africa) had at least one since World War II, and most have had several. The preparation of economic plans began under the colonial regimes and under the stimulus of the colonial powers. Both the British and the French decided that aid to their colonial territories after the war had to be provided within the context of development plans, worked out for each colony by the territorial governments themselves with help from London in the case of the British colonies and by Paris for the French colonies. Perhaps the one point upon which everybody now agrees is that these development plans were defective; they were prepared by administrators with little or no economic background; coordination of the investments in various sectors was largely non-existent; there was no consistent development strategy. In short, the plans were no more than list of projects.[1]

Nigeria's first plan, "The Ten Year Plan of Development and Welfare for Nigeria 1946" evolved as a result of a request from the colonial office in Britain that all colonies draw up development plans to help in the disbursements of colonial development and welfare funds. Dean, commenting on the plan, says:

> The plan was oriented toward the allocation of these funds; it emphasized education, health, water supplies and transport and communications; it was based on programs drawn up in individual government departments and was in part a set of schemes for the expansion of services and facilities based on departmental policies.[2]

---

[1]Andrew Karmarck, The Economics of African Development, (New York: Praeger, 1972), p. 264-265.

[2]Dean, Plan Implementation in Nigeria 1962-1966, p. 11.

The plan was hardly half way through when "A Revised Plan of Development and Welfare" for Nigeria 1950-1956 superseded it. This was basically the same in approach as the earlier plan as Adedeji notes:

> However neither the Ten Year Plan nor its successor, the revised Five Year Plan was comprehensive. Both were essentially series of development schemes devoted largely to the provision of basic social and economic services. Neither covered all of the intended development activities of the Nigerian governments. The limited scope of the plan became increasingly obvious as from 1949 when, the establishment of regional authorities, quasi governmental development institutions such as the Regional Production Development Boards were set up. As there were no overall economic goals, no serious effort was made to relate the projects to one another or to any overall objective. And no attempt was made to coordinate governmental activities with development in the private sector. Thus during this phase, planning was far from being comprehensive and integrated.[3]

In 1953, the Nigerian and British governments commissioned the International Bank for Reconstruction and Development to undertake a study of the Nigerian economy. The Bank was asked "to appraise the economic development prospects of Nigeria and recommend practical measures for their realization." The result of the mission was a report entitled, "The Economic Development of Nigeria", and apart from being a truly integrated approach to the development prospects of the Nigerian economy, the report is a reliable economic document on the economic state of Nigeria at this time.[4]

All efforts at development planning so far sought an integrated national approach to planning. However, in 1954 Nigeria became a federation, and the integrated approach came to an end. The 1954 constitution had given the regions considerably new responsibilities; in the economic sphere, this meant that the state were generally free to prepare their own development policies and strategies. The federal government was

---

[3]Adebayo Adedeji, "Federalism and Development Planning in Nigeria" in A.A. Ayida and H. M. A. Onitiri (eds.) Reconstruction and Development in Nigeria (Ibandan: Oxford University Press, 1971), p. 98-99.

[4]International Bank for Reconstruction and Development, "The Economic Development of Nigeria," (Baltimore: John Hopkins Press, 1955).

thus rendered practically powerless to organize development planning on a nation-wide scale. By 1955, each region was preparing its own plan, and it is interesting to note that the federal plan was overshadowed by the regional plans. This was simply a reflection of the political situation in Nigeria in which there was a built-in competition amongst the regions with each region trying to secure the material prosperity of its own peoples. Adedeji is once again instructive on this score:

> It should, however, be pointed out that it was not simply the introduction of a federal system of government in Nigeria in 1954 that made coordinated national planning impossible. It was the acrimonious rivalry amongst the regions that made cooperative effort extremely difficult. Unfortunately, the federal government failed to provide an effective leadership at both political and civil service levels. Lacking any coherent national social and economic objectives and guided by weak political leadership, it is not surprising that it was unable to perform effectively in any coordinating role. In fact, it was so anxious not to impinge on regional autonomy that the regional governments felt completely free to do whatever they liked. The attempts later during the plan period to coordinate the implementation of the various programs through the setting up of intergovernmental institutions, were so half-hearted that it was not surprising that they were ineffective.[5]

It has been our aim in this chapter, by examining the political background and framework and the early attempts at planning in Nigeria, to establish some sort of relationship between the two. According to Callaway,

> The principal motive of the British in creating Nigeria was not to advance the interest of Nigerians, but to serve Britain's own economic interests. Once her authority was firmly established in Nigeria, Britain had the orthodox colonial preoccupation of maintaining law and order while extracting raw materials for the home market and creating Nigerian demands for British manufactured goods. Under British colonial rule, export crops such as groundnut, cocoa, palm oil and cotton were introduced and Nigeria's timber, tin, and coal were fully exploited products

---

[5]Adedeji, Reconstruction and Development in Nigeria, 1971, p. 101.

which today (along with the more recently developed oil industry) are the mainstays of the Nigerian economy.[6]

The independent Nigerian State got her national flag but it inherited economic dependence. This dependence was used by the imperialist forces to further their objective. The dependence rests on two major stands, a continued colonial division of labor based on the capitalist law of comparative advantage and foreign control of key sectors of the economy. This pattern was summarized as follows: (1) As in colonial time a large part of production is sold for export. (2) Most of the goods exported are a few unprocessed raw materials. (3) More than four-fifths of Nigeria's exports is directed to the imperialist states. Three-fourths of Nigeria's imports originate from there. Britain still dominates Nigeria's business activities, but the United States, and to a lesser extent Japan, are also important trade partners. There is little or no trade transaction between Nigeria and other African States. (4) The big private companies which have dominated the exploitation of Nigerian raw materials are powerful actors on the Nigerian scene. For many of them their annual turnover is far larger than the total country's annual budget.

The Activities of Multinational Corporation in Nigeria: A Focus on UAC

Following the colonial trade wars and the consequent consolidation of the 1920, the Nigerian market was dominated by a small number of large and highly integrated foreign trading companies such as the United African Company (UAC), John Holt, Paterson, Zachonis, the Compagnie Francaise del 'Afrique Occidentale (CFAO) and Societe Commerciale de l'Quest Africainel (SCOA). These large merchant wholesalers provided credit to small scale Nigerian businessmen and market women who were committed to buying their products for their trade. In this way, the foreign firms in effect controlled even small-scale retail trade in Nigeria.

Even after Nigeria gained political independence, its socio-economic life remains firmly entrenched into the western capitalist system. Its economic planning efforts have been influenced largely by western advisers and

---

[6]Callaway, The Political Economy of Africa, p. 102.

consultants. In the country's development projects, western finance capital still plays a very significant role. The influence of western firms in Nigeria are equally great. The major trans-national corporation operating in Nigeria today include Standard Oil of California, Mobil Oil, Gulf, Imperial Chemicals Industries (ICI) of Britain, Texaco, Shell-BP, Agip, Uniler (owner of United African Company--U.A.C. and its subsidiaries), Farben, Krupps, Siemmens, Barclays Bank, Bank of America and Standard Bank of West Africa. Among these foreign firms, the U.A.C. is the largest. It has a host of subsidiaries and it is involved in almost every aspect of the Nigerian economy. After independence Western business interests have actively strengthened themselves at the expense of Nigerian businessmen. Within the first two years of independence, the two principal expatriate banks in Nigeria (Barclays and Bank of West Africa) opened some forty new branches. "The indigenous banks (African Continental Bank, National Bank of Nigeria, and Agbonmagbe Bank) opened only five branches during the same period.[7] No new banks, entirely Nigerian, were opened during the period, whereas, four new banks, in which foreign capital was the senior partner in association with Nigerian capital, were opened.   Another four new banks wholly foreign, were established in Nigeria including world giants such as Bank of America and Chase Manhattan Bank of New York. By 1962, there were some eight financial institutions in Nigeria including Lombard (Nigeria) Ltd., Commonwealth Finance Corporation, the United Dominion Trust, and some Swiss and other continental firms. None of these finance institutions was owned by Nigeria at that time.

Investments in the extraction of Nigeria's mineral resources is one of the major areas in which foreign investors are highly interested. Foreign investments in the Nigerian oil industry have grown considerably since the late 1950s. The oil companies dominate the industry from mining to retailing gasoline in the neighborhood petrol stations. Thousands of gasoline stations are opened by Shell-BP, Mobil Oil, Texaco, Exxon, Agip, Total and Chevron. Between 1960 and 1962, Shell-BP poured about $60 million into exploration and production of Nigerian crude oil. Other foreign oil companies which until independence were very insignificant also increased their activities and

---

[7]Africa, No. 49, (September 1975) p. 14.

expenses on prospecting for crude oil in Nigeria. This was especially true of the American oil companies and the Italian Agip.

Also, in the shipping industry, the dominance of foreign interests is still visible. A large and unbelievable proportion of Nigeria's exports and imports are still carried in ships which belong to foreign firms-Elder Dempster Lines, Palm Lines, Holland West Africa Line and others. The Nigerian National Shipping Line formed and managed by the Nigerian Federal Government operates as a junior partner with the foreign companies. Shipping on Nigerian rivers is largely controlled by Elder Dempster Agencies and U.A.C. with Nigerians handling short distances, smaller passenger crafts or working for the big foreign firms.

The Nigerian Railways are state-owned but the capital for railway extension was largely from foreign sources. For example, the N20 million for Bornu Railway extension came from the International Bank for Reconstruction and Development (World Bank)[8]. The loan was given to Nigeria at a rate of interest of eight and one-third percent. The Nigerian airways belong to the state. It was no less similarly dependent of foreign capital than the railways and other Nigerian public-owned corporations. The Nigerian Airways had depended largely on capital from the United Kingdom. Nigeria's airline is in partnership with Elder Dempster Lines Limited of Liverpool and the British Airways prior to 1970.

Furthermore, in the tin mining industry the foreign firms maintain a monopoly position. Nigerians act merely as subcontractors. Amalgamated Tin Miners of Nigeria (ATMN) a foreign company in which U.A.C., a subsidiary of Unilever, has controlling shares has remained a prominent influence and dominant factor in the mining industry at Jos in Nigeria.[9]

The picture which emerges in the area of large-scale plantation in agriculture is equally that of the domination of foreign capital by the multinational corporations. With the exception of a few estates owned and managed by statutory corporations (the Development Corporation), the large estates in Nigeria are owned by foreign firms. The United African Company, (U.A.C.) a subsidiary of the Anglo-Dutch Unilever, through its local subsidiary Pamol Limited, runs several large palm oil and rubber estates in the Mid-

---

[8]Federal Republic of Nigeria, Economic and Statistical Abstract, (Lagos 1970), p. 103.
[9]Ibid.

Western State and in Calabar area of the Southeastern state. Dunlop Rubber Company Limited, is running a rubber estate and factory in Calabar area while Elders and Fyfe are running banana plantations in what is now part of Cameroon Republic (that area was formerly a part of Nigeria). Other examples abound. In the timber and plywood industry, for instance, the only factory in the country which is located at Sapele is owned by African Timber and Plywood Limited, a subsidiary of the U.A.C.

In the case of light industries, the picture that emerges is not any different. The few assembly plants in Nigeria and those already negotiated are just other examples of foreign domination of the productive resources of the Nigerian economy. The Nigerian breweries, soap, cigarette, textile, car assembly, flour packing, and other factories are dominated by foreign influences.

However, of all businesses, road transport is the only big example which is almost entirely owned by Nigerians. However, few foreign firms are involved in road transport in Nigeria. Examples are Armel's Transport (which for a long time had been involved in hauling passengers, goods, and the Nigerian mail) and the Arab Transports (largely involved in hauling produce in the North). Again, even when road transport is largely in the hands of Nigerians, through monopoly of importation, sales, maintenance, credit arrangements and other business strategies of large firms, the multinational corporations have been able to extract a great deal of the profits of the Nigerians in road transport business.[10]

Again, in the few large industrial projects set up by statutory actions, owned by the state and manage by public corporations, foreign interests have conveniently secured influential position and firmly entrenched themselves in their management. Multinational corporations have secured a firm grip on those industrial projects through agreements which appoint persons from the multinational corporations as advisers, contractors, consultants, and managing agents.[11]   For example, Burham Cement Company of England has the managing agency for Knalagu Cement Factory in Eastern Nigeria. Portland Cement Company holds the managing agency for the Ewekore Cement Factory in Western Nigeria. Pepsi-Cola company of the United States of

---

[10]Ibid., p. 105

[11]Africa No 49, (September, 1975) p. 18.

America runs the Pepsi-Cola factories in Nigeria.[12] In conformity with the global decision-making and management policies of the international firms, the "multinationals" use their arrangements with the statutory corporations in the management of these industries to ensure that the managerial and marketing policies of the state-owned industries are brought under the effective control of the global enterprises. It should not be surprising that locally manufactured goods have been unable to compete effectively with strategies and intrigues of the multinational corporations operating in Nigeria-as is happening in all African countries.

In the field of trade-wholesale and retail-within Nigeria, the dominant role of the multinational organizations is also visible. The import trade of Nigeria is handled mainly by the international firms such as U.A.C., John Holts, United Trading Company (U.T.C.) G. B. Ollivant, McIver, and others. Leventine and Indian interests have also shown interests in trade in Nigeria. K. Chellarams, Nasser's Bhojsons, Leventis and others have been involved in Nigeria's trade.   Until the Nigerian Indigenization Decree of 1972, the Lebanese were heavily involved in retail trade in the major urban centers of Nigeria, particularly in Lagos and in Ibadan. The big retail stores also involve themselves vigorously in retailing on the local markets both in urban centers and in the remote parts of the rural areas. All these activities of the foreign firms have been detrimental to the survival of indigenous businessmen.[13]

Since its founding and involvement in Nigeria's economy, the U.A.C. had been the largest company in the country. By 1933 U.A.C. bought up G. B. Ollivant. In Nigeria, the U.A.C. is involved in virtually all aspects of trade and industry. Peter Kilby has documented in a very clear and elaborate manner the level of industrial and commercial involvement of U.A.C. in Nigeria's economy.[14] The industrial and commercial institutions owned by the international giant (U.A.C.) in Nigeria are shown in table 5. The number

---

[12]Ibid.

[13]The Indigenization Decree of 1972 proves the indignation of the Military government towards the continue domination of Nigeria's economic life by foreign elements-businesses and individuals.   See also the indignation expressed on the same issue by a former Nigerian politician Samuel G. Ikoku in his Nigeria for Nigerians (Takoradi, Ghana: A. I. Press, July 1962), Nicholas Balabkins, Indigenization and Economic Development: The Nigerian Experience, (London, England, Jal Press 1982).

[14]Peter Kilby, Industrialization in An Open Economy, Nigeria 1945-1966, (London: Cambridge University Press, 1967).

and diversified nature of the companies listed in the table show the great extent to which the United African Company had dominated the economy of Nigeria. Kilby's list was made up in the mid-1960s. Since that time, the power, wealth and dominance of U.A.C. in Nigeria's welfare have increased. As Nigeria grows, so does the U.A.C. grow, both in power, wealth and influence. In the early 1970s a study conducted by Professor Stanley Diamond indicates more clearly the extent of U.A.C. involvement and control of the Nigerian economy. In a table similar to that of Professor Kilby he indicates that the U.A.C. of Nigeria was split into three sectors: Lever Brother Limited; Plantation Group-rubber, banana and oil palm plantations; Van den Berghs and Jurgens Limited-handling the production of margarine.

Further, immediately after World War II, the British created monopolistic marketing boards to control Nigeria's export trade. In spite of Nigerian control of the marketing boards after independence in 1960, expatriate firms continued to monopolize both import and export trade. measures were taken to promote Nigerian industrializatior, but these measures in fact were designed to attract private foreign investment into Nigeria.

The result of these policies was continued foreign domination of the Nigerian economy through a network of structural relationships now termed neo-colonialism. However, the primary objective of neocolonialism in Nigeria as elsewhere in Africa is to maintain the former colony as a controlled source of raw materials as well as a market for investment and the sale of goods manufactured overseas by local subsidiaries of foreign firms.

Also, Nigeria is a neo-colonial state in that political independence did not significantly affect the country's economic dependency before and after the post 1970 development of the oil industry. Even the oil industry also experienced foreign domination until the early 1970s.

Table 6 indicates the concentration of private foreign capital in the oil industry from 1960 to 1968. However, this table shows that in 1967, private foreign investment in oil accounted for 92 percent of all private foreign investment in Nigeria. Hence, investment income earned by non-Nigerians (factor payments abroad) increased from N32.4 million in 1960 to N635 million by 1970.[15] Petroleum, therefore, remained a typical enclave industry whose contribution to the economy was limited largely to its contribution to government revenues and foreign exchange earnings.

Table 5

INDUSTRIAL INVESTMENTS OF THE U.A.C. IN NIGERIA 1948-1965

COMPANY U.A.C. BRANCH FIRM OR SUBSIDIARY	PRODUCT	YEAR BEGUN
African Timber and Plywood	Timber and Plywood	1948
Nigerian Breweries(3)	Beer and Minerals	1948
Taylor Woodrow	Building contractors	1953
Nigerian Joinery (3)	Woodwork and Furniture	1953
Prestress	Prestressed Concrete	1954
Nipol	Plastic Products	1957
Vehicle Assembly Plant	Bedford Lorries	1958
Raleigh Industries(3)	Cycle Assembly	1958
Mina Farm	Pigs	1959
Northern Construction Company	Building Contracts	1960
West African Trade	Sewing Thread	1961
West African Portland Cement	Cement	1961
West African Cold Storage	Meat Products	1961
Walls	Ice Cream	1961
Vono Products	Bed Mattresses	1961
Cement Paints	Cement Paint	1962
Guiness	Stout	1962

[15]Federal Republic of Nigeria, Annual Abstract of Statistics, (Lagos: Federal Office of Statistics, 1971), p. 113.

Fen Milk	Reconstituted Milk	1963
The Nigerian Sugar Company	Sugar and By-Products	1963
Narspin	Common Yarns	1963
Pye	Radio Assembly	1963
Vitafoam	Foam Rubber Products	1963
A.J. Seward	Perfumery and Cosmetics	1964
Bordpak	Fibre Board Cartoons	1964
Kwara Tobacco Company	Cigarettes	1964
Associated Battery Manufacturers	Vehicle Batteries	1965
Crocodile Machetes	Machetes	1965
Textile Printers	Printed Textiles	1965

Source: Peter Kilby, Industrialization in an Open Economy p. 69.

During the first ten years of Nigeria's existence as a nation, it followed a conservative monetary policy, avoiding foreign exchange restrictions and remaining open to foreign investment and foreign companies. Thus, at the beginning of the 1970s foreign interest still controlled savings, investments, the money supply and the prices of most consumer items.[16]   Also, before independence, the Nigerian economy was dominated by agricultural production. Agricultural exports were initially the engine of growth in the Nigerian economy. Between 1940 and 1960, changes in the agricultural sector occurred mainly as a result of farmers' responses to income incentives generated by the integration of the traditional agricultural economy into the International market.

The increase in output in this sector come from the employment of surplus land and labor, and from substitution of higher value export crops for food crops, without significant reorganization of the society or the introduction of new production techniques. After independence, the situation continued.

---

[16]Ibid.

Table 7 presents the GDP by sectoral origin for 1950-1960 and 1960-1970, and the average annual sectoral growth rate for 1960-1970. A critical examination of the table indicates that from 1960 to 1970, no growth actually took place in the agricultural sector. In fact, it declined at an average annual rate of 0.4 percent. For instance, in 1950-1960, agriculture as a share of GDP was 64.3 percent, but during 1960-1970, its share of GDP dropped to 56.7 percent. After 1967, the sector was seriously affected by the civil war. The table also indicates that while agriculture experienced stagnation during the 1960s, the manufacturing area expanded dramatically, at an average annual

Table 6

PRIVATE FOREIGN INVESTMENT IN THE OIL INDUSTRY
1960-1968

YEAR	MILLION	% INVESTED IN OIL
1960	24.0	-
1961	27.3	25.0
1962	17.7	42.0
1963	37.9	33.0
1964	63.0	57.0
1965	37.0	47.0
1966	34.0	83.0
1967	49.4	92.0
1968	60.8	71.0

Source: Edwin Dean, Plan Implementation in Nigeria, 1962-1968 (Ibadan: Oxford University Press, 1972).

Table 7

AVERAGE ANNUAL GROWTH RATE OF GDP
1960-1970
(PERCENT)

SECTOR	GDP BY SECTORAL ORIGIN 1950-1960 1960-1970		AVERAGE GROWTH RATE 1960-1970
Agriculture	64.3	56.7	-0.4
Mining Including Petroleum	1.2	3.5	20.0
Manufacturing	3.5	6.5	9.1
Construction	3.8	5.0	6.0
Electricity, gas, water	0.7	0.7	10.3
Trade, Finance	14.3	12.7	0
Transport or Communication	5.5	4.8	-0.3
Public Admn. Defense	3.3	3.9	13.6
Others	3.5	6.3	0
Total	100.0	100.0	3.1

Source: World Bank Statistical Abstract 1983 b:1, 134-135; Federal Office of Statistics Second National Development Plan: A Review of the First National Development Plan (Lagos 1975).

growth rate of 9.1 percent. However, increased demands generated by this rapid growth of industrial production, as well as export agriculture, led to very substantial growth in the public utilities and construction sectors. During the 1960s, the mining sector began to play the role of the potential leading growth sector in the economy. Table 8 provides the contribution of manufacturing to GNP for 1960-1975. In this table, manufacturing in GNP rose from 2.5 percent in 1960 to 9.1 percent in 1970. Thereafter, it started declining, chiefly as a result of sudden increases in oil revenues, a rise which reduces the percentage contribution of the entire non-oil sectors of the economy.

It grew at an average annual growth rate of 20 percent. The mining sector especially petroleum, thus became the dominant development area between 1960 and 1970, as oil production in Nigeria began on a significant scale. Our assessment is that Nigeria's economic development was, and remained in the first decade of independence, highly dependent upon conditions in world markets. This dependence quickly created problems for post colonial Nigeria. Table 9 shows Nigeria's exports and imports between 1950 and 1970. The table shows that between 1950 and 1955, Nigeria enjoyed favorable terms of trade. After 1955, however, the favorable terms of trade disappeared; prices of Nigeria's exports began to decline while import prices continued to increase.[17]   Imports expanded rapidly, from N219.3 million in 1950 to N934.7 million in 1970. Also, import-substitution industries in processed food, beverages, and textiles, and restrictive import policies during the civil war prevented further expansion of imports. Still food and raw materials imports as a percentage of all imports increased from 19.9 percent in 1960 to 21.5 percent in 1970.[18]

Furthermore, the rapid growth of the industrial sector caused imports of machinery and equipment to increase from 24 percent in 1960 to 37.4 percent in 1970.[19]   These changes in the trade pattern produced considerable fluctuations in Nigeria's balance of payments. Trade deficits continued annually until 1966, when import substitution and expanding petroleum export brought a surplus. Again, most of the import-substitution

---

[17]African Research Bulletin, Economic and Statistical Review, 1976, p. 178.

[18]Ibid., p. 183.

[19]Ibid.

industries were financed to a large extent by foreign capital. Added to this was the fact that petroleum production in Nigeria was controlled by foreign companies and, like many Nigerian exports in general, the return to Nigerians was very low.

Again, during that time, Nigeria was able to implement its First Development Plan (1962-1968). The First National Development Plan estimated an overall expenditure of N1.351 billion. "Out of that amount, 67.8 percent was reserved for the economic sector, 24.4 percent was allocated to the social services, and administrative services received 7.2 percent."[20] This plan resembled that of the colonial plans owing to the reality that the two expert planners W. F. Stolper and L. M. Hansen were foreigners, mainly American who favored the interest of the West and Western Capital at the

Table 8

CONTRIBUTION OF MANUFACTURING TO GNP
1960-1975
(millions)

YEAR	TOTAL GNP	VALUE OF MANUFACTURING & CRAFTS	PERCENTAGE OF MANUFACTURING & CRAFTS IN GNP
1960	2,224.6	80.6	3.5
1961	2,373.4	88.2	3.7
1962	2,630.8	93.4	3.6
1963	2,806.4	151.8	5.8
1964	2,914.0	157.8	5.6
1965	3,080.6	164.8	5.6
1966	3,210.0	192.2	6.2
1967	3,051.8	196.0	6.1
1968	3,140.8	231.2	7.6

[20]S. Tomori and F. O. Fajana. Development Planning F.A. Olaloki et al., Structure of the Nigerian Economy (New York: St. Martin's Press, 1979).

1969	3,278.2	270.4	8.6
1970	3,485.8	311.0	9.1
1971	9,442.1	475.1	5.0
1972	11,177.9	460.3	4.1
1973	11,993.1	570.1	4.8
1974	13,135.5	626.5	4.8
1975	14,410.7	683.9	4.7

Source: S.O. Olayide (ed.) Economic Survey of Nigeria, 1960-1975, (Ibadan: Aromolaran Publishing co., 1976), p. 54.

Table 9
EXPORTS AND IMPORTS, 1950-1970
(MILLION OF NAIRA)

YEAR	EXPORTS	IMPORTS
1950	266.7	219.3
1955	273.2	368.1
1960	278.5	481.0
1961	341.4	487.0
1962	366.8	456.4
1963	379.0	455.4
1964	423.3	547.0
1965	567.4	590.0
1966	585.5	572.2
1967	517.7	556.8
1968	452.4	517.9
1969	599.5	629.2
1970	890.5	934.7

Source: World Bank World Table 1976: 179; central Bank of Nigeria Annual Report, Lagos, 1971, 1972 and 1974.

expenses of Nigerian citizens. For example, in the plan, they required 50 percent of the planned expenditure to be financed through foreign aid. During its execution generally, only 25 percent was received.[21]   Also, because most foreign loans and grants had strings attached, they were tied to particular programs and therefore could not be used for other programs irrespective of their priorities and preferential arrangement in the plan.[22]

Particular demands of foreign aid donors had to be added into the program.   These conditionalities cause problems in raising the external financing needed for the First Plan. As for the internal source of financing for the program, the government had to depend on the revenue accruing from recurrent surpluses and the statutory corporations (including the marketing boards). Also, domestic borrowing contributed a large portion of the internal financing.   The First Plan projected an average annual growth rate of 4 percent.[23]

The two largest projects in the plan were the hydro-electric dam at Kainji, and the steel mill, both representing substantial amounts of federal expenditures on electricity and trade and industry respectively. At the end of the plan period, work had not progressed beyond the preliminary studies. The low rate of performance was caused by lack of a concrete list of projects and of clearly defined measures for their promotion.

Table 10 shows the distribution of public sector capital investment during 1962-1968.

The First National Development Plan reflected the colonial plans where infrastructure investment such as transport received high priority. In assessing the success of the plan, one ought to judge it on the basis of its objectives. The focus of the plan was on the productiveness of the economy and the autonomy of the country. On the basis of the productiveness of the economy and the sudden growth of GDP, the First Plan was right on time. It estimated an average annual growth rate of 4 percent, while the real annual

---

[21]Dean, as quoted in Economist, (September 13, 1982), p. 3.

[22]Olayiwola, Petroleum and Structural Change in A Developing Country.

[23]Federal Republic of Nigeria, 1964.

average growth rate of GDP between 1961 and 1966 (before the civil war) was 4.8 percent.[24] On the question of national autonomy, it did not succeed. The heavy investment in transport could not bring national autonomy. Investments in the transport and other infrastructure areas only served to increase trade expansion, to induce, and, as a result, subsidize foreign capital interest. Also, trade and capital accumulation do not in themselves promote national autonomy and self-reliant development.

The First plan indicates that even though Nigeria was independent, its national planning endeavors continued to be colonial in origin. Like the pre-independence plans, it was drawn up by foreigners who were from capitalist countries, and who lacked the knowledge of the historical background and local customs of Nigerian citizens. The First Plan was, therefore, a direct transfer of Western model and value. Again, by emphasizing programs that were generally complementary to rather than competitive with the private foreign direct investment, the plan was designed to encourage foreign investment, specifically in commercial areas. Hence, the emphasis on building infrastructure such as roads, bridges, electricity, transport railways and the like.[25] Agriculture which employed more than 75 percent labor force in Nigeria was virtually neglected.

The Second and Third National Development Plans 1970-1974, 1975-1980

Perhaps if nothing else, the Gowon regime must be credited with the post-war reconstruction. The war had done considerable damage to the national infrastructure. The Second National Development Plan was mainly a reconstruction plan which called attention to the reactivation of the national economy to previous levels of performance. This is made quite explicit throughout the plan itself as it is stated:

The basic problem facing development planning in Nigeria in the early 1970s is how to revive the post-war economy such that

---

[24]Douglas Rimmer, Development in Nigeria: An Overview", In Political Economy of Income Distribution, ed by Diejomaoh (New York: Homes & Meirer, 1981), pp. 28-87.

[25]Edwin Dean, Plan Implementation in Nigeria, 1962-1968 (Ibadan: Oxford University Press, 1972).

it grows with greater speed and more confidence in the future. That essentially, is what the present Reconstruction and

Table 10

FIRST NATIONAL DEVELOPMENT PLAN 1962-1968:
SECTORAL DISTRIBUTION OF PUBLIC
SECTOR CAPITAL INVESTMENT

SECTOR	% OF TOTAL
Agriculture	13.6
Transport	21.3
Electricity	15.1
Communication	4.4
Trade Industry (including mining)	13.4
Education	10.3
Health	2.5
Water	3.6
Town and Country Planning	6.2
Labor, Social Welfare, Sports	0.7
Cooperative and Community Development	0.6
Judicial	0.1
Information	0.5
General Administration Defense and Security	7.1
Financial Obligations	0.6

Source: Federation of Nigeria 1961:41, Federal Ministry of Economic
Development, First National Plan 1962-68: Sectoral Distribution, Lagos, 1965.

Development Plan of 1970-1974 is about. It starts from the position that the civil war only worsened an already defective economic structure both in terms of capital formation and resource utilization. It then seeks to correct, through comprehensive planning, the various defects by a combination of policy reforms and new direct public investment programs. Given the serious setback of 1966-1969, the Plan views the first half of the 1970s as one of progressive accelerating growth in output, income and employment.[26]

In view of the above mentioned problems, General Gowon, in a state of the nation policy broadcast on October 1, 1970, set out a nine-point program on which, according to him, lasting peace and political stability in Nigeria could be maintained.[27] These included the implementation of the National Development Plan and the repair of the damage and neglect of o war; the reorganization of the armed forces; the eradication of corruption from Nigeria's national life; the settlement of the question of the creation of more states; the introduction of a new formula for revenue allocation; the preparation and adoption of a new constitution; the conducting of a national population census; the organization of genuinely national political parties; and the organization of elections in the states and the nation. The hope to achieve these objectives was based from the revenue derived from the oil export.

This particular government benefitted most from oil wealth. For example, in 1960, oil export signified only 2.56 percent of all exports; by 1970, it signified 57.56 percent. A year later, it signified 74 percent, and by 1974, its share of all export had jumped to 92.97 percent (See Table 11).

A major distinguishing aspect of the planning process of the Second Plan (as well as the Third Plan) from the First Plan is the greater degree of centralization of planning under the Federal Government; this was opposed to the lack of coordination which characterized the pre-coup planning period. Table 12 indicates the total public sector capital investment (1970-1974). In this area the biggest single area of the plan was transportation where 23.7 percent of the total public investments were to be found. This indicates the priority given by the military government to the reconstruction of roads and

---

[26]Federal Republic of Nigeria, Second National Development Plan 1970-1974 (Lagos: Federal Ministry of Information, 1970), p. 37.

[27]Rimmer, Political Economy of Income Distribution, p. 4.

bridges destroyed in the war and ultimately necessary and sufficient for the reorganization of normal economic operations.

Secondly, as compared with the 1962-1968 plan in which 66.9 percent of planned investments were to go into the Economic Area (the area actually absorbed 71.4 percent of investment funds), the Second National Plan represented only 56.7 percent of total investments for the Economic Area. The shift was to social services and administration. The emphasis on social services emerged from the neglect of areas like education and health during the war periods. The increase relative importance of Administration, on the other hand, takes account of the twelve - state apparatus which

Table 11

OIL EXPORTS AS PERCENTAGE OF TOTAL EXPORTS
1960-1983
(MILLION NAIRA)

YEAR	TOTAL EXPORTS	PETROLEUM	% OF TOTAL
1960	339	9	2.65
1961	529	131	24.76
1970	886	510	57.56
1971	1,304	964	73.93
1972	1,433	1,175	82.00
1973	2,319	1,935	83.44
1974	6,104	5,892	93.25
1975	4,791	4,592	95.85
1976	6,322	5,895	93.25
1977	7,594	7,046	92.78
1978	6,707	6,033	90.00

1979	10,676	10,035	94.00
1980	14,640	13,999	95.00
1981	11,892	11,250	94.60
1982	11,145	10,503	94.24
1983	8,427	7,786	92.39

Source: International Monetary Fund. International Financial Statistics Yearbook, 1984, pp. 454-455. Central Bank of Nigeria Annual Reports and Economic and Financial Review, various issues posted prices (of API 34 crude) From UN Monthly Bulletin of Statistics November 1976.

considerably enlarged the ranks of the bureaucracy; also, defense appropriations increased significantly as compared to the First Plan, an indication of the army's new status.

The Plan, in those areas where new ground was broken as opposed to reconstruction efforts, was clearly capital intensive rather than labor intensive, considerable attention being give to the promotion of industries, as opposed to agriculture wherein lies the main opportunities for absorbing Nigeria's growing number of unemployed. Our evaluation and observation in this section is that the Second National Development Plan recognizes that agriculture is the mainstay of the Nigerian economy with about 75 percent of the country's labor force employed in the area. Agriculture has, however, seen a constant decline in its contribution to Gross Domestic Product (GDP) since 1960. Despite the strategic importance of the sector, the plan only represented 10.5 percent of capital investments for the sector.

The plan had emphasized capital-intensive projects, thus giving low priority to the creation of job opportunities in the rural areas.[28] Secondly, social amenities had been concentrated in the urban areas. Coupled with high wage rates in the cities, there was a continued rural migration to the urban areas. Inflation also dramatically reduced the real incomes of urban regions workers and took most consumer goods out of the control of the rural

---

[28]Ibid., p. 38.

Table 12

TOTAL PUBLIC SECTOR CAPITAL INVESTMENT 1970-74

Table 11

TOTAL PUBLIC SECTOR CAPITAL INVESTMENT 1970-74

SECTOR	TOTAL	FEDERAL GOVT.	ALL STATES	BENUE PLATEAU	EAST CENTRAL	KANO	KWARA	LAGOS	MID-WESTERN	NORTH-CENTRAL	NORTH-EASTERN	NORTH-WESTERN	RIVERS	SOUTH-EASTERN	WESTERN
A. ECONOMIC															
Agriculture, livestock, Fishing, Forestry	10.5	5.5	10.3	11.0	20.5	12.1	10.4	11.1	10.4	—	17.6	11.4	13.2	12.5	10.5
Mining	2.4	0.6	4.6	-3.4	4.4	2.6	2.8	—	2.8	2.2	—	6.6	6.1	2.7	4.2
Industry	0.3	0.5	—	—	—	—	—	—	—	—	—	—	—	—	—
Commerce and Finance	8.1	7.3	9.6	7.4	11.1	6.7	9.4	11.3	6.8	10.9	6.7	12.3	9.4	14.2	28.7
Fuel and Power	1.8	2.0	1.7	0.1	1.2	—	7.5	9.1	0.7	0.4	2.3	2.3	5.7	5.7	6.6
Transport	4.4	8.2	—	—	—	—	—	—	—	0.7	2.5	2.5	1.5	1.4	1.8
Communications	23.7	30.1	16.1	26.5	10.6	14.7	14.7	23.1	16.8	23.1	5.6	1.7	0.7	3.1	2.4
Resettlement Rehabilitation	1.0	1.8	—	—	—	—	—	—	—	—	—	—	21.1	6.8	1.5
SUBTOTAL	50.7	63.7	48.3	48.7	49.0	55.0	44.8	45.8	44.9	43.2	61.0	57.4	50.3	53.3	41.6
B. SOCIAL															
Education	13.5	6.8	19.1	19.8	15.7	15.6	11.4	14.0	17.6	24.3	12.3	24.6	16.4	14.2	28.7
Health	5.2	1.8	9.3	3.4	13.8	9.4	14.1	9.2	10.9	2.7	8.7	14.2	9.4	5.7	6.6
Information	1.1	0.9	1.5	1.5	2.0	0.1	0.5	0.4	1.3	2.3	2.3	2.5	1.5	1.4	1.8
Labour and Social Welfare	1.2	0.5	1.9	0.9	0.1	1.0	5.8	0.5	1.8	0.5	2.5	2.5	2.4	1.4	1.8
Town and Country Planning	1.9	2.9	2.9	1.1	3.4	3.1	5.8	1.3	6.8	5.6	2.6	1.7	0.7	3.1	2.4
Water and Sewage	5.0	1.0	11.0	16.3	6.7	8.6	13.3	16.1	9.6	20.0	7.5	6.8	7.4	6.8	13.5
SUBTOTAL	27.9	13.0	43.5	43.0	42.6	38.8	47.3	44.8	43.2	35.0	35.0	57.4	39.0	60.1	54.9
C. ADMINISTRATION															
General Administration	5.1	4.2	6.2	8.3	8.4	6.2	7.9	—	2.8	4.0	4.0	7.5	10.3	7.7	28.7
Defence and Security	9.4	17.4	—	—	—	—	—	—	—	—	—	—	—	—	6.6
SUBTOTAL	14.5	21.6	6.2	8.3	8.4	6.2	7.9	9.3	2.8	4.0	4.0	7.5	10.3	7.7	3.5
D. FINANCIAL															
Financial Obligations	0.9	1.7	—	—	—	—	—	—	—	—	—	—	—	3.2	3.5
SUBTOTAL	0.9	1.7	—	—	—	—	—	—	—	—	—	—	—	3.2	3.5
GRAND TOTAL	100.0	100.0	100.0	100.0	100.0	100.0	100.0	100.0	100.0	100.0	100.0	100.0	100.0	100.0	100.0

Source: Third National Plan, p. 23.

population. As a result, the increases paid to export crop produces proved to be insignificant. Agriculture on the whole experienced a severe downward trend in productive terms.

At the time the plan was launched, the economy was suffering from a fundamental imbalance which reflected its inability to absorb the new capital. The plan was, however, supported as the answer to Nigeria's numerous economic problems; it was expected to generate a radical transformation of Nigerian society. This chapter attempts to analyze the plan so as to enable us to see how far that claim has been met in the plan's provisions.

The Indigenization Policy: A Strategy For Development

The government officials had also come to the aid of Nigerian business interests over the Second Plan period by passing a decree reserving certain types of business enterprises mainly for indigence; the Enterprise Promotion Decree passed in 1972 was basically an attempt to transfer control and ownership of some areas of the economy into the hands of Nigerians citizens.[29] The policy was also linked to state ownership of industrial capital, largely through joint ventures with foreign capital, and through the naturalization (up to 60 percent) of the equity capital in certain strategic areas of the economy. Government participation in economic production has been expanding even before the decree. The second development plan (1970-1974) prescribed a minimum 55 percent government holdings in the equities of iron and steel, petrochemical and oil refining, and other capital intensive projects, while indigenous private ownership was set at, least, 35 percent in the other medium - and small -scale industries, such as retail trade and marketing.[30] The National Oil Corporation made its first acquisition in 1971, and later by obtaining a 35 percent interest in shell in 1973, which was later raised to 55 percent of equity of all oil producing businesses.[31]

---

[29]Federal Republic of Nigeria Official Gazette, No. 10, Vol. 59 (Lagos: The Federal Ministry of Information, February, 1972).

[30]Chima Nnadozie, "Investment in Nigeria: The Political Climate," Economist, 23 August 1981, p. 14.

[31]African Research Bulletin, March 1980, p 2015.

However, while the indigenization exercise has been furthered by three successive legal instruments - the decrees of 1972, 1976, and the revision of 1977 - the main objective remains somewhat the same. As the official decree stated:

> The intention of the federal Military government in promulgating the Decree referred to as the indigenization Decree, is first and foremost to promote greater and more effective life of the nation. Government also believes that through such participation Nigerians would acquire the entrepreneurial know-how and develop a better habit of saving and thrift, all of which are so essential for the economic independence of the country.[32]

For reasons, the provisions of the original (1972) decree restricted foreign ownership and participation in 55 industrial sectors, and reserved for Nigerians certain types of business, with effect from March 31, 1974. A list of 22 activities, listed as Schedule I of the decree, including retail trade (other than department stores and supermarkets), small-scale manufacturing, bakery and advertisement, were reserved for Nigerians (and other Africans whose governments gave reciprocal treatment to Nigerians). In a further 33 activities, listed as Schedule II, foreign enterprise was to be excluded unless (a) either the paid-up capital of the enterprise exceeded N400,000 or turnover exceed N1 million or (b) where these limits were exceeded, at least 40 percent of the equity was held by Nigerian citizens or associations. The decree set March 31, 1974 as the date of compliance, after which defaulting enterprises would be bought over by the government.

The 1977 amendment followed the recommendations of the Industrial Enterprises Panel, set up to review the indigenization process with a view to facilitating compliance to the provisions of the original decree.[33] The revised decree in 1977 reclassified enterprises into three schedules instead of two, as contained in the original decree. Schedule I enterprises are reserved exclusively for Nigerians. Among the 40 enterprises in this schedule were advertising and public relations blending and bottling of alcoholic drinks,

[32]Ibid.

[33]The Nigerian Enterprises Promotion Decree (Amendment No. 2.) 1977.

candle manufacture, casinos and gambling centers, commercial transportation, department stores with an annual turnover of less than N1 million, real estate agencies, printing and travel agencies.

Schedule II enterprises, which must have 60 percent (instead of the original 40 percent) Nigerian ownership, contained a list of 57 enterprises, among which were boat building; beer brewing; clearing and forwarding agencies; construction; commercial, merchant and development banking; manufacture of cement; insurance; mining and quarrying. Foreign capital participation in these enterprises is allowed only if Nigerian citizens' or associations' participation is not less than 60 percent of the total equity capital. Schedule III enterprises (i.e., all others) must have a minimum 40 percent local ownership. However, a minimum of 60 percent Nigerian ownership is necessary if the turnover of such enterprises exceed N25 million per year. This schedule contains 39 enterprises, including the manufacture of drugs and medicines, of engines and turbines, electrical appliances, and housewares; ship-building and repair; manufacture of motorcycles, vehicles, watches and clocks, aircraft and textile manufacturing industries. for more detailed list of businesses exclusively or partially reserved for Nigerian indigence see Table 13.[34]

Three new institutions were established by the Federal Government to implement the decree; these were namely the Nigerian Enterprises Promotion Board, the Capital Issues Commission and the Bank for Commerce and Industry, established to provide Nigerians with the capital to buy out foreign interests in the earmarked sectors. The Enterprises Promotion Board (NEPB) was responsible for identifying affected enterprises and monitoring them in order to verify transfers of share of company ownership, while the Federal Commissioner was vested with discretionary powers in granting extension and/or exemptions. Also, the issue of shares in public companies was handled separately by the capital issue commission and Lagos Stock Exchange. Later, the establishment or creation of the Nigerian Bank of Commerce and Industry, under Decree No. 22 of 1973, provide an institutional financial system to provide the finance necessary to buy equity share participation by Nigerians.

---

[34]Nicholas Balakins, Indigenization and Economic Development: The Nigeria Experience, (London: Jal Press, 1982).

Table 13
NIGERIA'S LIST OF RESTRICTED INDUSTRIAL SECTORS
Schedule I

Enterprises exclusively reserved for Nigerian ownership under the 1977 decree are as follows:

Distribution agencies, excluding motor vehicles, machinery, and equipment and spare parts.
Electrical repair shops, unless associated with distribution of electrical goods.
Film distribution.
Hairdressing.
Ice cream making.
Manufacture of suitcases, briefcases, handbags, purees, wallets, portfolios and shopping bags.
Manufacturers' representatives.
Office cleaning.
Pool betting and lotteries.
Poultry farming.
Printing of stationery.
Protective agencies.
Real estate agents.
Stevedoring and shorehanding.
Travel agencies.
Watch, clock and jewelry repairs.
Wholesale distribution of local manufactures and other locally produced goods.
Bread and cake making.
Candle manufacture.
Casinos and gaming centers.
Cinemas and other places of entertainment.
Commercial transportation (wet and dry cargo and fuel).
Commission agents.
Department stores and supermarkets with less that 2 million turnover.
Advertising and public relations.
Assembly of radios, record changers, television, tape recorders and other electric domestic appliance not combined with manufacture of comments.
Blending and bottling of alcoholic drinks.
Blocks and ordinary tiles manufactured for building and construction works.

Schedule II*[35]

According to the 1978/79 budget proposals, integrated agricultural production and processing will be transferred from Schedule II to Schedule III.

The following enterprises require 60% Nigerian ownership:

Canning and preserving of fruits and vegetables.
Cement manufacturing.
Clearing and forwarding agencies.
Coastal and inland waterways shipping.
Construction.
Department stores and supermarkets with a turnover of more than 2 million.
Distribution agencies for machines and technical equipment.
Distribution and servicing of motor vehicles, tractors and spare parts thereof, of other similar objects.
All undertaking with 25 million annual turnover.
Banking (commercial, merchant and development).
Beer brewing.
Bicycle and motorcycle tire manufacturing.
Boat building.
Soft-drink bottling.
Business services (management and consulting), but not machinery and equipment and rental and leasing.
Manufacture of basic iron and steel.
Manufacture of bicycles.
Manufacture of biscuits and similar dry bakery products.
Manufacture of cocoa, chocolate and sugar confectionery.
Manufacture of cosmetics and perfumery.
Manufacture of diary productions - butter, cheese, and other mild products.
Publishing of books, periodical, etc.
Pulp and paper mills.
Restaurants, cafes and other eating and drinking places.
Salt refining packaging.
Screen printing on cloth, dyeing.
Slaughtering and storage association with the industrial processing and distribution of meat.
Mining and quarrying.
Oil seed milling and crushing.
Paper conversion industries.
Petrochemical feedstock industries.
Photographic studios, including commercial and aerial photography.
Plantation cultivation of trees, grains and other cash crops.
Plantation sugar cultivation and processing.
Printing of books.
Production of sawed timber, plywood, veneers, and other wood conversions industries.
Fashion design.

Fertilizer production.
Fish and shrimp trawling and processing.
Grain mill products except rice milling.
Industrial cleaning.
Insecticides, pesticides and fungicides.
Insurance (all classes).
Internal air transportation.
Lighterage.
Manufacture of furniture and interior decoration.
Manufacture of leather footwear.
Manufacture of matches.
Manufacture of metal containers.
Manufacture of metal fixtures for household, office and public use.
Manufacture of food products such as yeast, starch, baking power; coffee roasting processing of tea leaves into black tea.
Manufacture of paints, varnishes or similar articles.
Manufacture of pens, pencils, umbrellas, canes, buttons, brooms, brushes, lamp shades, tobacco pipes, cigarette holders, toys.
Manufacture of plastic products.
Manufacture of rubber products.
Manufacture of sops and detergents.
Manufacture of tires and tubes for vehicles.
Manufacture of wire, nails, washers, bolts, nuts and similar articles.
Tanners and leather finishing.
Wholesale distribution of imported goods.

Schedule III

The ventures requiring a minimum 40% Nigerian ownership are all enterprises not included in Schedules I or III and not belonging to the public sector.

Nigeria's Industrial Priorities

Establishment of an automobile assembly industry.
Expansion of export-oriented industries.
Further import substitution in "areas of currency deficiency".
Establishment of a basic iron and steel industry to provide the input for manufacture of intermediate governmental-owned.
Establishment of liquified petroleum gas and petrochemical industries (production of raw materials may eventually be 100% government-owned.
Promotion of integration, forward linkage and diversification of the textile industry.

SOURCES: Nicholas Balakins. Indigenization and Economic Development: The Nigerian experience, London, England: Jal Press. p. 163-195. See The Nigerian Enterprises Promotion Decree (Amendment No. 2.) 1977.

Any interpretation of the Third National Plan must of necessity understand the climate of optimism (generated by the availability of funds) which accompanied its formulation. It is a large plan in terms of cost (N30 billion), and represents the most ambitious plan yet to be drawn in Nigeria. Furthermore, the feasibility of the plan was based on the substantial revenues being generated from the export of oil. As a result, the former reliance on agricultural exports and foreign loans thus gave way to revenues from oil exports. In fact, oil provided over 90 percent of total government earnings and about 70 percent of total government revenue during the Third National Plan period.

Again, our examination of the Third Plan shows that trade and industry (including mining) received the largest shares and transport and other infrastructures also received more attention. Contrary to all the rhetoric about agriculture being a key priority area, its share in the Third Plan was 7.7 percent compared to 10.5 percent in the second Plan, which when translated indicated a decline of 32 percent.[36]

Also, the Fourth National Development Plan (1981-1985) implemented by the Shagari administration relied heavily on the revenues from petroleum. Petroleum revenues were important and responsible for paying for imports as well as for financing Nigeria's Fourth Plan. The outline of the Fourth Plan, as presented in 1980, emphasized the promotion of self-reliance and the involvement of the masses in the development endeavor. The practical effects of greater self-reliance are not clearly defined, but one would expect it to include the substitution of Nigerian for foreign factors of production, products, services, techniques and tastes. The Fourth National Development Plan proposed public investment of N70.5 billion. And this was based on a estimated petroleum production of 3.0 million barrel per day (b/d) which never realized because of the reduction in world oil demand and more competition from non-OPEC oil suppliers such as Britain, Mexico and

---

[36]Federal Ministry of Economic Development. Third National Development Plan 1975-1980, Vol. 1 (Lagos: The Central Planning Office, 1979).

Norway. The result was a reduction in plan operations and reduction and in many cases, stoppage of many development plans.

Again, the highest priority was placed on transport, trade and industry, education, general administration and defense. Agriculture, which is the main engine of economic development was given less attention in the Fourth Plan. Our finding is that none of the National Development Plans had agriculture as the first priority. The Nigerian governments ranging from General Gowon to Shagari were paying lip service to agriculture and agricultural development.

The assumption in most less developed countries is that once a country has abundant supply of oil, then economic growth will be achieved in a relatively short time period. This is obvious because oil provides a source of energy which is so vital to industrialization and the improved living conditions of the oil producing economies. With a large deposit of crude petroleum, substantial foreign exchange could be earned through petroleum exports, and, consequently, capital formation in different sectors of the economy can proceed unhampered. One may therefore wish to ask whether this expectation happened and/or has been realized in Nigeria.

Also, between 1970s and 1980s the country had a strategy of indigenizing Nigerian economy. The two indigenization decrees were measures to increase Nigerian participation in the ownership and control of important business operations. The outcome had been the employment of Nigerians in every industry operating in the economy. There is no doubt that indigenization was seem as a essential part of economic development and was expected to produce a self-reliant and economically independent nation. Regrettably, that has prove to be absorptive. Instead, Nigeria became more dependent economically because of its world trade and oil export activity.

According to Olayiwola, furthermore, the oil boom and the indigenization program generally benefitted the middle class, while living conditions became more difficult for the lower class who happened to be the majority of the population who are marginalized. Despite the appearance of development, the large oil production of the 1970s did not result in economic and political autonomy and independent for Nigeria. Rather, the country became more dependent on oil revenues. Millions of naira were invested on physical infrastructure. Still, Nigeria had little to show for all the money because of waste and corruption on a large scale.

In addition, economic activities reserved for Nigerians were in spheres that did not exert a significant influence on the economy. These activities were originally run by Nigerian anyway. Foreigners were allowed to participate in the more vital areas like wholesale distribution, shipping, construction, boat building, furniture manufacturing, bicycle manufacturing and the like. In principle, Nigerians were allowed to purchase foreign businesses, and in effect, only well-established local business were credit worthy to receive bank loans for such endeavor. Moreover, the decree failed to bring the really big enterprises and transnational corporations, which dominate the economy, under Nigerian control.

Above all, one cannot say that the indigenization decree was made because of a strong ruling class commitment to put to an end, in a fundamental way foreign domination of the Nigerian economy. Nor was the decree designed primarily to improve the material well-being of the entire population.   In other words, the decree was less than nationalistic in implementation and operation.

However, the evidence of development was found everywhere during the 1970s and early part of the 1980s. For instance, road building in Nigeria experienced heavy growth rate. The total road network increased from 66,074 kilometers in 1960 to 95,374 kilometers in 1972, an increase of 44 percent.[37] Also, major programs have been undertaken to establish a national integrated highway system. It has been indicated that between April 1975 and December 1978, the combined lengths of roads, and bridges under construction increased from 4,800 kilometers to 14,500 kilometers.[38] However, the importance of roads in Nigeria cannot be over exaggerated when one realizes that between 1978 and 1980, the motor vehicles in use increased from 449,424 to 633,268, an increase of about 41 percent.[39]

Furthermore, education in Nigeria is viewed as an engine of development. This popularly held view was confirmed by late chief Obafemi

[37]Federal Republic of Nigeria, Second National Development Plan 1970-1974. Second Progress Report, (Lagos: Central Planning Office 1974). See Third National Development Plan 1975-1980. Special Launching Edition, (Lagos: Central Planning Office 1975).

[38]Federal Republic of Nigeria.   Economic and Statistical Review, (Lagos: Federal Government Press, 1979), p. xix.

[39]Ibid.

Awolowo, who in 1955 introduced free primary education into the Western Region. To quote Awolow:

> The provision of education and health in developing country such as Nigeria is as much an instrument of economic development as the provision of roads, water supply, electricity, and the like. To educate the children and enlighten the illiterate adults is to lay a solid foundation not only for future social and economic progress but also for political stability. A truly educated citizenry is, in my view, one of dictatorship, oligarchy and feudal autocracy.[40]

Furthermore, according to the Third Plan, grade school enrollment was expected to increase from 2.9 million on 1960 and 3.9 million in 1971 to 11.5 million during 1975-1980 as a result of the introduction of free universal primary education.[41] The increased enrollment created additional demands on the government, in the 1980s and above, for more secondary school, more universities, more jobs and other related socio-economic activities.

As we have seen in this chapter, most of Nigeria's investment had gone into physical infrastructural development rather than development of productive sectors. Physical infrastructural development means little to citizens if they cannot assume the positions of industrial leadership. National emphasis on trade and capital accumulation resulted in growth without development. Political and economic self-reliance, as expressed in the various National Development Plans, was focused on Nigerian ownership of businesses while neglecting the real definition of autonomy in an economic and political sense, which would emphasize the capacity of a country to stand on its own to be self-sufficient, and able to exist independently, without outside dominance. In 1980, despite political independence, the Nigerian economy was colonial in nature, dependent on foreign trade and capital attraction for its growth, development and expansion.

---

[40]Obafemi Awolow, The Autobiography of Chief Abafemi Awolow, (Cambridge: Cambridge University Press, 1960), p 268.

[41]Federal Republic of Nigeria. Third National Development Plan (1975-1980), p. 238.

CHAPTER 5

The Origin And Development
Of The
Economic Crisis In Nigeria

In this chapter, we examine the internal and external dimensions of the economic situation in Nigeria for Nigerian economic predicament for a particular purpose; to provide a description of the economic situation in Nigeria so as to clarify the environment in which the International Monetary Fund has functioned since the mid-80s.

In addition, this chapter addresses the following questions: Can Nigerian economic crisis be fully explained by internal political and socio-economic factors, such as the political dominance of the military activity, military and civilian government corruption, Nigerian nationalism, and the Nigerian-Biafran War and its impact? Or, to what point is its development strategy the product of a structural condition of dependence and underdevelopment created by its colonial past and continued by its export, oil economy? Can Nigeria's economic crisis be explained comprehensively by its decision to carry out unbalanced development, and/or must the role and influence of industrialized states be added to explain the crisis? These and other similar issues are the primary focus and concern of this chapter.

Nigeria is recently in a dangerous crisis, whose real severity, dimensions, and social and political implications are not fully appreciated by Nigerian Citizens. The major causes of this worsening economic crisis include a wide range of internal weakness, and a hostile external economic environment. It is important that the structure of this crisis be clearly understood by the Nigerian government, the multilateral institutions, and donor countries. Without a general understanding of the factors responsible for Nigerian economic crisis, it will be impossible to design economic measures and assistance programs to attack the crisis consistently and effectively.

Nigeria's economic condition, already serious, is deteriorating. In fact, unless effective or efficient are taken now, the already fragile fabric of the economic, social, and political system may break down in no distance time.

The International Monetary Fund, the World Bank and other international organizations have published materials on some aspects of the crisis and the complex range of issues resulting from it: mass poverty, unemployment, unsustainable population growth rates, high rate of inflation, the rapidly decreasing ability of the country to feed itself, mass poverty, havoc wreaked by drought, low rate of economic growth, and shortage of domestic savings.[1]   There are two major findings in this case. First, for many Nigerians, poverty and other hardships are more severe now than twenty years ago. Second, the interaction between rapidly increasing population, shortage of resources and skills, and weak or ineffective administrative machineries have in many cases led to greater human misery in Nigeria, while appropriate internal measures by the Nigerian government are necessary, the Nigerian economy is substantially influence by forces beyond its control. For example, six primary products alone such as cocoa, cotton, wheat, peanut, rubber and palm oil account for 75 percent of Nigeria's export earnings, making Nigeria's export earnings extremely vulnerable to changes in international demand. External economic disequilibrium is a manifestation of the dependence of Nigeria on industrial nations. Nigerian exports depend on the production of primary products (from agriculture and mining). The demand for these products is price inelastic in the short run.

In addition, the ambitious investment programs the country initiated after independence necessitated increased resort to external borrowing, thereby significantly increasing external indebtedness. The current economic crisis has led the country to experience payments difficulties so critical that it

---

[1]World Bank Annual Report "World Development Report" in Economist (16 May 1985), p. 11.

crisis has led the country to experience payments difficulties so critical that it has been unable to pursue the development efforts or plans initiated earlier.

On the domestic area, it is necessary to underline the significance of structural obstacles and their implications, which in turn derive from historical circumstance or from the physical environment, for instance, human resource underdevelopment inherited from colonial training policies, economic confusion accompanying decolonization, rapid population growth, the high cost of newly established institutions adapted to the new political realities and directed toward new requirements.

External Factors

The economic crisis recorded in Nigeria since the 1970s and 1980s originated from both external and internal factors. The economic growth of Nigeria depends on external resources in the form of both export revenues, whose level again, depends on world market terms and borrowed capital. The external interaction of Nigerian economy, also makes this country sensitive to external shocks and vulnerable in world market prices.

Furthermore, negative influence on Nigeria included the combined impacts of inflation and slackening economic activity (stagnation) in the developed countries. However, the rise in oil prices resulted in a slowdown in the productive operation of industrialized states at a period when inflation was high. With regard to Nigeria, these conditions led to the collapse of its export commodity prices and to higher prices for its imports, resulting in the deterioration of her terms of trade and widening current account imbalances.

Collectively, they constrained the possibilities for national development. Furthermore, as Nigeria came to realize, her socio-economic progress was not a matter of internal economic activity and policy alone. The pursuit of unbalanced growth stressing first agricultural development for export, and then petroleum export and the infrastructural sectors, led Nigeria into an economic environment influenced significantly by circumstances beyond her control. At this point, however, Olanyiwola indicates that Nigeria became dependent upon international supply and demand conditions that determined her export revenues, limited her ability to attract foreign investment in sectors other than her growth sectors, set the terms of foreign exchange, and as a result determined her direction and terms of trade. These factors are affected by events outside the control of Nigerian policy that have increasingly determined its success. As a result, Nigeria has been forced to balance internal demands for development with external conditions of trade, international politics, internationalization of capital, and the availability of substitutes for Nigeria's export commodities.[2]

However, Nigeria hoped to lessen these influences, through its active memberships in Organization of Petroleum Exporting Countries (OPEC). By encouraging a unified production and pricing policy, she aimed at turning the world market to her advantage. OPEC was supposed to provide economic security for her petroleum economy, and in the process strengthen the chances for success of her unbalanced growth strategy. It briefly worked as Nigeria intended.

One of the most significant external developments in the world market after the December 1973 price increase to work against Nigeria was the reaction of the oil importing industrial nations, especially the United States. In February 1974, the Washington Conference on Energy was held, attended by 13 major Western Capitalist States: Canada, West Germany, Denmark, Belgium, France, Norway, The United Kingdom, and the United States.[3] All, except France, agreed to established a new organization to manage their energy policies. That organization, named the International Energy Agency (IEA), was inaugurated in November 1974.

The formation of IEA was only a partial fulfillment of U.S. hopes. The United States was seeking a showdown between oil consumers and producers, while the other developed countries supported U.N. initiatives based on broader aspects of other issues than oil.[4] It is not surprising, therefore, that the desire of France to established a network of European-Third World relations independent of U.S. influence was an important force in turning

---

[2]Peter Olannyiwola, Petroleum and Structural Change in a Developing Country: The Case of Nigeria (New York: Praeger Publishers, 1987).

[3]For detailed account of the OPEC formation and its solidarity in the international economic order see: Robert A. Mortimer. The Third World Coalition in International Politics (Boulder, Colorado: Westview Press, 1984), pp. 43-71. J.E. Spero, The Politics of International Economic Relations (New York: St. Martin's Press, 1985), pp. 293-338. Bahgat Korany, How Foreign Policy Decisions are Made in the Third World: A comparative Analysis (Boulder, Colorado: Westview Press, 1984), pp. 138-164.

[4]Mortimer, p. 49.

common market partners away from confrontation. The Americans favored an anti-OPEC coalition operating outside the U.N. institutions because the

Table 13

GLOBAL ENERGY CONSUMPTION 1975 AND 1990
ACTUAL 1975   ESTIMATED 1990

	10^6 BTU	% of World Average	10^6 BTU	% of World Average	% Increase 1975-1990
Third World States	11	18	14	19	27
Second World States	58	97	65	90	12
Other Western Indust. States	136	227	234	325	72
United States	332	553	422	586	27

Sources: The Global 200 Report. Technical Section, Table 13-34.

Figure 7

NATIONAL LEVELS OF ENERGY CONSUMPTION

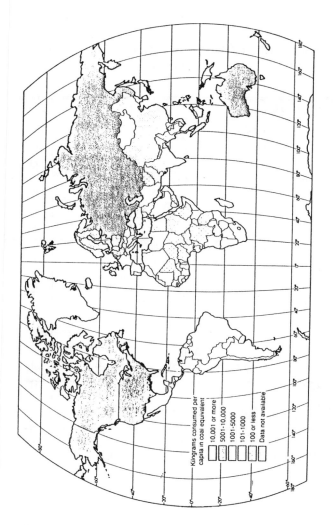

Source: National levels of energy consumption, rated by kilograms per captia. (Reprinted with the permission of Macmillian Publishing Company from Geography by Arthur Getis, Judith Getis, and Jerome Fellman, Copyright 1981 by Macmillian Publishing Company).

latter lent themselves to a show of Third World Unity. While the United States failed in its endeavors to isolate OPEC countries, the reaction underscored the fragile power OPEC members including Nigeria possessed during the 1970s.[5]

However, by the end of the 1970s, Nigeria's hoped-for OPEC buffer was under significant threat. Non-OPEC supplies were increasing rapidly as Britain, Norway, and Mexico offered petroleum at lower than OPEC prices. In 1982, the offer of non-OPEC petroleum by these countries began to put downward pressure on world prices. For example, "OPEC'S share of the world oil market fell from 63 percent in 1973 to 48 percent in 1979 to 33 percent in 1983".[6]   Cartel members saw an uneasy situation grow much worse. By 1983, members were neglecting OPEC pricing and quota policies, and the organization found itself unable to control its members.[7] In October 1984, in response to cuts by Britain, Norway, and Mexico, Nigeria reduced its oil price by $4 less than the OPEC of U.S. $34 per barrel.[8] Later that year, when OPEC prices reduced its production ceiling, and in effect the production quotas of its members, Nigeria had to seek and obtain exemption from further reduction in its quota of 1.3 million b/d. In December of 1984, Nigeria and Ecuador expressed their reluctance to support OPEC's plan for monitoring members' oil production levels, exports, and prices. Despite OPEC'S struggle to maintain harmony among its members and Nigeria crisis condition, one can expect Nigeria to remain a member of OPEC.   However, the economic security sought through OPEC is no longer feasible. For accurate account of major petroleum exporting countries see figure 8.

Again, in spite of the internal pressures with which Nigeria had to deal, there were also powerful external forces. These external factors contributed largely to the development and economic crisis now being experienced in Nigeria.

The enormous oil wealth of the 1970s that came from the industrialized states through Nigeria, but because of the structural nature of its economy, much of that wealth went back immediately to the developed

---

[5]Ibid., p. 50.
[6]Spero, p. 317.
[7]Ibid., p. 319.
[8]Ibid., p. 320.

Figure 8

MAJOR SOURCES OF PETROLEUM PRODUCTION AND REFINERY OPERATIONS OF THE WORLD

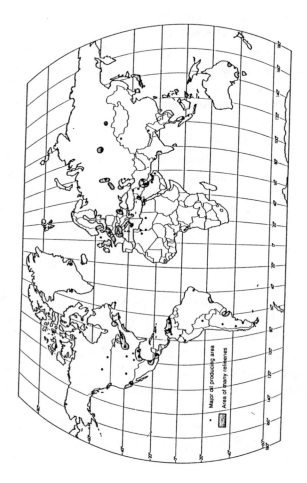

Source: Major sources of petroleum production and refinery operation of the world. (Reprinted with the permission of Macmillan Publishing Company from Geography by Arthur Getis, Judith Getis, and Jerome Fellman. Copyright 1981 by Macmillian Publishing Company.

countries to pay for her mounting import bill and MNC involvement in its development projects. Nigeria had little control over such factors. Her leaders and development planners should have expected the tactics of the various actors in her external environment and taken steps at least to minimize their effects. But such measures could not have solved Nigeria's fundamental problems, and cannot resolve them now. Without structural change in her political economy, Nigeria seems destined to move from crisis to crisis.

Added to this is the role of MNCs in Nigeria. After political independence in 1960, the subsidiaries of giant multinational corporations (MNCs) have emerged as the most powerful agents of multilateral imperialism in Nigeria. These are corporations whose monopoly capital and advanced technology, backed by tremendous political pressure from their national governments, constitutes the dominant mechanism for integrating countries more closely, into the international system of capitalist monopoly. With the ending of colonialism and the emergence of multilateral imperialism under the control of the United States after 1945, giant multinational corporations quickly emerged as the dominant catalysts of imperialism, particularly after the achievement of independence in the 1960s.[9]

As Baran and Sweezy in their book Monopoly Capital argue:

> One can no longer today speak of either industrialist or bankers as the leading echelon of the dominant capitalist classes. The big monopolistic corporations which were formed, and their early years controlled by bankers, proved to be enormously profitable and in due course through paying off their debts and plowing back their earnings, achieved financial independence, and indeed, in many cases acquired substantial control over banks and other financial institutions. These giant corporations are the basic units of monopoly capitalism in its present stage; their (big) owners and functionaries constitute the leading echelon of the ruling class. It is through analyzing these

---

[9]Archie Mafeje, "Neocolonialism, State Capitalism or Revolution?" in P. Gutkind and P. Waterman (eds) African Social Studies-A Radical Reader, (New York: Monthly Review Press, 1969), pp. 138-139.

corporate giants and their interests that we can best comprehend the functioning of imperialism today.[10]

In Nigeria, there has been a shift of foreign investment from trading and agriculture, to petroleum, other mineral products, monopoly finance and manufacturing industries. This shift in the input requirements for changing nature of industrial manufacturing, such as the emergence of the petro-chemical industry, has also meant concentrations of petroleum products and inputs for chemical product like artificial fibers and plastics.

Since 1960, these methods have been used in Nigeria to ensure monopoly and domination of such important economic areas as manufacturing, banking and insurance, petroleum and mining, transport and communication, construction, and import trade. According to Onimode, the exploitation of the areas by multinational corporations is based either on full foreign ownership, or on joint venture, with indigenous capitalists (private or government).[11]

For instance, by 1976, the petroleum area accounted for about 91 percent of Nigeria's foreign exchange earnings and about 96 percent of government revenue, at a period when the nation was the fifth largest exporter of oil in the world. This dependence on petroleum is also reflected by the fact that it contributed about 46 percent of Gross Domestic Product in 1974-1975 when the manufacturing share to GDP was only 4.7 percent (See Chapter 4, Table 7).

However, the historical foundation of multinational monopoly of petroleum industry in Nigeria originates back to 1937 when the British administration allocated Shell and British Petroleum the total land area of Nigeria as a petroleum concession. Petroleum was first exported from Nigeria by these corporations in 1958. After political independence in 1960, Shell BP surrendered its petroleum concession, some of which were inherited by the

---

[10]See Paul A. Baran and Paul M. Sweezy Monopoly Capital, quoted in Bade Onimode, Imperialism and Underdevelopment in Nigeria, (London: Zed Press, 1975), p.23.

[11]For an analysis of imperialism domination of these areas, see B. Onimode, "Imperialism and Multinational Corporations - A Case Study of Nigeria" in Y. Yansana (ed) Decolonization and Dependency: Problems of Development in African Society, (Greenwood Press, 1980), pp. 208-222. Ola Oni and B. Onimode, Economic Development of Nigeria: The Socialist Alternative, (Ibadan: The Nigerian Academy of Arts and Sciences and Technology, 1975), pp. 141-142.

American multinational corporation such as Gulf and Mobil. This is a reflection of a new multilateral imperialism under the United States domination in Nigeria. Table 15 and 16 summarize assets and profits of major oil companies in 1963 and yearly output of major oil companies operating in Nigeria, 1960-1972 respectively.

In Nigeria, the first oil refinery at Ememe near Port Harcourt is jointly owned by the multinational corporations. These corporations dominate oil distribution in the country. The marketing subsidiaries of the above mentioned giant companies dominate the country's import of petroleum products.

Also, Nigeria has other important minerals such as iron, ore limestone, lead, coal, columbite, marble, gold, and zinc. Again, British imperialist domination over "rich lands" ensured early monopoly of tin and columbite by multinational corporations in Nigeria. Before the indigenization policy,limestone was exploited for cement production by the West African Portland Cement Company, a joint stock company from Britain with 48 percent foreign and 52 percent local equity.[12]

The roles of multinational corporations in other areas include transport, communication, forestry and fishery operations. Shipping and handling are controlled and monopolized by Elder Dempster/West African Shipping Line. The activity of these companies accounted for about 54 percent of the 60 percent of the total United Kingdom West African Lines, traffic by origin or destination. However, the government's Nigerian National Shipping Line, which was formed in 1961, controls only about 10 percent of the nation's shipping.

Also, as regards communication, the American owned International Telephone and Telegraph (ITT) company came into the country after 1970. This giant corporation received a communication contract of over N802 million in Nigeria in 1971. It is important to note that air transport in Nigeria is also dominated by such multinational corporations as Pan America, KLM, British Caledonian, Lufthansa, Sabena, Swiss Air, and the like prior to 1970. Their large capacities, personnel and management, and monopoly capital

---

[12]Onimode, Imperialism and Multinational Corporations: A Case Study of Nigeria, p. 227.

Table 15

ASSETS AND PROFITS OF MAJOR OIL COMPANIES, 1963

COMPANY	ASSETS (MILLION)	PROFITS (MILLION)
Standard Oil of New Jersey	3,800	240
Royal Dutch/Shell BP	3,300	180
Gulf	1,700	120
Texaco	1,700	140
Second Mobil	1,500	68
Standard Oil of California	1,200	100
British Petroleum	900	65
Companies Francis Petroleum	600	42
Others	1,200	45
Total	16,500	1,000

Source: S.A. Aluko and M.O. Ijere "The Economics of Mineral Oil, "Nigerian Journal of Economic and Social Studies, 1965, Volume 7, p. 210.

enable them to monopolize and dominant the only nation's air line, Nigerian Airways, in both cargo traffic and passengers.[13]   Moreover, multinational corporations engage directly in forestry and fishery in Nigeria. The multinational corporations in forestry industry include Hushim Estates Ltd., Savannah Sugar Company, Ltd., with N35 million investment, the African

---

[13]Ibid.

Table 16

YEARLY OUTPUT OF OIL COMPANIES OPERATING IN NIGERIA
1960-72

Year	Shell-Bp	Gulf	Safrap	Mobil	Agip	Texaco
1960	6,367,187	—	—	—	—	—
1961	16,801,896	—	—	—	—	—
1962	24,623,691	—	—	—	—	—
1963	27,913,479	—	—	—	—	—
1964	43,996,895	—	—	—	—	—
1965	99,686,968	9,666,026	—	—	—	—
1966	129,527,559	18,614,765	—	—	—	—
1967	99,205,664	19,998,409	—	—	—	—
1968	135,311,067	35,992,227	—	—	—	—
1969	139,338,895	67,966,087	4,295,845	—	—	—
1970	209,827,680	84,551,243	7,327,021	19,787,820	1,776,492	867,784
1971	404,206,571	101,128,748	8,590,469	26,430,407	14,061,624	3,796,852
1972	442,195,656	119,101,841	20,230,307	60,953,145	19,101,052	3,701,330

Source: Oni and Onimode, Economic Development of Nigeria —
The Socialist Alternative, (Ibadan: The Nigerian
Academy of Arts, Sciences and Technology, 1975), p. 27.

Source: Oni and Onimode, Economic Development of Nigeria--The
Socialist Alternative, (Ibadan: The Nigerian Academy of Arts, Sciences
and Technology, 1975), 27.

Timber and Plywood Co., a branch of British Unilever, Tate and Lyle Swiss-Nigerian Wood Industries Ldt., and the South-Easter State Rubber Plantation owned jointly with Commonwealth Development Corporation. Table 15 summarizes the distribution of foreign monopoly capital in Nigeria, 1962-1974.

This table indicates three most attractive areas to multinational corporations as mining or petroleum after 1964, manufacturing particularly after 1970, and distribution, which dominated manufacturing before 1970. Building and construction is third, while agriculture and transport represent fourth and fifth position in preferential arrangement. With the construction boom of the enormous road projects of the military from 1974 to 1979, the share of building and construction might have well increased.

The consequences of multinational corporation in Nigeria are many and vary. The investment policies of these multinational corporations are biased against the development of capital goods industries in Africa including Nigeria, and biased in favor of the use of capital-intensive
technique in their extractive and export-oriented undertakings. Both of these biases hinder the balanced development of Nigeria. For instance, capital intensive techniques require less labor per level of output than labor-intensive techniques. They also require a small labor force composed of specialized management personnel and semi-skilled workers whereas labor intensive techniques tend to require a much larger labor force composed largely of skilled and unskilled workers.

The bias against development of the capital goods sector prevents a balanced growth of the internal market and, along with the use of capital intensive techniques, increases the dependence of Nigeria on the importation of specialized machinery and other capital goods from the developed capitalist countries. The latter aggravates the balance of payments problem experienced by the Nigerian government.

Furthermore, the impact of technological underdevelopment of Nigeria originated from colonial times. The imposition of import capitalist manufactures such as cotton goods, machinery and equipment, wines,utensils, and so on, and the export of Nigerian primary products for manufacturing of these products by capitalist states according to Onimode, have two major implications: (1) cheap import substitutes deprived Nigerian industrialists of their domestic markets and rendered domestic technologists like blacksmiths, cloth-weavers, miners and iron workers obsolete; and (2) the export of their

Table 17

CUMULATIVE DISTRIBUTION OF FOREIGN INVESTMENT BY ACTIVITY
(IN PERCENTAGES)

Year	Mining & Quarrying	Manufacturing & Processing	Agriculture Forestry & Fishing	Transport & Communications	Building & Construction Services	Trading & Business Services	Miscellaneous
1962	36.7	17.3	2.0	1.1	3.8	38.4	0.7
1963	36.1	19.1	1.0	1.0	4.2	37.2	0.5
1964	40.1	18.2	1.7	1.1	3.8	31.4	3.7
1965	43.7	18.5	1.5	1.5	5.3	24.6	4.9
1966	50.8	17.5	1.1	1.5	2.2	24.8	3.0
1967	45.9	22.2	1.2	1.1	2.5	24.8	2.3
1968	49.1	20.0	1.1	1.1	2.4	24.2	2.1
1969	44.2	22.2	1.3	1.3	2.5	26.2	2.3
1970	51.4	22.4	1.1	1.4	1.4	20.6	1.7
1971	52.5	28.6	1.2	0.9	1.2	14.1	1.5
1972	54.7	22.7	0.6	0.8	2.2	15.4	3.6
1973	52.5	23.2	0.4	0.6	2.6	16.7	4.0
1974	45.2	28.7	1.1	1.2	3.5	17.7	2.5
1975	41.6	22.4	0.8	1.0	5.0	25.2	4.0

Source: Central Bank of Nigeria, Economic and Financial Review, (Lagos, Government Printer, 1968.1976)

primary products deprived them of the necessary resources that would havehelped them to improve the traditional method of production and the quality of their products. "Hence, the patronage sought in order to 'transfer technology' has turned out to be a miserable disappointment at best."

In Nigeria, under the open door policy or industrialization in an open economy, multinational corporations have been left free to choose their lines of operation, location, production processes and the like. In effect, they have concentrated their investment in enclave industries such as petroleum and consumer goods manufacturing in urbanized areas like Lagos, Enugu, Kano, Ibadan, in order to ensure the quickest and highest possible profits. However, such industries and their production technologies are highly unrelated to the Nigerian development preferences.

The main objective of foreign investors in Nigeria as anywhere in the less developed countries of Africa, has been to invest only in the high profit sectors of the economy. The high profits which they realize from these areas are not reinvested for further development. Instead, these investors always send the profits back to their respective countries. Again, this practice not only prevents domestic capital formation but also results in a net outflow of capital from Nigeria to the developed capitalist countries in the form of repatriated profits, interest, or royalties. This practice also results in a drain on the nation's valuable foreign exchange earnings.

The effects of this include concentration of manufacturing on semi-luxury commodities such as lace, carpets, cigarettes, beer, and the importation of luxury products like television sets, cars, liquor and other consumer products. The consequence of this is much to Nigerians. Nigerians no longer believe that cars or television sets are luxury goods. Rather, they believe that these goods are necessity. The absence of these luxury goods as a result of scarcity of foreign exchange has increased tension by the masses especially those that were used to them but could not afford them now. The high demand of cars by Nigerians led to the building of expressways by the MNCs that crack up within four to five months of use. While large areas of the country remain inaccessible even by feeder roads. The emergence of petroleum has significantly turned the nation into a renter monocultural state, whereas agricultural decline had forced the country to become a net importer of food. Even with increasing food crisis in Nigeria, peasants are still encouraged to produce cash crops like tobacco for the Nigerian Tobacco

Company and Philip Morris of America, at the expense of needed food crops for Nigerian masses.

In addition, the multinational corporations have succeeded in introducing inappropriate pattern of consumption. In Nigeria today, the introduction of inappropriate modern substitutes by the MNCs is much more apparent. The introduction of powdered baby formulas into the country is a classic example of such endeavor. Nigerian consumers have been confronted with a barrage of advertising extolling the virtues of using powdered baby formulas in place of breast-feeding. The emphasis has been that the use of the formulas is more modern than breast-feeding. The product according to Sam Otuyelu, has clearly taken in the quantities of the natural status symbol of feeding a new baby.[14] This no doubt added more economic cost on the household budget. There is no clear concrete evidence to prove that powered formulas is more nutritious than the natural breast-feeding. Again, an additional cost is incurred when parents are unaware of the sanitary precautions needed for the preparation of this product, particularly, when such instructions are not provided by the distributors. This according to editorial comments of Daily Times November 5, 1975, posed a serious danger to the health of new-born babies in Nigeria.

A similar argument can be made about other food-related products such as breakfast cereals and toothpastes. Both products replace existing products with more costly commodities of lower substantial value. Processed breakfast cereals replace "porriages made from local grains, while the so called "modern" toothpastes take the place of the equally (often more) effective chewing sticks popularly used for cleaning and scraping the teeth and gums.

Again, economic policies in the industrialized countries have resulted in higher nominal and real interest rates. This has effect on debt servicing in Nigeria. The increase in interest rates especially that of the U.S. dollar has increased the cost of servicing external debts.

In addition, a surge in protectionism in the developed countries, manifested in a marked increase in tariff and non-tariff barriers, has resulted in a substantial reduction in the exports of Nigeria commodities to the industrial countries. In sum, this constellation of mutually reinforcing

---

[14]Sam Otuyelu, "How Safe is Bottle Feeding" Nigerian Daily Times, 22 October 1975, p.7.

problems has resulted in deterioration in the country's terms of trade and external payments position and has increased debt-service commitments, causing in turn a vicious circle of low income, savings, investments and output in Nigeria.

Internal Factors

The economic crisis has also been characterized by acute import contraction, which many Nigerians perceive as the main cause of domestic difficulties. Restricted access to imports particularly, during Shagari's second term in office has reduced output and caused excess capacity and increasing unemployment in industry, agriculture, and services and a consequent deterioration in sales tax and income tax collections by government. It has also undermined the export capacity of the country.

Furthermore, the rate of population growth in Nigeria is among the highest in the world. This trend has put pressure on land where average per hectare production has been lagging behind other developing regions. Also, population growth increases the need for additional social services and puts further pressure on government expenditure. In terms of the physical quality of life, Nigeria is among the Third World countries that have the lowest index, as well as highest infant mortality rate and the lowest average literacy rate. The vast majority of the people in Nigeria are living in abject poverty and social deprivation.

Moreover, rapid population growth rate has put pressure on arable land, thus, forcing marginal lands to be brought into cultivation, which in turn has drastically reduced agricultural outputs, income, and employment and has accentuated domestic inflation.

The expansion of the petroleum in Nigeria since 1964, even though its role as a source of government revenues and capital formation did not become visible until after the oil price increases of 1971, was the brain behind the Nigerian economic change and the origin of its unequal level of development. Table 17 presents the average annual growth rate of Nigeria's main economic sectors for the period 1960-1970 and 1970-1981. The table indicates that the greatest growth between 1960 and 1970 took place in the mining area, where petroleum is the predominant commodity. The table also points that between 1970-1981, mining grew at an average annual growth rate of only 2.5 percent, a rapid decline from an annual growth rate of 31.7 percent in 1960-1970.

Also, agriculture, the economic operation in which the majority of Nigerians are operated, indicated the lowest average annual growth rate during 1960-1970. It even declined to -1.3 percent and -0.4 percent during 1971-1977 and 1970-1981 respectively. The fall of agriculture has played a significant role in Nigeria's recent economic history. Before the oil increase of the 1970s, Nigeria depended on agriculture exports (cocoa, palm oil, palm kernels, cotton, timber and rubber) for 68 to 75 percent of its foreign exchange. By 1970, their value had dropped to 44 percent of total exports, and in 1978-1980, they accounted for only 6 percent of the total.[15] Since 1980, Nigeria has relied on oil for more than 90 percent of its foreign exchange. Nigeria, which was the second largest world producer of cocoa after Ghana has now lost its market share because of oil discovery.

The implication of agricultural decrease is serious for Nigeria. Agriculture provides employment for half of the country's work force. Its decrease since 1960 has been followed by a large decrease in the Nigeria's labor force participation rate. In 1960, the ratio of the labor in agriculture was 71 percent. However, by 1980 it had reduced to 54 percent. However, during the same period, the proportion of the labor force in industry increased from 10 percent to 19 percent. Overall, the nation's total labor force participation rate reduced from 42.2 percent in 1960 to 36.4 percent in 1980.[16] Apart from providing food for the population, and raw material for the industrial area, agriculture has originally generated most of the revenues and foreign exchange from exports. The decrease in this area not only has seriously affected the exports but also has led to increase in imports, which in turn affects Nigeria's foreign exchange reserves. This is true because in 1970, food constituted 7.6 percent of all imports. Between 1978 and 1982, it had increased to 12.4 and 19.6 percent of all imports respectively.[17]

For many years, the nation's oil marked the structural problems of the economy. Its foreign exchange reserves increased rapidly from $355 million

---

[15]Federal Ministry of Economic Development Third National Development Plan: 1975-1980, Vol.1, (Lagos: The Central Planning Office, 1979).

[16]World Bank: World Tables Third Edition, (New York: Oxford University Press, 1983).

[17]Ibid., p. 72.

at the end of 1972 to $5.602 million by 1974 (For clarification See Table 38). The main contributor to the increase was petroleum incomes. It was, therefore, not surprising that when petroleum production dropped in 1978, foreign exchange reserves fell to $1,887 million. With higher petroleum prices in 1979 and 1980, foreign exchange reserves recovered, but not so much. The sudden fluctuations and steep declines in petroleum revenues have destabilized Nigerian political, social and economic development.[18]

Also, many areas of the Nigerian economy rely on imports in order to produce goods, and thus increase in imports is to be foreseen. As Olannyiwola indicates:

> this means that the economy is structurally organized to exacerbate its foreign exchange problem; export earnings, determined by world oil market conditions, will vary greatly, while foreign exchange needs will continue to grow. Left on its own the Nigerian economy will drift from crisis to crisis. Yet the national government is unable to correct the imbalance through its revenues because its primary source of funds is the faltering petroleum economy. Federally collected revenues in 1983 were N8.6 billion, a drop of 21.8 percent from N10.9 billion in 1982. The decline in government revenues has compelled the federal and state governments to utilize deficit financing by borrowing heavily from the banking system internally and internationally. In a ten-year period, Nigeria has gone from high growth with extraordinary domestic capital reserves to a near bankrupt economy trying to borrow its way out of collapse.[19]

Another important factor that affected Nigerian development is the choice of development planning. For example, the planning strategy for industrialization in Nigeria involved the replacement of imported goods with machinery and equipment that produced the goods that previously were imported.

In Nigeria, the emergence of import substitution industrialization strategy corresponded with the post war boom around 1950, which was also

---

[18]Olayiwola, Petroleum and Structural Change in A Developing Country.

[19]Olannyiwola, Petroleum and Structural Changes in Developing Country, pp. 139.

Table 18

SECTORAL AVERAGE ANNUAL GROWTH RATE (1960-1981)

SECTOR	1960-1970	1971-1977	1960-1981
Agriculture	1.3	- 1.5	- 0.4
Mining	31.7	8.1	2.5
Manufacturing	12.8	13.4	12.4
Construction	9.0	24.7	13.1
Transport Communication	4.0	16.5	8.3
Imports of goods and services	4.0	24.7	15.9
Electricity, gas, water	16.7	18.2	16.3
Public Admn., Defense	4.8	24.7	15.9
Exports of goods and services	12.9	5.6	0.8
Gross Domestic Product at factor cost	4.3	6.2	4.5
Gross Domestic product at market prices	4.4	6.0	4.5

Source: World Bank Annual Report 1980: 150-151. World Bank 1983: 134-135, Central Bank of Nigeria, Annual Report, Various Issues Compiled in 1980

the beginning of the last phase of the nationalist struggle. At that time, there was a need for diversification of domestic production. As export demand declined in the capitalist states, there was a strong need to redistribute productive forces or factors of production to achieve a new domestic division of labor. Also, a change in import structure, through the shift of demand from the import of consumer commodities to industrial raw materials, capital goods and intermediate goods, was needed to preserve scarce foreign exchange earnings. In addition, the disintegration theory for development of the industrial area further demands import substitution for breaking pre-imperialist relations of production, reducing unemployment, reducing dependence on capitalist nations, and accelerating economic growth.[20]

However, these aims and objectives centered around increasing the rate of economic growth and creating more job opportunities in order to carry out the electoral promises of the newly emerged Nigerian ruling class after 1951. T.A. Oyejidi has this to say:

> Under neocolonial capitalism in Nigeria, industrialization has been highly perceived, as in other less developed countries, as a major opportunity to increase the rate of economic growth, create job opportunities, raise the low standard of living of the population, reduce import of manufacturing goods from the imperial powers, and decrease the trade deficits that result from such imports. Even if gains do not lead to the liquidation of structural underdevelopment they are seen by the domestic petty bourgeoisie in Nigeria and elsewhere as sufficient ends in themselves. Hence, industrialization becomes one of the critical bourgeois indices of modernization upon which the fragile legitimacy of their client dominance is based.[21]

During that period also, the government encouraged the growth of local industries by providing them with a high degree of protection, at least until they are enable to stand on their own. The declaration by the Federal Ministry of Finance, Chief Festus Okotie Eboh, in the first neo-colonial

---

[20]For an analysis of the origin of the strategy of import substitution industrialization in LDCs, see Onimode, Imperialism and Underdevelopment in Nigeria (London: 2nd ed., University Press, 1985).

[21]T.A. Oyejidi, Tariff Policy and Industrialization in Nigeria, (Ibadan University Press, 1975), p. 145.

budget laid the ground work for import-substitution industrialization in Nigeria. From then on tariff policy was actively used for protecting infant industries.

The policy of import substitution was used because it was assumed that by beginning with this kind of industrialization, a nation would generally be led by backward linkage results to establish domestic production of intermediate and basic industrial elements.   For this reason, import substitution industries received a high degree of protection from the country. However, this approach led to increase in the price of industrial products vis-a-vis that of agricultural products. Furthermore, the unreal high exchange rate punished agriculture and agricultural production by reducing the receipts in domestic currency from a given amount of agricultural exports. And this has resulted in the decline of agriculture. Instead of reducing the volume of imports, import substitution industrialization tended to increase it in Nigeria reality.[22]

Also, the planning method of import substitution industrialization led to the redistribution of population caused by migration of rural dwellers seeking employment to the urban areas, specifically to Lagos. Mabogunje in his book, The Development Process in Nigeria estimated that the population of Lagos grew from approximately 1.0 million in 1965 to about 2.5 million in 1975 which was an annual growth rate of 10.2 percent. However, because the apparatus utilized for import substitution industrialization in Nigeria seem to be capital-intensive rather than labor-intensive, most of the migrators to the urban areas remain unemployed.   Rather than decreasing poverty and unemployment, the policy has compounded the problem.   This policy also created an urbanization in which economic activities are growing too slowly to ensure employment for the rapidly accelerating urban dwellers.

In addition, the backward linkages expected from import-substitution industrialization did not materialize due largely to its enclave nature. The effect of this is that even though there may be progress in the urban centers, it does not generally produce effective economic activity at the periphery of the country. The majority of citizen depend heavily on agricultural revenue, which are declining. Hence, the majority of the population is becoming worse off, and the rural-urban income gap is increasing. Also, the oil industry, which

---

[22]Bade Onimode, Imperialism and Underdevelopment in Nigeria, p. 179.

had generated tremendous revenues for the economy during the 1970s and early 1980s, is capital-intensive and thus generates relatively few jobs for the citizens at large.

Furthermore, nationalism played a significant role in explaining Nigerian economic situation.   Anti colonial nationalist movements played a serious role in achieving Nigeria's political independence from Britain in 1960. Nationalism for the nationalist leaders and for the majority of people that followed them was not mere symbol.

For this reason, Brenton (1964) suggests that nationalism leads economies to invest resources in nationality or ethnicity, and that it encourages demands for changes in the international or inter-ethnic distribution of property and wealth of a nation.   These statements suggest that nationalist economic policies tend to emphasize activities such as manufacturing, especially in certain important industries, such as steel, that indicate the nation is modern and moving toward a condition of self-sufficiency.   Also, nationalist economic policy tends to encourage too much state control over, and public ownership of, the means of production. Also, according to Daly and Globerman (1976), "nationalist economic policies tend to redistribute material income from the lower class toward the middle class, especially the educated middle class."[23]

Also, the Indigenization Decrees of 1972 and 1977 represent nationalist policy.   The objective of the 1972 decree was to redistribute equity shares from foreigners to Nigerians.   The resultant wealth concentration was not seem.   The 1977 decree was an attempt to minimize the concentration of share equity ownership in a few individuals.   It is doubtful, however whether that goal was ever realized.   Many of the shares of foreign investors were sold by private placement or offer for sale.[24]   That gave the rich and the middle class who had political and business connections the opportunity to benefit most from this endeavor.   Active participation by the general population was limited because of the low rate of offer for prescription.

---

[23]D.J. Daly and S. Globerman, Tariff and Science Policies: Application of a Model of Nationalism, (Toronto: University of Toronto Press, 1976), p. 146.

[24]Federal Republic of Nigeria (FRN) Annual Abstract of Statistics, (Lagos Federal Office of Statistics, Vol. 13, No. 8, 1980).

Furthermore, the oil industry was seriously affected by the indigenization operation. In 1971, the state-owned Nigerian National Oil Corporation (NNOC) was created to own equity shares in the major oil corporations and to carry out exploration jointly with foreign firms. In 1977, the NNOC was incorporated with the Federal Ministry of Petroleum Resources to form the Nigerian National Petroleum Corporation (NNPC). In July 1979, the NNPC increased its equity shares in oil activities from 55 percent to 60 percent. On July 31, 1979, in revenge for shell-BP's oil arrangement that led to Nigerian oil being exported to South Africa, BP's interests in Nigeria were nationalized, effective August 1, 1979. Shell-BP's benefits amounted to more than 80 percent of all the oil benefits granted in Nigeria, and were yielding an average of 60 percent of the total oil production in Nigeria. No doubt the indigenization activities of 1972 and 1977 were designed to accomplish self-sufficiency and to change the equity ownership structure in the economy. They were also meant to increase Nigerian participation in the management of corporations, particularly the number of Nigerians employed in middle and top administrative management.

Indeed, the Nigerian economy of the 1980s is more dependent and open than ever. Its economic live is at the mercy of petroleum export, which provides over 90 percent of its foreign exchange earnings. The country has found that with lower oil sales, manufacturing seriously is adversely affected, and importation of food and other essential commodities is extremely costly expensive. Whatever indigenization was supposed to achieve, it did not dramatically affect the dependency of the economy. Nigeria is an independent political entity in a legal sense, but its social and economic structure remains fundamentally similar to that of its colonial origin. Adeoye Akinsanya has this to say:

> the indigenization of private foreign investments under the Nigerian Enterprises Promotion Decrees of 1972 and 1977 has not really enhanced national control over the economy nor does the Federal Government's majority equity interests in foreign owned oil producing and insurance companies and bank

> necessarily confer effective control (on the Federal Ministry Government) over the operations of the joint ventures.[25]

In describing the same decrees, Oyebode argues:

> the Nigerian Business Enterprises Decrease... when taken in a holistic framework amount to no more than the indigenization of the exploitation of the Nigerian nation and resources by the affluent members of the national bourgeoisie.[26]

In evaluating and assessing the role of nationalism in Nigerian development, one has to distinguish between the results of political nationalism and economic nationalism. There can be little no doubt that political nationalism in Nigeria was instrumental in the realization of political independence in 1960. Economic nationalism, however, was less successful. Rather than producing economic independence it may have been an impediment to economic independence insofar as it fostered the view that economic independence, can be achieved by the simple act of Nigerians acquiring ownership and management of private foreign companies operating in Nigeria. In this manner, economic nationalism prevented Nigerian planners and leaders from focusing on the structural problems of the petroleum economy. Being patriotic is one thing; being responsive to economic reality is another. But while economic nationalism deflected leadership attention from the real causes of the dependent structure of the Nigerian economy, it mainly was not the major obstacle barriers to achieving autonomous development and economic nationalism.[27]

Added to these factors is the Nigerian civil war. Six years after Nigeria had gained political independence, the January 1966 military coup took place, not because of economic problems of the nation but because of political issues. The main aim was to stabilize the political system of the nation. The July 1966 military coup, which brought General Gowon to power, had a similar goal. Despite the oil revenues, which provided the funds for reconstruction and development, the civil war proved to be a big waste not

---

[25] Adeoye Akinsanya, as quoted in William Zartman, The Political Economy of Nigeria, (New York: Praeger, 1983), p. 179.

[26] A. Oyebode, as quoted in Zartman, The Political Economy of Nigeria, Ibid.

[27] Olayiwola, Petroleum and Structural in A Developing Country.

only on the nation's physical and economic resources but on its human resources as well. Resources that could have been productive elsewhere in the country were converted to war operation. During the war period, also, agriculture and other economic activities were greatly affected. Politically, the Nigerian-Biafra war brought ethnic rivalry into practice. The civil war also established the beginning of the rise of the military with respect to the power and capability of that institution to chart a course for Nigeria. Again, with the oil boom following the civil war, the military was placed in the advantageous position of controlling the large wealth of the country.   The Gowon administration affected by civil war, happened to be at the right place at the right time during the oil bonzer. Yet, its policies contributed to the scarcity of essential product in the midst of unlimited revenue. Nigeria, at this point, has not recovered from the scarcities of goods since 1974. As Olannyiwola put it: "In the event of such scarcity, a "get rich quick" mentality emerged. The next administration, that of Murtala Mohammed and Obasanjo, came to power because the nation lacked effective leadership." Also, when the civilian administration came to power in 1979, they were not elected for economic development objectives, but to restore democracy in Nigeria. As West Africa indicate:

> The very first deliberations in the various legislatures were on issues of personal remuneration and terms of service rather than on the more pressing issues of stabilizing the nation's industry and agriculture.   The irony is that the civilian politicians may have been trying to avoid hurting feelings when they ignored the clear signs of economic distress which they inherited from an era of economic extravagance generated by previous military governments.[28]

Furthermore, the expectations generated in the 1970-1979 period during which most Nigerians believed that Nigeria was a rich country also created a major problem to the government. These expectations generated internal demands and pressures for economic self-sufficiency, economic autonomy industrialization, modernity, equitable distribution of income and national resources. These demands also created a financial burden to the

---

[28]"The Return of the Nigerian Military: 1, The Pattern of Military Rule, " West Africa, 9 July 1984, pp. 1394.

government. The substantial growth of road development contracts and import substitution industrialization left the nation with large debts and more dependent on the importation of raw materials, components and parts, even food (For reference purpose, see Table 19). This, however, has pushed Nigeria into a debt trap. Nigeria's total external debts account $88 billion in 1988. In addition, Olkoshi, has this to comment:

> The quadrupling of oil prices in 1973 generated a change from the agrarian basis of accumulation in Nigeria to that of crude petroleum. Petroleum exports which accounted for only 10 per cent of the country's export earnings in 1962 rose to 82.7 per cent in 1973 and , for the second half of the 1970's, peaked at between 90 and 93 percent.   By 1980, the country was producing 2.05 million barrels of oil per day. The massive oil earnings were used to finance the expansion of the country's industrial sector, commercial enterprises, numerous agricultural projects and the construction of many infrastructure facilities. This massive expenditure was instrumental to the rapid development of the Nigerian petitbourgeoisie, the expansion of the foreign corporate presence in the country and the growth of state capital to an unprecedented level. The increased tempo of economic activities from the oil boom was accompanied by an expansion of corrupt practices such as contract inflation 10 percent kick-backs, over-invoicing, and outright stealing of public funds.[29]

While the windfall from oil exports led to a considerable expansion of the economy, it did little to increase the country's self-reliance. If anything, the country's dependence on external sources for crucial inputs and various commodities increased. The structure of the country's import substitution industries entailed a high import profile for machinery and spare parts.

Also, corruption is another internal factor that affected the political economy of Nigeria. Many Nigerians knew that there was corruption from the highest level to the lowest level. The federal military government, for example, has been waging a campaign against corruption, indiscipline, the inflation of contracts and mismanagement. In 1970, every contract in Nigeria

---

[29]Adebayo Lukuoshi, Impact of IMF-World Bank Programs on Nigeria (eds) in Bade Onimode, The IMF, The World Bank and the African Debt: The Economic Impacts (London 2nd ed 1989), p. 222.

Table 19

IMPORTS BY END USE AT CURRENT (1983) PRICES (N million)

	1974	1975	1976	1977	1978	1979	1980	1981
Consumer Goods:								
1. Non-durable								
a) Food	166.4	353.7	526.7	912.6	1,006.1	1,040.1	1,416.8	2,198.3
b) Textiles	31.5	81.3	65.0	58.9	41.9	73.2	92.6	202.6
c) Others	173.6	353.5	476.7	612.1	720.5	705.8	567.4	822.0
2) Durable	65.8	191.3	282.0	421.7	370.2	380.7	473.7	674.1
Sub-total	437.3	979.8	1,350.4	1,985.3	2,136.7	2,199.8	2,550.3	3,897.0
Passenger car	97.0	220.3	261.0	397.4	350.1	169.7	206.1	1,316.9
Capital Goods:								
Capital equipment	490.1	1,136.6	1,515.0	2,129.8	2,529.8	1,576.0	2,228.0	2,661.3
Transport equipment	124.9	371.1	729.6	1,012.5	1,233.8	988.7	1,770.2	1,818.7
Raw material	519.3	903.0	1,094.0	1,543.0	1,880.1	1,115.7	2,156.9	3,038.5
Fuel	55.4	100.2	175.0	128.6	156.7	112.4	195.4	187.2
Sub-total	1,289.7	2,731.2	3,774.6	5,111.3	6,150.5	3,966.5	6,545.3	9,022.6
Grand total	1,727.0	3,711.0	5,135.0	7,096.6	8,287.2	6,106.3	9,095.6	12,923.6

Source: National Economic Council Expert Committee Report, The State
of the Nigerian Economy, 1983.

was undertaken with inflated price. Many public servants, politicians, private business companies and individuals have been implicated in the on-going probes established by the Buhari regime.[30]

Again, the contract system has been abused in Nigeria. For instance, three senior civil servants in Benue State have been dismissed following the recommendation of a panel which probed the N3.2 billion chalk deal and other irregularities in some local governments between 1980 and 1983. It has also been reported that three former politicians in Bendel State confessed to sharing $146,000 public funds from the Delta Boat yard company which was unable to pay salaries for eighteen months.[31] In the area of debt probes, it has been established that many fraudulent devices, such as forgeries of such documents as bills of lading, import licenses and letters of credit, have been used. Furthermore, various ex-state governors have been sent to prison with terms ranging from 12 to 22 years because of corruption. Certainly, no discussion of Nigeria's crisis will be complete without the role of corruption and mismanagement.

Even development strategies in Nigeria often exhibited the political motives and self-interests of political leaders and public administrators rather than the objective of development as we see it. For example, location of industries tended to be based on political rather than economic objective. In Nigeria, the location of industries is not always determined by needs, but rather by the ability to bribe the federal or state government.

Again, development in Nigeria has been prevented by ethnicity and fear of domination. As we discussed early in our introduction, the country Nigeria was a British creation. Given the differences in culture, language, lifestyle background, lifestyle, and education, there is a tendency for certain ethnic units within the country to feel that they are being swallowed upon by the major ethnic units. Even among the major ethnic units such as the Ibo, Hausa and Yoruba, there has always been insecurity. The job of nation building is made more difficult in such an atmosphere. In response to ethnic rivalry, Nigerian government have sought to geographically balance economic development with the result that location of industries has tended to be based more on political motives than on national goals and objectives.

---

[30]The Guardian (18 August 1985).

[31]Africa South of the Sahara (London: Europe Publication. 1983) p. 16.

Above all, both internal and external factors had serious implications on Nigerian development measures. Most of these factors also had intensified the economic crisis in Nigeria. In this chapter, a critical analysis of the origin and development of the economic crisis in Nigeria was provided. Also, examined were the role of certain external and internal factors that exacerbated the economic crisis. Overall, our examination has led to the conclusion that both the external and internal factors were responsible for Nigerian economic crisis. However, the major cause of the economic crisis is the structural condition of Nigerian underdevelopment. This condition derives from its colonial past, which created an industrial and export agriculture economy dependent upon foreign capital and trade. Faced with mounting economic and financial difficulties, Nigeria was forced to embark on adjustment programs supported by the International Monetary Fund. The decision by Nigeria's leaders and planners to accept and implement the IMF stabilization adjustment programs for its economic development only reinforced the structural condition of neocolonialism, new imperialism and external economic dependency.

CHAPTER 6

The History And Evolution Of The International Monetary Fund, Its Operations And Policy Conditionalities

The International Monetary Fund was established at Brenton Woods, New Hampshire, in 1944, near the end of World War II. The establishment of the Fund was not an easy act. It was preceded by five years of intensive planning within the governments of the United States and the United Kingdom. The experience of the 1920s and 1930s influenced this planning. U.S. officials saw the practices of 1930s that affected trade patterns such as competitive currency devaluations, the use of multiple currency practices whereby a currency would be exchange at one rate for one purpose and at a different rate for another, the wide use of exchange regulations and import licensing, and bilateral trade deals- as causes of unemployment in export industries, the world-wide depression, and even World War II. One of the "inescapable problems" of the postwar period as seen by the U.S. was " to prevent the disruption of foreign exchange and the collapse of monetary and credit system."[1]   The overriding goal of the U.S. was the reconstruction of a

---

[1]See Ragner Nurkse, International Currency Experience: Lessons of Inter-War Period (Geneva: League of Nations, Princeton: Princeton University Press, 1944), pp. 7-8; and Kenneth Dan, The Rules of the Game: Reform and Evolution in the International Monetary System (Chicago: Chicago University Press, 1982), pp.44-70. See also Alfred Eckes, Jr., A Search for Solvency (Texas: Austin University Press, Wittkopf, World Politics: Trend and Transformation, Second Edition, (New York: St. Martin's Press, 1985), pp. 174-175. J.E. Spero, The Politics of International Economic Relations, (New York: St. Martin's Press, 1985), pp. 35-46.

genuinely multilateral system of international trade. This contemplated that countries would agree to cooperate to reduce barriers to trade and barriers to payments.[2] Barriers would be reduced to moderate levels and made nondiscriminatory in application. Currencies would become convertible. In particular, exporters receiving a foreign currency in exchange for goods or services would be able to convert that currency and utilize its proceeds in other nations.[3]

The British idea on postwar monetary institutions was set fourth by the Chancellor of the Exchequer on the floor of the House of Commons in early 1943:

> We want an orderly and agreed method of determining the value of national currency units, to eliminate unilateral action and the danger which it involves that each nation will seek to restore its competitive positions by exchange depreciation. Above all, we want to free the international monetary system from those arbitrary, unpredictable and undesirable influences which have operated in the past as a result of large-scale speculative movements of capital. We want to secure an economic policy agreed between the nations and the international monetary system which will be the instrument of that policy. This means that if any one Government were tempted to move too far either in an inflationary direction, it would be subject to the check of consultations with the other Governments, and it would be part of the agreed policy to measures for correcting tendencies to dis-equilibrium in the balance of payments of each separate country. Our long-term policy must ensure that countries which conduct their affairs with prudence need not be afraid that they will be prevented

International Monetary Fund, The Role and Function of the International Monetary Fund, (Washington, D.C.: IMF, 1985), pp. 1-3.

[2]Statement of H.D. White in the Introduction to his Preliminary Draft Proposal for a United Nations Stabilization Fund and a Bank for Reconstruction and Development of the United Associated Nations (April 1942), in Margaret Garrisen de Vries and Keith Horsefield, The IMF, 1945-1965: Twenty years of International Monetary Cooperation 3 vols. (Washington: IMF, 1969), p. 37.

[3]Richard Gardner, Sterling-Dollar Diplomacy rev. ed. (New York: McGraw-Hill Book Co., 1969), Chapter I.

from meeting their international liabilities by causes outside their own control.[4]

As we have earlier raised the question of in whose interest are these policies formulated in our introduction; the answer to this question will be provided in this chapter as we go along.

The Bretton Wood Conference was essentially a conference about the monetary and financial problems of the industrialized capitalist countries. Although the latter were in a numerical minority, their views and interests-particularly those of the United Kingdom and above all, the United States - were predominant.[5]

The United Kingdom's economy was dependent upon trade, and London had been the center of international finance. The United States would emerge from the war with both political influences and economic strength.

The Soviet Union was present but chose not to join the IMF; the few of its Eastern Europeans allies which did join the Fund later withdrew. Africa and Asia were represented by only seven countries apart from China, all of which were in one way or another under British or U.S. sphere of influence. The remainder of Africa, Asia and the Caribbean was represented by proxy; that is, by colonial powers.[6]

The only major less developing countries presence was that of the Latin American Countries. Hence, the Third World delegates at Bretton Woods, despite some attempts to bring development strategies and matters on the table were overwhelmed by the weight and influence of the big powers. As Abdalla puts it:

---

[4]House of Commons, Parliamentary Debates (Hansard), 5th Series Vol. 386 Column 826, February 2, 1943, quoted in Gardner, p. 78.

[5]Ismail-Sabril Abdalla, "The Inadequacy and Loss of Legitimacy of the IMF "Development Dialogue, (Sweden: Dag Hammarjold Foundations, 1980-1982) , p. 37.

[6]Ibid.

The national liberation movements struggling to achieve political independence were not fully conscious of the need for Third World solidarity, nor of the tough demands of development. Thus, it is by no means an exaggeration to state that the spirit of the Group of 77, born some 20 years later, was completely absent from the Bretton Woods.[7]

The International Monetary System had been in disarray since World War I. British hegemony in world trade and the gold standard functioned well from 1870-1914. The First World War caused a total collapse of that system. During the 1920s the attempt to return to a gold standard failed. The 1930s saw a period of fluctuating exchange rates and the use of dollar, pound and francs to back gold, but these efforts also failed.

However, the major industrialized countries met at Bretton Woods, New Hampshire to work out an international agreement that would deal with exchange control, balance of trade deficit, economic growth, and monetary and fiscal policy.[8] Two plans were in operation: The White Plan and the Keynes Plan. "Both plans accepted the need for a new international institution and both contemplated that it be staffed by professional economists who would be international civil servants."[9] Also, both plans started from the premise of relatively stable exchange rates. Changes in currency exchange values should be reserved for subject to a measure of international control, would be orderly, and should not spurt competitive devaluations. Finally, both plans assumed that countries must adopt policies that would achieve balance of payment equilibrium over the long term.[10]

Charles Kegley quoted Block in this way:

Exchange rate alterations proved to be traumatic politically and economically under the Bretton Woods system. Devaluations were taken as indications of weakness and economic failure by states and, thus, were resisted. Exchange rates became more rigid than the founders of the IMF had anticipated. When

---

[7]Ibid.

[8]For detailed explanation of the reason for the formation of the IMF, See Rick Edelson, International Monetary Fund, (New York: Praeger, Inc., 1980), p. 6.

[9]Ibid.

[10]Edelson, International Monetary Fund, p. 8.

states, nevertheless, were compelled to devalue their currencies, it was usually done without consultation with the IMF, because negotiations prior to the fact invited heavy speculation against the weakening currency in international money markets.[11]

The major serious differences between the two plans related to the manner in which resources would be provided to nations facing balance of payments deficits and the magnitude of the resources to be provided. Lord Keynes, representing a prospective deficit country, wanted a large volume of credit available at the request of a member state. In his plan, entitled "Proposals for an International Currency (or clearing) Union," the international institution would provide this credit by creating a new form of international money called bancor".[12] The Currency Union was conceived as a central bank for government central banks. The Union would extend overdraft rights to deficit nations and would credit surplus nations with an equivalent amount in bancor. Then, when a surplus nation went into deficit, it could use its bancor balance to offset this deficit. The aggregate total of overdraft rights to be authorized under Keynes' plan was estimated at U.S. $ 26 billion.[13] However, in reality the only major nation likely to run a significant surplus in the immediate postwar period was the U.S., the plan was, in effect, a prescription for a $26 billion long-term line of credit from the U.S. to the rest of the international community.

The United States being the prime potential creditor, the idea of a $ 26 billion line of credit was unacceptable. It feared that an overdraft approach, even with safeguards, might cause the U.S. to lose control over the size of its responsibilities. The United States wanted to limit the magnitude of its liability to finance the adjustment processes of other nations. It wanted authority in the international organization to require deficit nations to implement policies that would restore their international accounts to balance the limited liability that would be protected by deficit nations obtaining the currencies they needed to settle international accounts, not simply by means

---

[11]Kegley and Wittkopf, World Politics, p. 180.

[12]Economic Journal, Vol. 87,(fall 1979), P. 30; Also see Fred Block, The Origins of International Economic Disorder, (Los Angeles: University of California Press, 1977), p.48.

[13]Lord Keynes, as quoted in Joan Robinson, "The International Currency Proposals", Economic Journal, vol.53, (1943), p.161.

of credits from other members monitored by an international institution, but instead from a finite fund owned and managed by the international institution itself and composed of gold and national currencies.[14] Each member of the organization according to White Plan could contribute an agreed amount of its own currency and gold. These resources would form a pool on which a deficit country could draw if it were prepared to comply with the conditions imposed by the international authority. The total amount of the Fund would be at least U.S.$ 5 billion. The contributions of the member countries would be determined by a formula related to an appraisal of their general economic strength, with the obligation of the U.S. being less than $ 3.5 billion. After a long series of debates, the White Plan was adopted.

However, the White Plan had to take into consideration the position and mood of the American Congress and the public. America was influenced by the need to protect its industries which had prospered during World War II. Hence, the White Plan focused at setting up of exchange rates to ensure an orderly and stable world exchange of the major currencies. It did not address the need for development or trade; it merely wanted the "status quo" to remain and for countries to trade on the given parities that were worked out. The British, represented by Keynes, who together with other European nations expected to need the IMF after the War, argued that its resources would be made available unconditionally.[15] The U.S. government disagreed and the principle of conditionality became in the early years of the Fund's operations, firmly established at the heart of Fund.

The IMF, from its inception, had problems of too much influence by America, Britain and Canada (ABC). Over the years, the Group of Ten, led by the United States, United Kingdom, Canada, France, West Germany, Italy, Sweden, Belgium, Japan and Netherlands dominated the Organization.[16] The United States in 1946 loaned Britain a substantial sum of money outside of the auspices of the IMF in return for trading areas. This had the effect of undermining the multilateral transactions that the IMF was founded to perform. Thus, the precedent was set for bilateral arrangements between

---

[14]Ibid., p. 170.

[15]Fred Block, The Origin of International Economic Disorder (Los Angles: University of California Press, 1977), pp. 42-48.

[16]Spero, The Politics of International Economic Relations, pp. 43-46.

friendly developed countries operating outside the IMF, indicating that the old system among developed countries was the order of the day. Not that bilateral arrangements would be outlawed, but for the IMF to be functional, a better initial example by the two major powers was needed.

Consequently, the U.S. dollar became the dominant monetary force because of the weakened economies of Europe and Japan. The United States started to rebuild and lend monies to these depressed economies. The United States dollar, therefore, became the major world currency. It had become so powerful that the U.S. was able to insist that the dollar be backed by gold at thirty five dollars an ounce.[17] This and the dollar as major currency laid the foundation for the international monetary crisis of 1970.[18]

Although the United States was both the chief proponent and supporter of the various management techniques devised during the 1960s, none proved sufficient enough to counter the dollar crises that began in the late 1960s and early 1970s. However, following the devaluation of the British pound in late 1967 and the resulting massive speculation against the dollar in the form of gold purchases, the United States began to act unilaterally to protect the dollar. According to Block:

> In March 1968, the United States simply announced that it would no longer support the prices of gold at #35 an ounce in the free market. From that point on, there would be a two-tier gold market allowed to reach its own level. This amounted to renunciation of a U.S. obligation under the Bretton Woods Agreement. It stopped short, however, of a unilateral U.S. refusal to redeem all dollars held by a foreign central banks for gold.[19]

How can these developments be explained? Among the main elements of the explanation are the following: The very successes of the Bretton Woods System proved to be a major source of its later difficulties. The system was one of the elements that permitted and encouraged the rapid postwar growth in the economic and financial power of European countries

---

[17]Kegley and Wittkopf, World Politics: Trend and Transformation, p. 175.

[18]Robert Trifflin, as quoted in Kegley and Wittkpof, World Politics: Trend and Transformation, pp. 177-178.

[19]Fred Block, The Origins of International Economic Disorder, p. 194.

and Japan. It thus also contributed to the concomitant loss by the U.S. of its position of overwhelming predominance in international economic affairs.[20] An indication of the size of the shifts in the U.S. trade and payments relationships with Europe, Japan and other major areas is provided in Table 20.

Most striking is the fact that the overall U.S. trade position shifted from a surplus of $4.9 billion in 1965 to a deficit of $ 6.8 billion in 1972. In turn, the major structural changes that lay behind these shifts called for far more frequent and extensive changes in adjustment policies and particularly in exchange rates than the system seemed able to bring about.

The recovery of the European and Japanese economies adversely affected United States supremacy in industrial production. The early American deficits of the late 1950s and early 1960s became chronic by the mid-1960s. The recovered economies of Europe and Japan were not willing to revalue their currencies because in so doing they would lose their trade advantage. According to Kegley:

> If too few dollars were the problem in the immediate postwar years, by the 1960s too many dollars became the problem. The costs of overseas military activities, foreign economic and military aid, and massive private investments produced increasing balance -of-payments deficits, which earlier had been encouraged but later ran out of control. Furthermore, American gold holdings in relation to the growing number of foreign-held dollars fell precipitously. Given these circumstances, the possibility that the United States might devalue the dollar led to a loss of confidence by others and hence an unwillingness to continue to hold dollars as reserve currency. The French under the leadership of Charles de Gaulle even went so far as to insist on exchanging dollars for gold.[21]

The United States responded to the situation by printing more dollars and floating the U.S. dollar in the international market.

---

[20]Spero, pp.25-30.

[21]Kegley, p. 178

Table 20

U.S. BALANCE OF PAYMENTS BY AREA,
1965 AND 1972 (in billions of dollars)

		Western Europe		Japan		Canada		Developing Countries	
	1965	1972	1965	1972	1965	1972	1965	1972	
Trade Balance	4.9	-6.8	2.7	-0.6	-0.4	-4.1	0.6	-1.8	1.3	-0.9
Exports	26.4	48.8	8.9	15.0	2.1	5.0	5.4	12.6	8.4	13.9
Imports	-21.5	-55.7	-6.2	15.6	-2.4	-9.	-4.8	-14.5	-7.2	-14.8
Current Account Balance	4.3	-8.0	1.2	-4.5	-0.4	-4.8	1.4	-0.4	1.5	0.8
Total Long-term Capital(net)	-6.1	-1.2	-1.3	3.4	-0.1	0.3	-1.4	-1.1	-2.8	-3.3
Private Long-term Capital	-4.6	0.1	-1.2	3.5	-0.1	0.3	-1.4	-1.1	-1.3	-2.2
Basic Balance	-1.8	-9.2	-0.1	-1.1	-0.5	-4.5	–	-1.5	-1.3	-2.4
Official Settlements Balance	-1.3	-10.3	–	–	–	–	–	–	–	–

Source: U.S Department of Commerce, Survey of Current
Business, 1985.

The reasons for the inability of the United States to control its balance-of-payments deficits are many, including an unwillingness to pull back from costly, globalist foreign policy posture the nation had assumed since World War II and a lag in the modernization of its economic productive facilities growing out of the decision of American-based multinational corporations to build branch plants abroad rather than new facilities at home. These ideas are seriously elaborated by Fred Block, whose revisionist analysis of the roots of the American payments deficits concludes thus:

> The exercise of American political and military power on a global basis has been designed to gain foreign acceptance of an international monetary order that institutionalizes an open world economy, giving maximum opportunities to American businessmen. It would be absurd for the United States to abandon its global ambitions simply to live within the rules of an international monetary order that was shaped for the purpose of achieving these ambitions. So it is hardly surprising that the United States continued to pursue its global ambitions despite the increasing strains on the international monetary order. The fundamental contradiction was that the United States had created an international monetary order that worked only when American political and economic dominance in the capitalist world was absolute. That absolute dominance disappeared as a result of the reconstruction of Western Europe and Japan, on the one hand, and the accumulated domestic costs of the global extension of U.S power, on the other. With the fading of the absolute dominance, the international monetary order began to crumble. The U.S. deficit was simply the most dramatic symptom of the terminal disease that plagued the postwar international monetary order.[22]

This has led to the emergency of free floating currency values, one in which currency values were determined by market forces rather than government imposed regulations. The theory underlying the new system of floating exchange rates was that a nation experiencing adverse economic conditions would see the value of its currency in the market place decline in response to the preferences of its traders, bankers, and business people. This would make its exports cheaper and its imports more expensive, which in turn

---

[22]Fred Block, The Origins of International Economic Disorder, p. 163.

would move the value of its currency back toward equilibrium. In this way, it was hoped, the politically humiliating devaluation of the past could be avoided. These actions had led to the suspension of the 1944 Bretton Woods fixed exchange rates agreements, under which the international monetary system had operated for nearly three decades.[23]

The actions of the United States in 1971 came as a serious shock to other members of international monetary system.

> They represented a new stridency in America's approach to international economic issues that perhaps reflected the American's simultaneous perception of their dependence on the rest of the world and their realization that the United States alone could no longer determine the course of international monetary matters. Hence, the political bases on which the Bretton Woods system had been built lay in ruins. American leadership was no longer accepted willingly by others nor exercised willingly by the United States. Power had come to be more widely dispersed among the countries making up the international monetary system, and the shared interest that once bound them together had dissipated.[24]

The other developed countries became concerned about accepting U.S. dollars; they were, in effect, supporting its deficit spending. France, under De Gaulle in 1966, made the first real objections to that policy by demanding gold for the United States dollar, a proposition that was realistic, but which the United States thought preposterous and ungrateful of the French. From that point on, everyone questioned the strength of the United States' economy and the dollar.

The IMF was adversely affected by these developments. The U.S. dollar had taken over the role that the IMF should have played. (loans were given bilaterally to the other industrial countries rather than under the auspices of the IMF). The General Agreement on Tariffs and Trade (GATT)

---

[23]Spero, The Politics of International Economic Relations, pp.54-55.

[24]Kegley, World Politics Trends and Transformation.

was activated to relieve the pressure. It made some gains for the industrial countries, but the Third World was not included.[25]

In addition, the membership of the IMF was changing; its initial forty-four members grew to one hundred and fifty-one by 1986. The majority of new members were small, dependent states that were relying on the generosity of European and North American developed countries. The IMF goals and principles were not directed at these nations and any adjustments to aid them have been minuscule. The problem was compounded by those small states demanding true independence and an end to their dependence on the North.

Also, the main concerns of the Bretton Woods negotiators were the avoidance of competitive rate manipulation and the maintenance of stable exchange rates among the major trading currencies, so as to promote international commerce and payments. Currency devaluation was suggested as a last resort to be approved by the International Monetary Fund only in cases of fundamental disequilibrium and to be avoided if possible by the use of the Fund Credits.[26] In dealing with the monetary and debt problems of the Third World countries, one has to question its fundamental strategy of emphasizing devaluation of national currency in favor of other available alternative solutions to Third World problems.

The History of Fund Conditionality

The International Monetary Fund was jointly created by forty-four member nations in an effort to promote international monetary stability and to facilitate the expansion and balanced growth of the world trade. Article one of the IMF's charter called on the Fund to make financial resources available to members, on a temporary basis and with adequate safeguards, to permit them to correct payments imbalances. In 1952, the principle of

---

[25]Secretary of State Hull had proposed an International Trade Organization (ITO) to solve the world's problem. But the IMF concept won over the (ITO). However, it was felt that there should be a systematic international trading body in the GATT. It functions to provide guidelines regarding international trade and tariff restrictions.

[26]Economist, 2 January 1985, p. 13.

conditionality was implicitly incorporated into the IMF's lending policies.[27] Conditionality was perceived to encourage policies that would make it more likely for a member country to cope with its balance of payments problem and to repay the Fund within four to five years.

The evolution of the practice of conditionality accompanies the birth of the "standby arrangement". In the early stage, the standby arrangement was intended to be a precautionary device used to ensure access on the part of members that had no immediate need for such resources in the near future. The standby arrangement, however, matured suddenly into a means for linking economic policies to financial assistance.[28] The standby arrangement can be described as a "line of credit outlining the circumstances under which a member can make drawings on the Fund".[29]

On September 20, 1968, the IMF decided to explicitly add the practice of conditionality into its charter. Before to this date, the idea of conditionality had generally been referred to in a vague manner. The amendments to the IMF's Article of Agreement in 1968 ended this confusion by defining for the first time, clear language which outlined the IMF's position with respect to conditionality.

Since the mid-1970s, the typical conditionalities placed on the use of Fund resources involved policies that influenced the level and composition of aggregate demand. During this period, excess demand was seen as the most important cause of inflation, currency overvaluation, and ultimately payment disequilibrium. The expeditious eradication of excess demand was viewed as an important condition for restoring payments equilibrium. This position has often been referred to as the 'monetarist instrument'.

The monetarist instrument views excess demand as the main cause of inflation and exchange rate destabilization. Its objectives is the rapid alleviation, typically in one year or less, of inflation and the restoration of exchange rate equilibrium vis-a-vis policies that alter the size and composition of aggregate demand.

---

[27]Manual Guitian, Fund conditionality Evolution of Principles and Practices, (Washington, D.C.: International Monetary Fund, 1981), pp. 13-14.

[28]Ibid

[29]Ibid

Demand management usually implies restraining or reducing budget deficits by cutting expenditures, by abolishing subsidies on such items as urban food consumption, or by the raising of taxes or user fees on government services. Price adjustments entail introducing 'realistic' exchange rates, 'adequate' prices for producers and exporters, the reform of price-distorting tariff and subsidy schemes, the use of interest rates to mobilize savings and allocate investment and the "liberalization" or decontrol of exchange and trade systems.[30]

In the mid-1970s, also the monetarist policy gave way to a more structural, long-run approach. The emergence of this new instrument to payment adjustments was precipitated by the growing recognition, both within and outside of the IMF, that payment imbalances could no longer be expected to be corrected within one year's time. In response to this recognition, the IMF increased its support for policies that called for adjustment over a longer period. In 1974, the IMF established the "Extended Fund Facility(EFF), which was designed to provide members with up to three years of financial assistance. In addition, the IMF decided in 1979 to allow stand-by agreements to be extended for up to three years.[31] This development was accompanied by growing support for more comprehensive policies that were designed to influence the balance of payments through changes in supply as well as in demand. These policies continued to rely on the typical monetarist instruments, but in a more gradual fashion.

In addition, they called for more structural supply oriented policies such as reducing the size of the public sector, channelling resources away from the public sector and into the private sector, creating financial intermediates, promoting savings, and discouraging wasteful investment by increasing real interest rates.[32]

---

[30]Alejandro Foxley, Stabilization Policies and Their Effects on Employment and Income Distribution: A Latin American Perspective in W. Cline and S. Weintraub (eds.) Economic Stabilization in Developing Countries (Washington, D.C.: Brookings Institute, 1981), p.194.

[31]Guitian, Fund Conditionality Evolution of Principle and Practices, pp. 18-22.

[32]A.W. Hooks, The International Monetary Fund: Its Evolution, Organization, and Activities, (Washington, D.C.: International Monetary Fund, 1982), p. 11.

However, drawings from the Fund are made in intrench. Drawings under the first tranche (25 per cent of a member's quota) can be made free of conditions; under subsequent tranche and under the Extended Fund Facility and Supplementary Financing Facility, conditions for drawing become progressively more strict.   Since 1953, the Fund has made stand-by arrangements under which it is agreed that a government can make drawings from the Fund, when and if it needs to, up to a stated amount over a stated period, one year under ordinary credit tranche facilities and three years under EFF, provided that it complies with agreed conditions.[33]   These conditions are embodied in a Letter of Intent, which is usually drafted by IMF officials but signed by the country's Minister of Finance. Other sources of the Fund's finance, include the oil facility, Compensatory Financing Facility, and the Trust Fund.   These were set up in the 1970s to ease the Fund's conditionalities.

How The IMF Operates

The operating structure of the IMF is such that member countries are allocated quotas, the size of which are reviewed every five years. Members deposit currency to the amount of these quotas with the IMF, 25 per cent being in reserve assets, the remainder in domestic currency. Quotas are measured in Special Drawing Rights (SDRs), with, at present, an SDR worth slightly more than one U.S. dollar.[34]

The control of the International Monetary Fund is determined by its voting rights. Each member is allocated 250 votes, plus one vote for every 100,000 of SDRs in its quota (See also Appendix 13 for Executive Directors and Voting Power in IMF on April 30, 1989). Table 20 indicates the SDRS and votes of the 18 industrialized countries, 43 African and 80 other LDCs members of the IMF. Quota is the amount of money the member nations contribute to the Fund in accordance with the members economic position. This means that the wealthier or stable a country, the more it contributes to the Fund. This is why the industrial nations especially, the United States, have greater influence on the IMF operations. But more important, voting

---

[33]Ibid.

[34]Boddie, "Africa, the IMF and the World Bank", Africa Research Bulletin, p. 87.

power is also weighted by quota, and the amount of resources a member can draw from the Fund is predicted on the size of the member's quota.

Table 21

THE INTERNATIONAL MONETARY FUND QUOTAS AND VOTES

COUNTRY	GROUPING	QUOTAS SDR(m)	VOTES	% OF VOTES
Industrial Countries	18	62,240	626,900	67.5
African Countries	43	3,734	48,090	5.2
Other LDCs Countries	80	23,267	252,670	27.3

Source: IMF Annual Report, 1984.

Although the determinant of the power structure and access to the resources of the Fund is the quota, the formula on which quota are based takes little explicit recognition of export instability, structural imbalance, or dependence on imported inputs and therefore tends to   underestimate the financial requirements of the African and other Third World countries for balance of payments assistance. Since the African countries as a whole have a relatively small share of total quotas in the Fund (See Table 21), they have been mere onlookers in the system with little or no leverage.[35]

A major problem in the flow of funds to the African countries is the IMF's standard conditionality that still puts rigid emphasis on demand contraction and exchange rate devaluation.[36]Currently, there has been a burdening of the IMF's conditionality, including a proliferation of cross-conditionality with other sources of finance, and growing practice of tying drawings under the compensatory financing facility to other conditional

---

[35]G.K. Helleiner, "Africa and the IMF", (Washington, DC).
[36]Ibid., p. 60.

agreements.[37] The Fund's compensatory facility, according to Helleiner in any case, supplied only about 4 per cent of the finance that would have been required to offset the worsening of developing African countries terms of trade in 1980-1982. Many agreements or arrangement have been canceled, a significant number of them in developing Africa on the grounds that members had failed to meet the Fund's rigid performance criteria.[38]

The IMF's conditionality is viewed in Africa as onetous in relation to the magnitude of the loans and, for this reason, members have shied away from using the Fund's resources, unless in dire circumstances. It is, therefore, not entirely correct to say that countries failed to approach the IMF early; in fact, they have been discouraged by the conditionality that they perceived to be stringent.[39]

Also more important is the reality that the adjustment problems in the developing African nations have been compounded by the policies of the IMF. The reality of the IMF's stabilization programs have been to focus more sharply on reducing aggregate demands than on stimulating aggregate supply. Given this fact, according to Helleiner: the Fund has treated the balance of payments objective as overriding and has not been sufficiently accommodating to other government objectives in designing stabilization policies.[40] As a result of the peculiar case of the African countries including Nigeria:

> restoration of a healthy payments position requires long-term changes in the structure of production and demand. Although the Fund offers some financial support, there is still scope for substantial improvement to reflect the influences of deteriorating terms of trade and other exogenous factors that have worsened the balance of payments situation in most developing countries. Admittedly, over the years, there has been some liberalization of the Fund's conditionality, including the introduction of the new lending facilities mentioned earlier. Nevertheless, the Fund's current approach offers only a high-cost solution, as the conventional stand-by arrangements of

---

[37]Ibid.
[38]Ibid., p. 31.
[39]Ibid., p. 61.
[40]Ibid.

one-to-three years duration are ill suited to address the problem of structural adjustment in developing countries.[41]

It is important to mention that the IMF's Articles of Agreement refer to the maintenance of high levels of employment, income, and economic development as "the primary objectives of economic policy", objectives that the IMF can help through balance of payments assistance. In reality, the IMF would appear to have treated these objectives as secondary to the restoration of payments equilibrium and has tended to neglect the potentially negative implication of its macro economic policies on the"primary objective" set out in the Articles of Agreement.[42]

Also, similar to the Fund, access to the resources of the World Bank is largely conditioned by its operational ideology. The Bank has traditionally conceived its major role as that of providing finance for projects and not for correcting external payments difficulties. This philosophy has, to a certain extent, hindered the effectiveness of the Bank's response to the resource requirements of the developing African countries. It is, also, important to note that the Bank has recently implemented programs aimed at expanding imports. While it is outside the scope of our research and too early to assess their effectiveness, these programs are nevertheless a step in the right direction.

The unnecessary emphasis which the Bank places on per capita income, reserve position, savings rates, and terms of trade in evaluating credit worthiness generally counts heavily against African countries because, given the nature of their economic problems, they score low marks on these criteria.[43]

The principle of conditionality is embodied in the statutes of the Fund, which have been used as the legal basis for its subsequent great expansion. Hence, the Fund's Articles of Agreement state, among other things, that it should promote exchange stability; assist in the elimination of the foreign exchange restriction; and made its resources available under adequate safeguards. So, the balance of payments equilibria could be maintained.

---

[41]Ibid.
[42]Ibid.
[43]Ibid., pp. 61-62.

Keyne's original idea of a clearing union, providing automatic access to resources in effect four times the size of those agreed for the IMF at Bretton Woods, and with supervisory powers of a technical nature only in the field of exchange rates, was abandoned. Thus, access to the Fund's resources were made conditional, under Article V.[44]

In practice, the operations of Fund conditionality soon went beyond even what was implied in its Articles of Agreement. The United States' view was that the IMF should not, as its Articles state, merely provide more or less automatic access to its resources to help them to deal with their balance of payments problems without resorting to severe deflation, but that it should exercise control over all drawings and should have discretion to promote what is considered to be appropriate domestic policies in its member countries. The Fund, clearly reflecting the interests of the U.S. as the dominant industrial power, began to see one of its major objectives as the promotion of multi lateralization in trade, in other words, the achievement of free trade and free access to the markets of Europe and Third World, including protected colonial markets.[45]

Thus, agreements with the IMF now invariably conclude with the standard undertaking that the government will not introduce new, or intensify existing exchange or import controls. Some go further and specify measure of trade liberalization and devaluation. The IMF conditionality takes three forms: "preconditions" or the action a government must take before the Fund will consider lending to it; performance criteria, which are quantified target at the end of Letter of Intent and which the government must meet or renegotiate if it is to remain eligible for the IMF money; and other measures which are embodied in the program set out in the letter of intent, but which are not specified as conditions which must be adhered to on pain of cancellation of the IMF stand-by arrangements.[46]

The IMF was not set up to lend to the Third World nations. As late as the 1970s over half of the drawings from the Fund were made by developed countries, including Britain and Italy, and 60 per cent of drawings

---

[44]Boddie, "Africa, The IMF and The World Bank", p.87.

[45]Raymond F. Mikesell, "IMF and Industrialization Strategies in Less Developed Countries: Some Lessons of Historical Experience", Concord International, vol. 20., No. 2., (August, 1983).

[46]Hayter, Aid As Imperialism.

between 1974 and 1976 were from low conditionality oil facility, most of whose funds were contributed by Third World OPEC nations. But, except in the early period and in part of the 1970s the main users of the Fund's resources have been developing countries and its pressures have become increasingly familiar, and unpopular in these nations. At first, Third World Countries have recourse that the
IMF was mainly for Latin America, where balance of payments problems became acute as a result of their attempts to grow rapidly. But by now practically every less developed country has made drawings from the IMF at one time or another, and nearly all of them have also been subjected to Fund conditionality.

Between 1982 and present, more than twenty-five countries in Africa had taken IMF loans involving conditionality because of their financial and economic difficulties of the 1980s. Nigeria which is one of the major African countries currently resisting the Fund imposed adjustment programs, by 1985 and 1986 started to implement the IMF's conditionalities, with the aim of qualifying Nigeria for IMF loan and rescheduling of extent debts from Western creditors. Since the Paris Club negotiations to commence cannot take place without the implementation of Fund adjustment programs.

CHAPTER 7

The International Monetary Fund, The World Bank And Sudanese Economy

In the year 1978, the government of Sudan accepted the stringent fiscal controls introduced by the International Monetary Fund and World Bank to receive a loan. Immediately the International Monetary Fund stabilization and World Bank structural adjustment policies were accepted by the government, the right-wing faction voiced criticisms of the agreement, and so did centrists, for the same reasons. At the same time, those groups politically affiliated with the left spoke seriously against the IMF/World Bank program in Sudan. Their argument was that IMF and World Bank's policy conditions could be reduced to a simple formula: Lower wages for Sudanese workers and larger profits for multinational corporations. Eventually, the IMF/World Bank Macroeconomic policies were implemented and effectively locked the Sudanese economy into the international capitalist system, and the evaluations and assessments of the left became true as the citizens struggled against the adverse effects of the policies at all aspects.

At this point, however, the Sudanese economy becomes a suitable case study for the implications of International Monetary Fund and World Bank programs on developing economies of Africa. The six year period of an economic stabilization program implemented by the Sudanese government on the advice of the International Monetary Fund and World Bank allows an assessment and evaluation of its effectiveness to the problems of a low income

LDC in economic predicaments. To make the assessment easy, I will provide the summary of the Sudan's macroeconomic policy from 1970-1978 in order to indicate the major causes for the serious economic crisis which resulted to the IMF and World Bank presences in Sudan. The next section is designed to a diagnosis of the International Monetary Fund/world Bank and their policy alternatives.

Evolution of the Economic Crisis in Sudan

Sudan like most former colonies, is characterized by a structural crisis of unprecented scale. Its economic activities are attached to the international market such as export of agricultural products and import of capital goods and consumer goods. However, given that this structure was a colonial origin, none of the federal government policies have addressed this structural deformity since political independence.

In the recent international economy, nations as agents of productions are divided into two main categories: Those who possess instruments of production and those, like sudan, who possess mainly raw materials. The result of the increasingly intensified struggle between the two is the domination of the latter by the former. Given this scenario, the idea of economic policy becomes, for developing countries, an important force, constituting the impetus for pulling out of the exploitative international division of labor and securing for their citizens the benefits from their natural wealth.

However, in order to be able to construct more adequate economic policies and strategies, peripheral capitalism needs constantly to evaluate and assess the effects of its macroeconomic policies. Nevertheless, there have been some major achievements, they do not result to Sudan's disengagement from international capitalism. The problems of underdevelopment and dependence, feature of peripheral participation in the world capitalist system, are therefore not being fundamentally resolved in Sudan. Again, the Sudanese economic policy has been essentially bourgeois in nature. The state instrument has been used to secure larger concession from foreign monopoly capital. However, such concessions accrue only to the few privilege groups of the bourgeois ruling class.

There was no consistent policy towards the development of traditional agricultural area which provide more than 85 percent of labor force participation, nor the development of the economy based on the use of domestic resources. The 1970s saw the introduction of an ambitious development strategy known as the "Breadbasket Plan" by the Sudanese government. This plan resulted to massive restructuring of production and trade in order to take advantage of a regional Arabic division of labor. This program depends on large-scale investments by the oil producing Arab nations. The strategy was to overcome the external economic dependence based on the export of a few raw materials or agricultural products such as cotton, sesame, grains, groundnut, gum arabic and sugar in the world market.

For this reason, however, the primary aims of the six year strategy (1978-1983) seem to indicate the need to overcome the unilateral dependence and underdevelopment that characterized the economy. The aims included but not limited to the development of traditional area and self-reliance in food production, balanced growth and improved standard of living of the nation that has been marginalized. Although, these goals were not reflected in the main allocation of resources. The strong emphasis on agricultural export production and on the modern sector of the economy was encouraged. As indicated by Lawrence:

> While the government concentrated on investments in irrigated agriculture, the Arab investments were directed to the Sub-Sectors of mechanized cereals production. Large-Scale cattle husbandry and various agro-industrial branches.   The concentration on the east-central region was maintained as well.[1]

Again, the execution of the Breadbasket Plan depended on external capital to a greater extent. This program was planned to cover 52 percent of total investment of which 38 percent of the domestic share of public sector investment was to be financed by foreign aid.[2]

---

[1]Peter Lawrence, World Recession and The Food Crisis in Africa (London: James Currey, 1986) p. 153.

[2]Federal Ministry of Planning and Development Sudan (1977), The Six Year Plan of Economic and Social Development, Vol. 1; pp. 55-56.

In the mid-1970s, the over ambitious and ineffective character of the Breadbasket Plan became visible.   Between 1971-1979, the import value increased by 318.7 percent compared with a 66 percent increase of export value. At the same time, the government deficit rose by 1,004 percent. From 1973-1978, Sudaneses debtedness also increased by 387 percent.[3]

At this point, however, it becomes very clear that the main aim on which the Breadbasket Plan was based did not materialize. In fact, the Arab nations were willing to invest in the projects but not to help Sudan efficiently with its balance of payments position. Instead, they began to make their loans to Sudan conditional on International Monetary Fund approval.   Also, because of declining international financial assistance and shortage of foreign exchange reserve, Sudan had to rely on commercial credits with higher interest rates. In addition to the above serious problems, there was a shift from project loans to balance of payment loans and from long-term to short-term loans. This vicious cyle in the final analysis reduced the government options.

Furthermore, as a result of rising import costs and rising deficit financing made possible by increasing the money supply, the inflation rate was recording officially 17.7 percent per annum from 1974-1978, which is believed to be highly underestimated by independent studies.[4]   The high rate of inflation affected the middle income, low income groups and the rural populations; it reflected on the standard of living. While the terms of trade were calculated to move against Sudan at an annual rate 15.4 percent. The major cause for Sudan's lack of satisfactory export performance was the declining quantities of exports. The export of the major commodity, cotton, felled persistently. In the overall, exports recorded a decline of 13 percent in 1970 and 1977. The fall in productivity was a result of shortages in imported inputs needed for agricultural and industrial development.[5]

Another essential factor for weak production performance was the high import dependence of irrigated and mechanized rain-fed agriculture and

---

[3]World Bank (1984) World Debt Tables 1983-1984, Washington, DC, p. 98.

[4]B.O.M. FadLalla, Problems and Perspective of the Socio-Economic Development of the Sudan, Hamburg: 1983.

[5]S. Umbadda and E. Shaaelain, IMF Stabilization Policies: The Experience of Sudan 1978-1982, (Hamburg: 1983) p. 8.

industry. In reality, the quantity of some important imported goods was decreasing seriously.[6]

More seriously is the lack of infrastructural development. Lack of infrastructure is a serious handicap for most projects which had been extremely underestimated. It eventually led to dependence on foreign inputs for most of the new projects. Added to this were shortages of raw materials and power supply. As a result of these factors most industries were operating at less than full capacity utilization. This has resulted in production losses and high unemployment rate.

Again, Sudan further experienced shortage of skilled and unskilled labor. Lack of labor supply registered in most of the important sectors (both in agriculture and industry) acted as a severe constraint to production. This is debatable in that the main cause of the shortage of labor in the first place was lack of satisfactory minimum wage. In reality, wages have been declining since 1950s upwards. Thus, for skilled labor there is a serious labor drain to Arab oil-labor producing nations; for unskilled labor many people turn to subsistence income.[7]

In spite of financial problems with which Sudan has found itself, the over ambitious development projects had gone beyond the federal government planning and implementation capability. Hence the main plan objectives were not shown in a consistent approach at plan implementation.

The Sudan's payments for essential inputs including technology in 1974-1980 amounted to nearly $515 billion - more than a third of the increase in its external debt during that year. In fact, far from enabling the Sudanese economy to reach its development objectives, it imports of technologies and other inputs, add to the factors that reinforce the situation of foreign domination from which most of the Third World nations suffer and which contributes to the reproduction of backwardness and underdevelopment. Again, the Sudan's participation in the world technology market has seriously consolidated its subordinate, dependent position in the system of international economic relations. Finally in Sudan, the effects of the crisis have been

---

[6]UNDP/World Bank, Cost of Production and Comparative Advantage of Crops in Sudan Khartoum, (1982), p. 32.

[7]D. Hansohm and H. Wolterdorff, Determining Factor of Working Behavior in Traditional Societies: A Case Study From Western Sudan, The Far and the Bagguru, Bremen, 1984.

transmitted in a very dramatic way worsening the already precarious situation characterized by poor development of its productive forces and deformation of its socio economic structures.

The Implementation of the IMF/World Bank Program in Sudan

The balance of payments problem culminated in the government of Sudan's turning to the International Monetary Fund for financial assistance. In 1978, the Sudanese government persured an economic stabilization program comprising of exchange and trade reform program, a financial stabilization policy and restructuring in the agricultural area to promote export crops. At first, the Sudanese government refused to accept the IMF macroeconomic policies because of the negative socio-economic and political implications.   In 1979, the Sudaneses government fell in line with the International Monetary Fund conditionalities.   And as such, Sudan experienced a six year intensive period of austerity measure comprising of restraint of expenditures, a reduction of subsidies on imported food, petroleum, medicines and other essential commodities, five devaluations of national currency and a moratorium on most of the new schemes and rehabilitation of existing projects.[8]

Also, included as a part of the IMF stabilization or anti-inflation program were strict controls on lines of credit given by commercial banks, requirements for the Bank of Sudan to maintain a certain level of foreign exchange, liberalization of import controls, control of wage increases, weakening of consumer price controls, and greater hospitality to foreign investment. Furthermore, agricultural land was redistributed to the traditional export crops of groundnut and cotton, foreign exchange market was liberalized, and privatization initiated.

The main aim behind the design of the IMF policy was to force Sudan to remain in the international capitalist system by controlling the flow of its international trade.   The Fund dictated that the total value of Sudan's imported commodities already in excess of its exports-had to be increased

---

[8]Lawrence, World Recession and the Food Crisis in Africa, p. 154.

even further in proportion to exports, the IMF maintaining all the while that this policy would be the one most beneficial for the Sudanese economy. This area of the program was to be accelerated by infusing additional foreign exchange into the Sudan's economy, therefore allowing the government to continue to import.

Also, by devaluation of local currency and frozen wages, the Sudan's export would become inexpensive on the world market. Obviously, according to the Fund, production and earning would generally increase due largely to the lower export price resulting from devaluation process. Increase in export earning would make the economy a better risk for foreign investors.

It is not just a question of these stabilization policies-the alchemy of the "monetary-fiscal mix" - having served merely to maintain and even intensify the crisis, in addition to taking a tragic social toll. The major problem is that these deflationary policies have disastrous economic impacts on the Sudanese economy. What is more the imposition of these policies on Sudan has sharpened the impact of the crisis and has subjected it to truly intolerable political, economic and social domestic tensions.

IMF Prescriptions: A Problematic Solution

Regardless of success or failure in the growth situation, however, the IMF stabilization policy and the World Bank structural adjustment plan in Sudan have been disastrous in terms of development that might benefit the poor citizens. This is not an accident of history. Stabilization and structural adjustment are not designed for these particular, social group. Soon after the results were observed, the IMF and World Bank refused to accept any blame from the Sudanese economic failure - its negative economic growth rate, its foundering light manufactured-export earning and its soaring, unpayable debt service. Instead, the IMF and World Bank, the international purveyors of stabilization and structural adjustment, blame the failure of their Sudanese experiment on the political turmoil that engulfed the economy.

The six year period of intensive austerity measure had been series of economic stabilization, economic rehabilitation and economic recovery which could not accomplish the desired objective of reversing trend of economic turmoil. Conversely, the economic indicators showed that the situation has been worse following the application of World Bank/IMF policy measures.

The deterioration of the Sudan's foreign economic relations is summarized in the growing deficits in the current accounts of its balance of payments which amounted to more than $10 billion in 1978-1982. Such negative balance of payments could not be met under these IMF and World Bank policy conditionalities except through more loans which began the spiral of indebtedness from which the Sudanese economy suffers.

Hence, the external debt grew at an average annual rate of 109 percent or $6.5 billion between 1980-1981, while debt servicing grew at unprecedented annual rate. Similar conclusion may also be drawn from the deterioration in the inflation rate, which increased to an average of 25.7 percent yearly.[9] What was more important according to Lawrence was:

> That the GDP growth rate was 3.9 percent annum and the real interest rates are estimated to be 10 percent or more. At the same time, the shift to rather unproductive branches of the services sector was enforced. The efforts to restrain government expenditures implied a bias against development expenditures: its share in total budgeted expenditures declined from 38.5 percent in 1978 to 24.8 percent in 1984.[10]

However, the burden of this policy was placed on the shoulders of the common men on the street via higher prices for consumer goods and services coupled with higher taxes and wage controls.[11] For the IMF's stabilization or the World Bank's structural adjustment to function effectively, both the control of foreign exchange and domestic policies had to operate hand in hand. If either one did not work, then the Fund applied more severe strigents through government budgeting.

To maintain control over the functions of the Sudanese economy, the Fund surveyed the situation on a monthly basis. Thus, passing the IMF test became the main criterion for credit rating. On the basis of the credit rating realized, Sudan received loans and line of credit, which in the first place has led to increase in its indebtedness and external dependency. The situation Payer described as "The Debt Trap".

---

[9]Ahmed and Fadlla, App. X.

[10]Lawrence, World Recession and Food Crisis in Africa, p. 154.

[11]Payer, The Debt Trap.

Also, the Fund's program had serious implication for Sudan's manufacturing sector. The depression cut deeply into domestic sales because of higher consumer prices. Devaluation increased costs in local currency commitment of imported parts needed for production process. Paying for and buying imported materials became more and more difficult. While high interest rates increased bank loans beyond the reach of potential manufacturers. Again, increases in the cost of petroleum on the international market acted as another drain on the finances of industrial development.

The existence of these industries depended on the availability of foreign exchange on every stage of production. These problems have significant impact on the masses. The situations of business in turn affected the wider population by putting many people out of work and setting limits on pay increase for wage receivers. The situation was further exacerbated by the already high rate of national unemployment. As Lawrence put it:

> The heavily import-dependent industrial sector had to suffer very much from devaluation. Prices for industrial commodities rose considerably, production declined for most commodities and the capacity utilization rate for most factories was between 20 and 40 percent. Under conditions of liberalized foreign trade regulations the economic stabilization programs implied, a bias against industrialization and a commitment of Sudan to a role of supplier of raw materials to the world market. In spite of these disastrous figures about Sudan's economic development, the government and the IMF/World Bank maintain their judgement that the economic performance is encouraging. This surprising evaluation is substantiated by the rise of export production, which is interpreted as a result of the incentives reform and the technical rehabilitation. While cotton yields could be increased, an overall view on agricultural production gives a less positive result. Furthermore, the rise in absolute agricultural production was not reflected in a parallel rise in export earnings: for the whole stabilization period export earnings decreased by 15 percent.[12]

---

[12]Lawrence, P. 154.

Perspective of IMF/World Bank In Sudan

The evaluation of the International Monetary Fund and the World Bank shows that these organizations' policy have not responded accurately to the crying needs and/or demands of Sudan, since they have completely ignored the structural nature of the Sudan's balance of payments problems; limited all except short-term, compensatory financing; and attached strings that entail a high social, economic and political price and go against citizens' interests.

Hence the IMF's traditional inflexibility is revealed today more explicit than ever in the tremendous gap between the scarce resources it contributes and the immense needs of the Sudaneses economy; between meager, barely, short-term solutions and the serious depth and historic nature of the crisis; and between what it offers and what it demands in exchange. It is a prescription that does not get to the bottom of the economic tragedy of the Sudanese economy.

At this point, however, many Third World leaders have perceived the urgent need to replace the neocolonialist "petty cash bag", that is, the International Monetary Fund, with a new equitable and universal international monetary and financial system. In fact, the uncontrollable growth of the Sudanese external debts is not a clear reflection of logical consequences of a development process which necessarily involves foreign financing imbalances.

Development requires large efforts and great cost. Only by eliminating the neocolonial nature of the international monetary system-particularly that of such instrument as the International Monetary Fund - will it be possible to undertake the transformation that are absolutely necessary. Objective analysis shows that no international institution in which a small group of five capitalist nations provides the capital, controls more than 44 percent of the votes and hence imposes its will on more than 152 less developed countries can serve the interests of the latter.

CHAPTER 8

The International Monetary Fund And The Zambian Debt Problems

Zambia, like most other Third World nations, has not been able to establish an autonomous economy or achieve self-reliance development due largely to external forces beyond its control. The Zambian economy is manifested by commercial copper's reliance on the world market, which absorbs more than 85 percent of the nation's entire cash crop production. This problem is exacerbated by a type of industrialization whose reproduction and expansionism structurally depend on imports. It is not an exaggeration to group Zambia's economy as open and dependent on International economic environment.

However, Zambia's growing interest in International Monetary Fund induced macroeconomic policy derives from the precarious financial and economic situation in which Zambia has found itself for many years. In addressing to its problems, Zambian government has resorted to the IMF's financial assistance, which is given under certain conditions. Some of the conditionalities have had significance impact on both the political, economic and social environment of Zambia. Most of the conditions attached to the IMF programs have also been justified in terms of the need to promote economic development in the Third World countries. Of course, supporters of the Fund program argue that promoting economic development in poor nations is in the long-term interests of the industrialized nations. Hence, they should endeavor to ensure that development occurs. The aim of development itself can be interpreted or viewed in different ways; some types of development in less developed countries are more likely to benefit advanced industrialized countries, or at least to be compatible with their interest. The subject of the IMF program has been, and presumably will continue to be peculiarly obfuscated by confusion about the ultimate objective.

To understand the dynamic of the economy and the economic impacts of the ongoing negotiation Zambia has had with the Fund, it is essential to examine and analyze the role of the IMF and its socio political perspective. At this point, we will address or indicate the main causes of the Zambian economic problems. To this end, the origin of the IMF negotiations will be examined along with the implications IF Zambia does default.

Socio Political Perspective of IMF

The basic issue this study addresses is the International Monetary Fund and the Zambian Debt Problems, with particular reference to Zambia debt moratorium. Many countries in the Third World are disintegrating under the almighty weight or burden of their respective debts. It has been largely argued that this state of affairs was the result of the tremendous hardship which has been imposed on the debtor nations through the draconian measures devised by the International Monetary Fund.

In the recent London conference organized by the Institute for African Alternative; the overriding theme was "The Impact of the IMF and World Bank Policies on the People of Africa." Among the conclusions reached at this conference was that the "consequences of the measures by the Fund and Bank have been dire for many in Africa. Globally they have meant that fewer are formally employed, more are landless and greater numbers, especially infant children, are confronted with starvation from social rather than natural causes."[1] The level of indebtedness by these less developing countries are enormous. Literally, almost all Third World countries owe the Fund. Among a host of the reasons cited for this indebtedness has been summarized as:

> The combination of sluggish growth worldwide, lagging purchasing power of commodity exports and the high burden of

---

[1]"The Bank, the Fund, and the People of Africa." West Africa, September 1987, p. 1832.

servicing the interest on external debt spells a sobering and perhaps bleak outlook for commodity exporters in general, and for the highly indebted among the developing countries in particular.[2]

Writing in Foreign Affairs, Pedro-Pablo Kuczynski put it bluntly:

No simple scheme will 'solve' the debt problem; there is no alternative.   However, to some mix of reform of debtor economics and fresh capital. Unfortunately, the clock is ticking and progress on new action has been limited.   Among the debtors the siren song of default is gaining new supporters.[3]

It is this default phenomenon which is increasingly gaining ground among the debtor nations that is the explicit focus of this study.

The International Monetary Fund and its twin institution, the World Bank came into existence as a result of a conference that was held at Bretton Woods, New Hampshire in July 1944.[4] The purpose was to discuss proposal for a more regulated international monetary system.   Following this conference a year later, the IMF and its coconspirator (the World Bank) became formally established.

The Fund's primary responsibility was to deal with monetary matters and particularly with countries suffering from short-term balance of payments problems. On the other hand, the Bank was established to provide "long-term developmental assistance to both developed and developing countries, especially in infrastructure and agriculture."[5]

Over the years, the Fund has done quite a few things in the Third World which are worthy of applause as well as thing equally worth of castigation. For example, since its inception, the Fund has assisted various development programs or projects in these countries:

---

[2]Pedro-Pablo Kuczynski, "The Outlook for Latin Amercian Debt," Foreign Affairs, Fall 1987, p. 136.

[3]Ibid. p. 143.

[4]Cheryl Payer, The Debt Trap: The International Monetary Fund and the Third World, New York, Monthly Review Press, 1974, p. 22.

[5]The Poverty Brokers: The IMF and Latin America, London, Latin America Bureau (Research and Action) Ltd., 1983, p. vii.

  i   the Fund's loans enable a country to continue to import items for longer period than would have been the case of the loans were not available;

  ii   without the Funds loans abrupt cuts in spending and investment would have to be made to reduce the deficit of a particular borrowing country;

  iii   IMF assistance allows debtor countries to adopt policies that lead to a more gradual reduction in the deficit of a country.[6]

However, all of these alleged merits of the Fund are open to dispute which will be explored critically in the next pages.

On the other hand, critics (particularly the LDCs) charge that because of the degree of power the Fund possesses, it often acts like a colonial power disciplining countries that failed to comply with its rule. Further, the economic development policies of the World Bank and IMF are perceived by the developing nations as reflecting the priorities of the principal capitalist donor states. It was largely because of this reason, in July of 1980, a North-South conference was held in Arusha, Tanzania, to discuss among other things the international monetary system. Delegates from twenty or so countries, mostly LDCs concluded that the IMF had lost its legitimacy and called for its replacement by a new world monetary order."[7] The Arusha Initiative maintained that "far from being scientific and generating economic progress, the performance tests which the Fund imposes lack scientific basis and that the Fund policies conceived to achieve stabilization have in fact contributed to destabilization and to the limitation of democratic process."[8]

Structural Deformity: Zambia
and the
International Economic System

Increasingly, the widening gap between the progressively impoverished masses and the privileged few is generating an explosive social crisis in

---

[6]Ibid. p. 34.

[7]Ibid., p. 31.

[8]As quoted in The Poverty Brokers, p. 31.

Zambian society, and it is in this context that both the present character of the regime and the role of IMF in Zambian reality can be best understood. The Present ruling class inherited a state structure, created by her former colonial predecessor, which it has maintained largely intact.   To quote Nkrumah:

> At the end of the colonial period there was in most African state a highly developed state machine and veneer of parliamentary democracy concealing a coercive state run by an elite of bureaucrats with practically unlimited power...a professional army and a police force with an officer sorbs largely retained in Western military academies and chieftaincy used to administering at the local level on behalf of the colonial government.[9]

In Zambia, the state structure has serve as the main instrument by which the Zambian bourgeoisie have imposed their domination on the subordinate classes and secured the privileged position in the present neo-colonial system.

No one has done a better work of accurately describing the character of the present regimes in Africa than Fanon.   His contribution is all the more remarkable because his observations were made in the late fifties before the present state of Africa had yet gained her formal independence.   Fanon indicated that the African bourgeoisie, including Zambians who led the national independence movements, would increasingly turn their backs on the masses and ally themselves with foreign interests.   They are forced to collaborate with foreign capital and erect an authoritarian regime around popular leader because they lack the economic power to secure their domination in any other fashion.[10]   Fanon further believed that:

> The bourgeoisie turns its back more and more on the interior and on the real facts of its underdeveloped country and tends to look toward the former mother country and the foreign capitalists who count on its obligating compliance.   As it does

---

[9]Kwame Nkruah, Class Struggle in Africa, (New York: International publisher, 1970), p. 55-56.

[10]Frantz Fanon, The Wretched of the Earth, (New York: Grove Press) 1963. p. 165-166.

not share its profits with the people, and in no way allows them to enjoy any of the dues that are paid to it by the big foreign companies, it will discover the need for a popular leader to whom will fall the dual role of stabilizing the regime and of the perpetuating the domination of the bourgeoisie.[11]

Again, without an economic power base of its own the Zambian ruling class has no choice but to become the willing accomplice of neocolonialism and to depend on an authoritarian dictatorship to maintain its domination and privileges.   After established themselves as a ruling class, they generally enriched themselves at the public, expense through bribery and corruption as well as deals with foreign capital.   Fanon prosaically describes this situation in the following words:

By dint of yearly loans concessions are snatched up by foreigners; scandals are numerous, ministers grow rich, their wives doll themselves up, the member of parliament either their nests and there is not a soul down to the simple policeman or the customs officer who does not join in the great process of corruption.[12]

As a result, the Zambian bourgeoisie have become increasingly obligated to foreign interests who are only very happy to give grants, loans, and credits which will place them in debt with foreign nations, organizations, institutions and/or banks.   Hence, in order to finance their conspicuous consumption, the ruling classes have mortgaged both the local economy and the state to foreign capital. Today, the operating budgets of Zambian state are totally dependent upon loans and grants from one or more of the major industrialized countries, while the local entrepreneurs and businessmen are dependent upon loans and credits from foreign banks and firms to finance their operations.   The end results is a neocolonial state tied in a varieties of ways to foreign capital.

---

[11]Ibid., p. 165.
[12]Ibid., p. 172.

The History of Debt Crisis

In the first instance, the Zambian economy was faced with economic and debt crisis because of the structure and nature of industrialization in Zambia. Industrialization in Zambia has derived the whole society of development, and thus growth has had to be financed by increasing foreign indebtedness, a problem exacerbated by the growing deficit between exports and imports. The economy was highly depended on export of copper, the price of which fluctuated seriously on the world market.

Zambia's per capita food production has fallen by a quarter since the 1970s, and its energy consumption per house hold is among the highest in the less developed countries of Africa. Other agricultural production such as maize has fluctuated since political independence. Demand has increased, but many peasant farmers have left the land and moved to urban areas in search of wage employment. As a result, large areas of land now lie fallow begging commercial farming that could turn the economy into a breadbasket for Africa in general and Zambia in particular.

The Zambia's debt was a classic example of a Third World country that, because of misguided policies of its own making as well as external economic factors beyond its control, finds itself in an economic guagmire. This bring us to the question where did Zambia go wrong? As Joseph Makokha put its:

Zambians soon will want to know where the national wealth is; they will want to know who gets what, when, where, and how. There is nothing so frustrating as struggling to share poverty.[13]

Prior to 1974, there was a great demand for copper, and prices were high. With this high price, Zambia had a huge capital reserves which became the envy or model of most African stats. As Kenneth W. Grundy asserts: "copper money flowed throughout the economy and nourished the state's social services."[14] Grundy maintains that the cycle of economic dislocation began after 1974. This was partly due to poor management because mostly

---

[13]Joseph Makokha, "Zambia: No More Loyalty to IMF" African World News, (January 1988), p. 22.

[14]The Atlanta Journal and Constitution, October 4, 1987, p. 6D.

the price of copper plummeted. The immediate effect was that the foreign exchange earning dipped and there was very little or no funds for maintaining the productivity of the copper mines and other enterprises declined.[15]   To complicate matters, Zambia, like any other Third World country, failed to diversify its economy at the boom period or cut spending to compensate for the decline in world copper prices. The price of oil and other essentials rose. For this reason, the government began to incur balance of payment deficits and was compelled to borrow from the IMF as well as other lenders, leading to a total foreign debt of $13 billion according to the Africa Report of October 1987, which it can longer service. Zambia's population is 6 million. If its massive foreign debt were to be shared among its citizenry, it will be translated "into nearly $120 to every woman, man and child in that country."[16]   A deficit country is one that has been unable to earn enough foreign currency to meet all its overseas commitments. If Zambia were to pay its debt, it means that Zambia has to continually transfer a hugh amount of resources into the hands of the Bankers in Europe, Japan, and the United States. As Harry Magdoff puts it: "Within the market system, the debtor countries cover their deficit by attracting more foreign investment or borrowing from international bankers, the IMF, and the World Bank. But all that does is to intensify the problem, since still more is going to have to be paid abroad for interest and profits. There lies the trap of debt peonage."[17] By the debt standards of most Latin American countries, Zambia's debt is not horrendous. What makes a world of difference is the Zambia's minisule economy. The main factor affecting Zambia's recovery is the debt situation, which has become so serious, not in terms of the quantum of the debt because Zambia's total debt is probably less than that of Brazil but in terms of the extremely heavy impact the debt burden has on the economy of this country, given the fragity of Zambia's very fragile economy.

---

[15]Ibid. p. 6D.

[16]Ibid. p. 6D.

[17]Harry Magdoff, Monthly Review, Volume 38, February 1987.

The Emergence of the IMF

Zambia started with the IMF supported programs in 1973 at the height of its booming copper economy, and stuck with it until as recently as May 1986.[18] Zambia decided to abandon the Fund policies and implemented its own package when it began to feel the razor's edge of the IMF dictated austerity measures inching closer and closer to its neck. IMF bitter medicine was largely borne by peasants and the urban workforce, the most vulnerable segment of society. The impact of the IMF cruel policies brought about riots in some major cities which eventually resulted in the death of fifteen or more people.

Zambia receives 90 percent of its export earnings on copper. As is very typical of most Third World nations which rely totally on a single export item such as the case of Nigeria which generates 95 percent of this export earnings on oil. In such economies, whenever there is a fluctuation in that country's principal foreign exchange rate, it usually has disastrous consequences on the poor. This was exactly the case with Zambia.

In 1973, the Zambian government had pursued an economic stabilization program comprising a financial stabilization policy, an exchange rate and trade reform program and a restructuring in the agricultural sector to promote export production. Between 1980 and 1984, Zambia has witnessed a series of long history of austerity measure comprising devaluation; cutting of subsidies on imported medicines, food, petrol, and other essential commodities; and credit ceiling.

The IMF's "austerity" measures have been a bitter medicine to swallow for Zambia, since they involve drastic changes which have an immediate impact on economic reality. These measures also pose political dangers because they involve explosive changes which are likely to heat up social unrest (for example government spending, cuts in Subsidies).

> This reaction is understandable: in the over indebted LDCs the
> majority of the people, i.e. the poor, have generally not reaped
> any fruits from the expansion of the economies in the seventies,
> and now that the price for previous policies must be paid, it is

---

[18]"The Bank, the Fund, and the People of Africa, "West Africa, September 1987, p. 1833.

the poor who must sacrifice most, as a consequence of tight fiscal policies, reduction in government spending and in subsidies, devaluation of the currency, increasing unemployment and cuts in real wages.   The economic objectives of IMF programs are actually often met (e.g. reduction of public debt to GDP), but there are political and social limits to which LDCs can be squeezed. These countries have critized the IMF as being inflexible, always using the same standard policy set, showing little appreciation of the political and social constraints on the individual countries.[19]

In Zambia, President Kaunda announced that Zambia would not continue with the IMF stabilization programs for economic recovery. According to Kaunda, the IMF medicine is stronger than the sickness it seeks to cure. For example, the foreign exchange auction system introduced in October 1985 - supposedly designed to stabilize the Kwacha and reduce black market dealings resulted in a fall in value of the Kwacha from K2.50 = $1.00 at the beginning of the year to K13.48 by November of the same.[20] Not only have the auctions market resulted in a rapid devaluation of the Kwacha, Kaunda proceeds;

> They have opened the door wide to nonessential imports and deprived the country of precious foreign exchange.   It is patently irresponsible for the IMF to preach that, faced with a major economic crisis, Zambia or any other debt-ridden country can toy with a free market experiments such as this. One of the few ways in which a sovereign government can master national resources for economic revival is through the prudent allocation of foreign exchange for essential, productive inputs.[21]

Zambian Prime Minister Kebby Musokotwane further added that:

> Shortages of both essential and luxury goods have grown worse. Beer shortages resulted in a "riot" on Christmas Eve at Zambia Breweries which police had to be called to quell as bar

---

[19]Manzsche Verlage, External Debt Rescheduling (Austria: Wienmanz, Vienna Inc., Horn, 1985), p. 42.

[20]EASA: Trade and Investment in Eastern and Southern Africa, Vol. I, No 2, (January 1987), p. 2.

[21]Ibid.

operators clamored for supplies. Although Zambia Breweries blamed the shortage on seasonal high consumption, but from the published list of bidders at the weekly foreign exchange auctions, the company has for sometimes bid too low to obtain foreign exchange for malt and other raw material inputs.[22]

Kaunda further states that the Fund-supported programs are generally standard and do not take into account the specific situation of African states. He further rejects the Fund idea that places much emphasis on the inadequacy of internal policies as the main factor for Africa's economic crisis. According to him, the hostile world economic environment has been the dominant factor in the problems now facing African states. The rapid increase in oil prices in the 1970s, followed by recession, protectionism, and high interest rates in industrialized states, set in motion forces that are still straining the economies of African countries. The subsequent decline in prices of their export commodities and the higher import prices have led to sharp falls in the terms of trade; hence the current economic crisis.[23]

Furthermore, in Zambian, the implementation of the Fund austerity programs have had adverse effects on lower and middle income Zambians. The number of civil servants and teachers employed by the state fell from 160,000 to 131,000.[24]

The education and health budgets have been pared down to a level whereby they have virtually no effect on Zambia's population of about 6 million. President Kaunda also set a limit to wage increase of 25 percent in 1985, whilst the rate of inflation was running at about 40 percent.[25]

Also, it has to be remembered that debt service is currently running at 26 percent of export earnings and the numerous rescheduling accorded to Zambia will only exacerbate this situation. Apparently, the 1985 Paris Club rescheduling has added $1.0 billion to debt service falling due in the period 1986-1991. However, a leading aid donor has calculated that, even if sufficient Zambian debt is rescheduled to keep debt service down to 15 percent over the next five years, minimum aid of $380 million per annum

---

[22]Ibid.

[23]Botswana Daily News, (6 March 1985), p. 43.

[24]Financial Times Survey, (September 1984), p. 47.

[25]Financial Times Survey, (31 March 1985), p. 49.

would be needed to keep net transfers at zero. This is obviously a situation incompatible with recovery of development.[26]

Furthermore, low returns for agricultural producers and the question of subsidies for rice and petrol have been a major concern of the IMF. Increasing prices paid to agricultural producers has been a major policy suggestion of the IMF negotiators in recent years. In this they are reflecting the view of their fellow Washington institution, World Bank, and in particular the perspective upon sub-Sahara Africa found in the Berg Report.[27] Producer prices were raised 120 and 100 percent in March and July 1983 for coffee and cocoa respectively. Unfortunately, the desired results did not emerge. Despite two increases in the price paid to producers, the volume of purchases almost halved.[28]

The cost of rice subsidies was questioned, but, in addition, the Fund has pressed for a reduction in the subsidy for petrol and other oil products. Zambian Finance Minister stated in 1984 that the state subsidy for pertrol resulted in the lowest consumer price. The subsequently increased petrol prices by 50 percent in the 1984 budget. Petrol prices were further raised both in January 1985 and 1986. However, erratic supplies and price increases have led to hoarding, queuing, political manipulation of distribution, and increased prices on public transport.[29] Petrol shortages and price increases have led to protests by urban workers and school children and have reinforced existing social and economic inequalities.

Zambia's recent decision to object an macroeconomic policy supported by the International Monetary Fund in favor of a "go it alone policy" reveals two unpleasant realities: The first is that after twenty-three years, President Kaunda has not transformed the productive forces he inherited from the colonial power, Great Britain, into a vibrant, multifacted economy for the independent state of Zambia, thus perpetuating a neocolonial situation. Second, the Organization of African Unity and its Economic Commission for

---

[26]EASA p. 4.

[27]World Bank, "Accelerated Development in sub-Saharan Africa: An Agenda for Action", African Review, (16 May 1982), p. 32.

[28]Financial Times Survey, p. 48.

[29]Sierra Leone National News Bulletin, (December, 1984), p. 13.

Africa, have failed to build a pan African approach to the continent's economic crisis since last year's United Nations Special Session on Africa.[30]

An examination of the Fund stabilization since 1979 points to the fact that this program failed to achieve its own targets, and more significantly improvement in the direction of structural changes needed for the long-run sustained development of the Zambian economy. Available data indicated that the large import-dependent industries had suffered heavily from devaluation. Also, prices for industrial commodities increased rapidly, the production of most commodities declined significantly, and the capacity utilization of certain factories was between 25-40 percent.[31]   In addition Zambia experienced high rate of inflation, unemployment and low rate of economic growth. External indebtedness increased by 110 percent in 1982 as opposed to 71 percent in 1974.[32]   In Zambian the macroeconomic stabilization policy of the IMF/World Bank has reinforced the country's unilateral dependence on the world market without necessarily improving the well being of the producers as advocated by the Fund.

Implication if Zambia Does Default

To begin with, if a debtor nation cannot obtain much loans to finance its domestic obligations, the chances are that, such a nation will be succumbed to the temptation of default on interest payments as a last resort. Defaults on debt payment is not unique only to the developing nations. Some center nations had defaulted on debt payments as it suited their interest. For example:

> The United States itself effectively canceled a foreign debt obligation of $68 billion in 1971 (equal to $80 billion in 1985 dollars) when it unilaterally renounced its commitment under the Bretton Woods agreements to convert foreign holdings of dollars into gold at $35 an ounce. The justification for this

---

[30]Joseph Makokha, "Zambia: No More Loyalty to IMF", African World News, (January 1988), p. 22.

[31]S. Umbadda and E. Shaacladin, as quoted in Peter Lawrence, World Recession and the Food Crisis in Africa, (London: James Currey, 1986), p. 154-156.

[32]Ibid., p. 154.

action is debatable. But given this experience, the U. S. government can hardly claim to be opposed in principle to debt cancellations when circumstances appear to require them.[33]

Kuczynski argues that for a debtor nation to follow the path of default implies that, that nation's economy would gradually become disconnected from the international financial system, thereby credit would be difficult if not impossible to obtain, and foreign trade would be reduced to bare essentials.[34] Further, if a nation defaults, it will be black-listed by the entire Western financial establishment. As that country runs out of foreign currency needed to pay for its imports, it means that in the final analysis, that nation will stop trading. As a final outcome, the world's banking system will be dislocated in the event of an outright default. "American banks hold about one third of the Latin American's debt and the same holds true for Africa."[35]

On the other hand, according to the Nicaraguan Vice President Sergio Ramirez, "when it comes to choosing between the necessities of our people and paying the debt, we prefer to take care of our people".[36] In the words of Isebill V. Gruhn, a correspondent for Africa Today:

> For African states the situation is quite different. Debts are relatively small by international standards. Defaulting would not place the international system at risk and thus a threat to default carries little leverage.   Even a collective African defaulting--which is not politically imaginable--would not give much international leverage.[37]

Fidel Castro believes that the Latin America's debt or any Third World debt for that matter is unpayable.[38] This view is increasingly shared by the

---

[33]Monthly Review, vol. 38, February 1987, p. 15.

[34]Foreign Affairs, Fall 1987, p. 130.

[35]Phillip A. Cartwright, "Latin Debt Problems Handled Best on the International Level," The Atlanta Journal and Constitution, March 29, 1987, p. 3E.

[36]"Nicaragua Plans to Skip Debt Payments Next Year", The Atlanta Journal WEEKEND The Atlanta Constitution, December 21, 1985, p. 19A.

[37]Isebill V. Gruhn, "The Recolonization of Africa: International Organizations on the March, "Africa Today", vol. 30, no 4, 1983, p. 39.

[38]The Atlanta Journal WEEKEND The Atlanta Constitution, December 21, 1985, p. 19A.

U.S. bishops, and other Third World leaders such as the Zambia's Head of State, Kenneth Kaunda, and the Peruvian President, Alan Garcia. Both have equivocally stated that should they decide to pay on their loans, they will designate no more than 10 percent of export income for debt servicing. Most Third World governments are beginning to realize that a great deal can be gained from a moratorium. Pollin and Zepeda maintained that moratorium: (i) would bring immediate and deserved relief from the punishing austerity of the past four years; (ii) would allow the domestic industries to recover some momentum; (iii) and it would also, ultimately, force more reasonable financial agreements from the creditors cartel.[39]

As a matter of fact, financial institutions or commercial banks such as the Citibank, Chase Manhattan, Pan American, just to name a few cannot foreclose on a nation as they can easily do so on an individual. This is because of the "doctrine of sovereign immunity," which simply means that commercial transactions of a nation cannot be sued.

By way of conclusion, it seems that many developing nations would join Zambia's debt club, if drastic or meaningful changes are not instituted by the IMF with the way it does business. The weight of these nations debt problems are so hugh that it is adversely affecting life's in these countries. Under the present structure, some countries have no choice than to declare moratorium or outright default. In a recent interview with Africa Report, President Kaunda puts Zambia's case this way:

> The IMF program has been with us for close to 12 years now and we began to see nothing but a contraction of the economy, contracting. In the end, we were living to pay the IMF, nothing else! And we were not developing, the economy was not expanding, it was contracting. Therefore, it got to the stage where nothing was going to happen, except the death of our economy.[40]

---

[39]Monthly Review, vol. 38, February 1987, p. 13-14.

[40]Africa's Economies: Debt, Exports, and Development", Africa Report, November-December, 1987, p. 13.

Solution to the Debt Crisis

A number of suggestions have been advanced to solve Africa's or the Third World debt crisis. At the recent Organization of African Unity (OAU) Summit in Addis Ababa this on July 1987, Africa's debt dominated their agenda. They came to the realization that many of them cannot service their debt and or finance development plans or economic reforms even the type prescribed by the IMF and World Bank. For this reason, they called for the establishment of an African debt club in order to coordinate activities such as appealing and rescheduling for continued help from the West.[41]   They affirmed the fact that:

> much of the debt will not and cannot be paid back in any real sense. What is needed is new loans on concessionary terms, new investments, and economic reforms. New policies must include debt relief, long-term rescheduling and conversion to softer terms.[42]

Another of the solutions suggested was liberalization and privatization of economies as urgent priorities for the debtor nations.   Cheryl Payer proposed the privatization of the Fund:

> a measure which would oblige Fund policies to compete with others in the international marketplace of ideas and, no doubt in the mind of the proposer, lead to their marginalization.[43]

Deferral of part of the interest burden was also suggested. Deferral is not a forgiveness or debt pardon. It simply means that the resumption of the payment of that debt be extended over a considerable length of time until circumstances are favorable to the debtor nation.

It was also suggested that for these countries to come out of their debts, a repatriation of capital is a necessity. It is said that, without it, foreign direct investment will be slow to revive from the low levels it has reached.

---

[41]"Assessing the OAU Summit," Africa Report, September-October 1987, p. 28-29.

[42]Ibid. p. 29.

[43]West Africa, September 1987, p. 1890.

Without this, it is said, foreign corporations are understandably reluctant to put money into countries from which their local partners are withdrawing.[44]

The Baker's plan is another strategy as a panacea for the debt problems. It calls for private banks to extend $20 billion in new credit to 14 heavily indebted Third World countries through 1988, and the World Bank would contribute an additional $9 billion.[45] Many Third World nations have not wholeheartedly embraced this plan, because they think the suggested sum was a drop in the bucket.   Owing to this uproar by the developing nations, The Christian Science Monitor reported that the Reagan Administration has changed its position on a package of new capital for the World Bank. The report says "the shift is good news for the bank, which has been seeking $40 billion to $80 billion in fresh capital, and the Third World nations, which would benefit from an increase in lending by the bank.[46]   However, it remains to be seen if this will be enthusiastically welcomed by the developing nations.

---

[44]Ibid.

[45]Ibid., 1982.

[46]Christian Science Monitor, (April 23, 1987).

CHAPTER 9

African Economic Crisis And The International Monetary Fund Response

African countries are recently in the last stage of an economic and social crisis of an unprecedented scale. To begin with, the crisis did not suddenly occur. It is the product of adverse developments in the International economic environment such as the economic recession in industrial nations, oil price shocks, rapid increase in international interest rates, and the fall of prices of raw materials. The effect of these external imbalances was aggravated by inadequate domestic economic and financial policies pursued by many African states. However, the convergence of these variable factors hence resulted in large growing internal and external imbalances, high rates of inflation and unemployment, and slackening economic growth in most African states. In addition, the situation was compounded by structural weakness created by colonialism and later neocolonialism. This particular section of the research examines the nature and causes of African economic problems and how the International Monetary Fund has responded to the crisis. The objective is to find out whether African countries have benefitted with the IMF policy measures.

The Nature and Causes of the Crisis

In Africa, internal structural rigidity and acts of nature has exacerbated by decreasing international economic relations. These factors have been responsible for generating the problems that constitute the current economic and social crisis in the continent.

Among the nations grouped by the United Nations as "the least developed" nations, two thirds are in African continent. As compared with other third world nations, social and economic indicators of development, such as health, output growth, per capita annual income, standard of living, and literacy have indicated persistently weak performance in this continent. Economic growth rates in Africa in the 1970s averaged 4-5 per cent as compared with 6-7 per cent recorded by Latin America. Average per capita income in 1981 was $ 770, as compared with $ 973 for Asia, and $ 2044 for Latin America.[1]

The economic and financial position of many African states deteriorated markedly in the mid-1970s and early 1980s. The annual rate of economic growth in the non-oil Africa states, which reached 6.9 per cent in 1974 and 5.8 per cent in 1976, fell to less than 2.5 per cent in 1977-1980 and to only 1.3 per cent in 1981-1983 (See Table 22), a rate strongly lower than the 3 per cent annual increase in population, resulting in a serious reduction in real per capita income. At this time, their combined external current account deficit increased largely, rising from $ 4.9 billion in 1973 to $ 14.1 billion in 1981, or from an average of about 10 per cent respectively.[2] To finance these enormous and growing deficits, a number of African states depended on foreign borrowing which was facilitated in the second half of the 1970s, by relatively easy access to external sources of financing. At this point, the heavy borrowing, combined with the rapid increase in interest rates led to a serious debt crisis in most African states.[3] The weakening in economic growth and the large external payments disequilibria were accompanied by an intensification of inflationary pressure. The average annual rate of inflation in the non-oil African states rapidly increased continuously, from 10 per cent

---

[1]J.O. Sanusi, quoted in Africa and The International Monetary Fund, ed. by Helleiner, (Washington, DC IMF 1980), pp.53.

[2]International Monetary Fund, "World Economic Outlook".

[3]J.B. Bhatia and Amor Tahari, "External Debt Management and Macroeconomic Variables: Problems of African Countries in the 1980s", (unpublished International Monetary Fund, 1984); presented at a Seminar on External Debt Problems of African Countries Organized by the African Center for Monetary Studies, (Tunis, Tunisia, September, 1983), As quoted in Africa and The IMF, (9 March 1984), p. 13.

Table 22

AFRICA; SELECTED ECONOMIC INDICATORS, 1973-84

	1873	1975	1977	1979	1981	1983	1984
				(Percent)			
Economic growth	2.19	2.75	2.30	2.00	1.70	0.80	3.20
Inflation	9.86	15.84	24.30	22.90	28.00	26.50	17.00
Terms of trade	8.30	-12.19	18.10	2.70	-3.00	-0.10	3.50
Ratio of external debt to GDP	24.90	27.50	36.00	37.90	43.40	54.60	57.70
Debt service ratio		9.50	11.90	15.50	18.70	22.60	24.90
				(billions of dollars)			
Current account	-4.50	-7.20	-6.60	-9.60	-14.10	-10.20	-9.40
Net official transfers	1.10	1.70	2.30	3.00	3.40	3.30	3.40
Net capital inflows	3.80	4.90	5.00	6.40	8.40	5.40	5.10
Overall balance of payments	0.50	-0.60	0.70	-0.20	-2.30	-1.50	-0.90
Total outstanding debt	11.60	18.40	31.00	45.10	56.30	62.20	69.30

Source:International Monetary Fund, Current Studies Division, Research Department, and World Economic Outlook (Occasional Paper No.27, 1984).

in 1973 to over 20 percent during 1977-1983.[4] Furthermore, the serious implication of external variable factors was exacebated by inefficient domestic demand management and structural measures. These in turn, contributed to the worsening in the balance of payments position of African states.

Also, the economic arrangement in Africa is mainly dualistic in nature with a large subsistence sector accounting for over 80 per cent of the gross domestic product, and relatively small "modern sector" often dominated by mining and other extractive industries operated by multinational enterprises. The production arrangement in the modern sector is largely export oriented and comprises a narrow range of primary products-mainly mining and agriculture.

---

[4]Helleiner, Africa and The International Monetary Fund.

However, the development of African countries has been restrained by their primary export-oriented economic structure that has been historically determined, and after more than twenty years of political independence, remains virtually the same. Also, as open economies, African nations are more affected by the changes in international economic events.

Further, in the early 1970s, the terms of trade of African states have decreased sharply due largely to unequal movements in the prices of imports and exports. As the African countries have been beset with large increases in the prices of their imports (for instance, intermediate and capital goods, oil, and food), the prices of their exports (such as cocoa, coffee, cotton, and tea) have decreased dratically.[5]   With deficits in current accounts and the worsening terms of trade, African countries have minted in the debt trap. Table 23 summarizes Sub-Sahara African external debt.

The Table indicates that for Africa as a whole, the ratio of debt-service payments to exports of goods and services doubled to over 30 per cent in 1984 from about 14 per cent in 1980. While for Sub-Sahara Africa, the ratio reached 27 per cent in 1985-1986. The widespread and prolonged debt servicing difficulties among African countries are the financial reflection of the disappointments and problems encountered in many sectors of the real economy. Policies directed at achieving sustained improvement in underlying economic trends are therefore the first step to improving the debt-servicing ability, and thus the credit worthiness of many African countries. However, such policies only are insufficient to address adequately with existing debt-servicing difficulty or to establish a framework for improved policy on external indebtedness.[6] While it is not the purpose of this Chapter to trace the macroeconomic causes leading to past and present debt-servicing difficulties, a consensus seems to be emerging among scholars and observers that inadequate policies on resources allocation, relative prices and demand management aggravated by negative external economic influences - are at the root of the problems. Lancaster has this to say:

> The economic crisis in Africa involves problems much deeper than those posed by short-term financial obligations. It is a

---

[5]Harris, The Political Economy of Africa, p. 13.

[6]For accurate discussion of these issues, see Onyema Ogochukwu, "And Now For The IMF", West Africa, (23 April 1984), p.866-867.

Table 23

SUB-SAHARAN AFRICAN EXTERNAL DEBT - IMF ESTIMATES

A. Amounts 1977-1984 (amounts in $ billions)

	1975	1977	1979	1981	1982	1983	1984
Medium and Long Term	15.3	23.6	38.4	51.7	61.4	64.8	64.8
% Share thereos	(17)	(18)	(18)	(20)	(19)	(21)	(22)
Bilateral	(44)	(41)	(40)	(41)	(43)	(44)	(45)
Financial Inst.	(16)	(20)	(26)	(27)	(28)	(27)	(25)
Others	(23)	(20)	(15)	(13)	(9)	(9)	(8)
Short Term	0.1	1.2	1.5	2.2	2.5	6.1	4.8
Arrears	1.5	1.5	2.0	4.6	9.7	9.3	9.4
IMF Credit	1.7	1.3	1.5	2.0	3.4	4.0	5.1
Total	18.6	27.6	43.6	60.5	75.0	84.1	88.1

B. Debt Ratios 1977-1986 (Percentages)

	1977	1979	1981	1982	1983	1984	1986
To Exports	120.0	141.7	168.3	199.8	216.8	223.2	230.9
To GDP	33.8	36.7	43.5	49.7	54.2	72.6	68.0

C. Debt Service 1980-1986 (Amount in $ billions)

	1980	1981	1982	1983	1984	1985	1986
Sub-Saharan	2.6	2.7	3.2	3.5	4.3	4.8	4.6
Interest							
Amortization	2.9	3.1	3.0	3.9	5.7	6.2	6.2
Total	5.5	5.8	6.2	7.4	10.0	11.0	10.8
% of Exports	9.5	12.3	15.5	20.6	26.2	28.1	26.0
Africa	10.9			14.1	17.4	19.2	18.9
Interest	4.7			5.5	6.5	6.8	6.6
Amortization	6.2			8.6	10.9	12.4	12.3
% of Exports	13.9			25.5	30.3	32.4	30.0

D. Average Terms New Public Sector Debt Commitments 1975-1982

	1975	1977	1979	1980	1981	1982
Interest (%)	5.6	5.6	7.6	7.4	9.5	7.7
Maturity (Years)	19.9	18.1	15.5	17.6	15.3	19.9
Grace (Years)	5.2	4.8	4.5	4.8	4.3	5.0
Grant Element (%)	30.0	29.1	17.5	20.2	8.4	19.6

Of which Low Income Africa

	1975	1977	1979	1980	1981	1982
Interest (%)	4.2	3.8	5.2	4.5	4.8	4.2
Maturity (Years)	23.7	23.7	20.7	22.8	25.1	28.1
Grace (Years)	6.1	5.8	5.5	5.8	6.1	6.6
Grant Element (%)	41.8	44.0	34.1	40.0	40.3	45.9

Source: International Monetary Fund, World Economic outlook, (Washington, D.C., April 1985).

result of fundamental economic ills for which there are no sure solutions... Perhaps the most intractable problems in Africa involve: the population, which increasing rapidly; the small scale of man national economies (24 African countries have populations of less than 5 million), which limits the opportunities for growth through industrialization; and political instability, which continues to disrupt economies in various parts of the continent... How many financial crises, devastating droughts, political upheavals, or foreign interventions must occur before the political leaders in Africa and in the developed world realize that the human as well as political costs of ignoring the crisis are greater than the costs of acting?[7]

Adedeji further comments that:

The future that emerges from the historical trends scenario... is horrendous. To imagine that the African region will be more dependent on other regions in all critical areas is a cause for alarm...riots, crimes and misery would be the order of 2008 if present trends continue without conscious change. With the weak and fragile socio-political systems, the sovereignty of African states will, then, be at stake. As such, self-reliance and independence will, to the generation of 2008, sound like slogans of the past....another future must be designed. Hence, the normative development scenario.... of self-determination, self-confidence, collective self-reliance and self-sustainment. This 'willed future' (consists of) a will to establish, today, a genuine development process.[8]

The agitation and advocacy which led to the articulation of the Lagos Plan of Action have their roots in a number of factors and levels which came together in the "Conjuncture" of the mid-1970s. First, at the global level, the combination of fluctuating exchange rates, inter-imperial rivalries, and energy shocks marked the end of the Bretton Woods era. The contours of the crisis are now quite familiar. Africa has been the hardest hit of all developing countries in 1970s. Given the abundant natural resources, Africa still

---

[7]Carol Lancaster, "Africa's Economic Crisis", Foreign Policy", 52, (Fall 1983), pp. 149-151, 166.

[8]Adebayo Adedeji, "Introduction to ECA and Africa's Development, 1983-2008: A Preliminary Perspective Study", Africa News, (17 November 1983), p. 2.

contributes least to global trade and product in terms of both primary product and manufactured commodities.

The nature and character of the African crisis have become increasingly clear as relentless and exponential setbacks have hit most countries on the continent over the last decade or so. As the latest IBRO World Development Report indicates:

> Low income countries in Africa being more dependent on primary commodity exports, have suffered badly from the world recession. Their per capita income has continued to fall, and there is a real possibility that it will be lower by the end of the 1980s than it was in 1960s.[9]

However, as in the case of Nigeria, the World Bank also asserts that internal rather than external factors were responsible for the causes of African economic underdevelopment. As the World Bank puts it:

> When the sub-Saharan states won independence some 20 years ago, they faced formidable constraints to development. These included under-developed human resources, political fragility, insecurely rooted and ill-suited institutions, a climate and geography hostile to development, and rapid population growth. And while the governments have scored considerable achievements, the legacy of history and the facts of geography continue to hamper African progress.[10]

Such an "imperialist" perspective is compatible with the kind of development strategy it prescribes for Africa. Known fully well that external rather than internal factors are more serious in aggravating African economic problems, the Plan adopts a more "radical paradigm" compatible with dependency analysis. The Plan points out that:

> Africa, despite all efforts made by its leaders, remains the least developed continent....Indeed, Africa was directly exploited during the colonial period and for the past two decades; this exploitation has been carried out through neocolonialist

---

[9]World Bank, World Development Report, Washington, D.C., 1983, p,.2

[10]"Accelerated Development in sub-Sahara Africa" African Review, (3 December 1980), p.29.

external forces which seek to influence the economic policies and directions of African states......We view, with disquiet, the over-dependence of the economy of our continent on the export of basic raw materials and minerals. This phenomenon has made African economies highly susceptible to external developments and with detrimental effects on the interests of the continent.[11]

Given the above mentioned economic and financial problems, a number of African states embarked, especially since the 1980s, on adjustment programs supported by the International Monetary Fund.

The Function of the IMF in the Adjustment Efforts in Africa

For many years, the International Monetary Fund has been playing a significant role in helping a number of African states in the design and financing of their stabilization programs. The IMF's function in Africa, as elsewhere, is guided with its Articles of Agreement, which stipulated at the beginning (Article I) that its objectivities are:

(ii) to facilitate the expansion and balanced growth of international trade, and to contribute thereby to the promotion and maintenance of high levels of employment. Prolonged debt servicing difficulties among African countries are the financial reflection of the disappointments and problems encountered in many sectors of the real economy. Policies directed at achieving sustained improvement in underlying economic trends are therefore the first step to improving the debt-servicing ability,and thus the credit worthiness of many African countries. However, net and real income and the development of the productive resources of all members as primary objectives of economic policy; (iii).... to maintain orderly exchange arrangements.....; (iv) to give confidence to members by making the general resources of Fund temporarily available to them under adequate safeguards, thus providing them with opportunity to correct maladjustments in their balance payments without resorting to measures destructive of national or international prosperity; and (v)...to shorten the duration and

---

[11]Lagos Plan of Action, p.7.

lessen the degree of disequilibrium in the international balance of payments of members.[12]

With respect to these aims and objectives, the IMF has established a more pragmatic and flexible method in assisting member nations in their adjustment endeavors and in providing them with financial and technical assistance. In reality, the IMF has persistently adopted its macroeconomic policies and procedures in response to the changing international economic relations and the needs of member states. For example, to solve the problem of the balance of payments disequilibria that are temporary and beyond the control of the authorities, the IMF has introduced certain special facilities with low conditionality. These include as we stated earlier, the oil facilities, the Trust Fund, the subsidy accounts, the compensatory financing facility; and, more recently, the so-called cereal facility. The oil facilities were implemented in 1974-1975 to enable members rebuild their economies against the adverse effect of the sharp increases in oil prices in 1973-1974. The Trust Fund was established in 1976 to give low interest loans to low-income countries out of profits realized from sales of a part of the Fund's gold holdings. The subsidy accounts were introduced in 1975 and 1980 to enable the same group of countries to meet the higher charges on amounts given to them from resources borrowed by the International Monetary Fund at market-directed interest rates. Also, in 1979, the maximum requirement for the compensatory financing facility, which was created in 1963 to enable nations finance balance of payment deficits due largely to temporary export decrease, was increased to over 100 per cent of quota. Furthermore, in 1981 the IMF established the cereal facility, to provide help to member states experiencing temporary increases in the cost of cereal imports. Many countries benefitted from these special facilities. Purchases under the oil facility by African States amounted to SDR 465 million in 1974-1976, and Trust Fund loans disbursed to them totalled SDR 962 million over the period 1977-1981.[13] The drawings under the compensatory financing facility increased from SDR 968 million during 1974-1979 to SDR 1,620 million in 1980-1984 (See Table 24.)

---

[12]International Monetary Fund, The Role and Function of the IMF, (Washington, D.C., 1985), p.ix.

[13]Helleiner, International Monetary Fund.

TABLE 24
COMPENSATORY FINANCING FACILITY PURCHASES BY AFRICAN COUNTRIES, 1980-1984
(millions of SDRs)

	1980		1981		1982		1983		1984	
	Export short-falls	Cereal import excesses	Export short-falls	Cereal import excesses	Export short-falls	Cereal import excesses	Export short-falls	Cereal import excesses	Export short-falls	Cereal import excesses
Central African Republic										
Chad										
Côte d'Ivoire								130.5		
Egypt	6.4								92.3	
Equatorial Guinea										
Ethiopia					135.0	135.4	12.2			9.0
Gambia, The										
Ghana			40.8				34.0			
Guinea-Bissau										
Kenya							20.7		14.4	
Liberia				9.0			39.1		12.9	
Madagascar	39.3			1.9						
Malawi			16.0		21.4					
Mali	10.5		18.0		24.7		12.1			
Mauritania	8.1		15.0		26.9		27.3			
Mauritius	21.8		42.0		102.9					
Morocco										
Niger	15.0		45.7							
Senegal	25.0		13.9							
Sierra Leone			6.7							
Sudan			7.2							
Swaziland			9.0							
Tanzania			16.0							
Uganda										
Zaïre										
Zambia										
Zimbabwe										
Total (both facilities)	233.0		434.1		469.2		493.3		92.3	
Total (excluding Egypt and Sudan)	91.3		378.4		89.3		454.3		95.4	

Source: International Monetary Fund Bureau of Statistics, 1985.

Furthermore, while given the usefulness of facilities to African states, it was reality that many nations in Africa were suffering fundamental in balance that can only be solved by many years through the implementation of effective measures, designed in the context of comprehensive stabilization programs. According to Helleiner's table, the number of African states that carried out such stabilization programs and were supported by stand-by and extended facilities from the Fund increased from 8 in 1974-1979 to 27 in 1980-1984. The amount of IMF assistance received under these agreements increased from SDR 600 million to over SDR 5 billion, respectively.[14] As indicated in Table 25, at the end of 1980, there were 11 stand-by agreements and 5 extended facilites as result; the two combined amounted to SDR 2,685 million, of which SDR 685 million was drawn. By the mid of 1981, the number of stand-by agreements and extended arrangements increased to 13 and 7 respectively. However, because of some cancellations of the arrangements, the number of extended Fund facilities declined in 1982 to only 1 while the number of stand-by arrangements remained unchanged, with a total amount of SDR 1,583 million drawn. During the end of 1983, the number of stand-by arrangements increased again to 16, while that of extended arrangements rose to 2; the total amount was SDR 2,629 million, and the total amount drawn increased to SDR 1,298 million.[15] However, at the end of 1984, there were 14 stand-by arrangements and 1 extended Fund facility, with a total sum of SDR 1,435 million committed and SDR 719 million drawn under these agreements. Again, it is important to note that Nigeria has not been a recipient of the IMF's Extended Fund Facility and Stand-by Arrangement until 1987-1989 (See Table 26). Between 1988 to 1989, Nigeria has received a total number of 18 Stand by and Extended Fund Facility Arrangements.[16]

---

[14]Ibid., p. 76.

[15]Ibid.

[16]See International Monetary Fund Annual Report, (Washington, D.C., 1989), p. 62.

Table 25

STAND-BY ARRANGEMENTS AND ARRANGEMENTS UNDER EXTENDED FUND FACILITY AT END OF YEAR, 1980-84

	Stand-By or Extended Fund Facility	Date of Agreement	Expiration Date	Amount Agreed	Amount Purchased	Undrawn Balance
1980						
Central African Republic	SBA	Feb. 15, 1980	Feb. 14, 1981	4.00	4.00	. . .
Egypt	EFF	July 28, 1978	June 30, 1980	425.00	75.00	350.00
Equatorial Guinea	SBA	July 1, 1980	June 30, 1981	5.50	3.00	2.50
Gabon	EFF	July 27, 1980	Dec. 31, 1982	34.00	. . .	34.00
Kenya	SBA	Oct. 15, 1980	Oct. 14, 1982	241.50	60.00	181.80
Liberia	SBA	Sept 15, 1980	Sept 14, 1982	65.00	18.40	46.60
Madagascar	SBA	June 27, 1980	June 26, 1982	64.50	10.00	54.50
Malawi	SBA	May 9, 1980	Mar. 31, 1982	49.90	22.00	27.90
Mauritania	SBA	July 23, 1980	Mar. 31, 1982	29.70	8.90	20.80
Mauritius	SBA	Sept. 5, 1980	Sept. 4, 1981	35.00	15.00	20.00
Morocco	EFF	Oct. 8, 1980	Oct. 7, 1983	810.00	147.00	663.00
Senegal	EFF	Aug. 8, 1980	Aug. 7, 1983	184.80	41.10	143.70
Somalia	SBA	Feb. 27, 1980	Feb. 26, 1981	11.50	6.00	5.50
Sudan	EFF	May 4, 1979	May 3, 1982	427.00	150.00	276.00
Tanzania	SBA	Sept 15, 1980	June 30, 1982	179.60	25.00	154.60
Zaïre	SBA	Aug. 27, 1979	Feb. 26, 1981	118.00	98.40	19.60
Total				2,685.00	684.80	2,000.00
Total (excluding Egypt and Sudan)				1,833.00	458.80	1,374.20

Stand-By Arrangements and Arrangements Under Extended Fund Facility at End of Year, 1980-84

	Stand-By or Extended Fund Facility	Date of Agreement	Expiration Date	Amount Agreed	Amount Purchased	Undrawn Balance
1981						
Côte d'Ivoire	EFF	Feb. 27, 1981	Feb. 22, 1984	484.50	176.70	307.80
Ethiopia	SBA	May 8, 1981	June 30, 1982	67.50	44.00	23.50
Gabon	EFF	June 27, 1980	Dec. 31, 1982	34.00	. . .	34.00
Kenya	SBA	Oct. 15, 1980	Oct. 14, 1982	241.50	90.00	151.50
Liberia	SBA	Aug. 16, 1981	Sept 15, 1982	55.00	33.00	22.00
Madagascar	SBA	Apr. 13, 1981	June 26, 1982	109.00	39.00	70.00
Malawi	SBA	May 9, 1980	Mar. 31, 1982	49.90	40.00	9.90
Mauritania	SBA	June 1, 1981	Mar. 31, 1982	25.80	10.30	15.50
Mauritius	SBA	Dec. 21, 1981	Dec. 20, 1982	30.00	7.50	22.50
Morocco	EFF	Mar. 9, 1981	Oct. 7, 1983	817.10	136.50	680.60
Senegal	SBA	Sept 11, 1981	Sept 10, 1982	63.10	15.70	47.30
Sierra Leone	EFF	Mar. 30, 1981	Feb. 22, 1984	186.00	33.50	152.50
Somalia	SBA	July 15, 1981	July 14, 1982	43.10	25.90	17.20
Sudan	EFF	May 4, 1979	May 3, 1982	427.00	251.00	176.00
Tanzania	SBA	Sept 15, 1980	June 30, 1982	179.60	25.00	154.60
Togo	SBA	Feb. 13, 1981	June 10, 1982	47.50	7.25	40.25
Uganda	SBA	June 5, 1981	June 30, 1982	112.50	77.50	35.00
Zaïre	EFF	June 22, 1981	June 21, 1984	912.00	175.00	737.00
Zambia	EFF	May 8, 1981	May 7, 1984	800.00	300.00	500.00
Zimbabwe	SBA	April 8, 1981	April 7, 1982	37.50	37.50	. . .
Total				4,722.50	1,525.35	3,197.15
Total (excluding Sudan)				4,295.50	1,274.35	3,021.15

Stand-By Arrangements and Arrangements Under Extended Fund Facility at End of Year, 1980-84

	Stand-By or Extended Fund Facility	Date of Agreement	Expiration Date	Amount Agreed	Amount Purchased	Undrawn Balance
1982						
Côte d'Ivoire	EFF	Feb. 27, 1981	Feb. 22, 1984	484.50	292.14	192.36
Gambia, The	SBA	Feb. 22, 1982	Feb. 21, 1983	16.90	16.90	. . .
Guinea	SBA	Dec. 1, 1982	Nov. 30, 1983	25.00	11.50	13.50
Kenya	SBA	Jan. 8, 1982	Jan. 7, 1983	151.50	90.00	61.50
Liberia	SBA	Sept 29, 1982	Sept 28, 1983	55.00	5.00	50.00
Madagascar	SBA	July 9, 1982	July 8, 1983	51.00	30.60	20.40
Malawi	SBA	Aug. 6, 1982	Aug. 5, 1983	22.00	10.00	12.00
Mali	SBA	May 21, 1982	May 20, 1983	30.40	25.40	5.00
Morocco	SBA	Apr. 26, 1982	Apr. 25, 1983	281.30	196.90	84.40
Senegal	SBA	Nov. 24, 1982	Nov. 23, 1983	47.30	6.00	41.30
Somalia	SBA	July 15, 1982	Jan. 14, 1984	60.00	15.00	45.00
Sudan	SBA	Feb. 22, 1982	Feb. 21, 1983	198.00	70.00	128.00
Togo	SBA	Feb. 13, 1981	Feb. 12, 1983	47.50	7.25	40.25
Uganda	SBA	Aug. 11, 1982	Aug. 10, 1983	112.50	50.00	62.50
Total				1,582.90	826.69	756.21
Total (excluding Sudan				1,384.90	756.69	628,21

Stand-By Arrangements and Arrangements Under Extended Fund Facility at End of Year, 1980-84

	Stand-By or Extended Fund Facility	Date of Agreement	Expiration Date	Amount Agreed	Amount Purchased	Undrawn Balance
1983						
Central African Republic	SBA	Apr. 22, 1983	Apr. 21, 1984	18.00	4.50	13.50
Côte d'Ivoire	EFF	Feb. 27, 1981	Feb. 22, 1984	484.50	446.00	38.50
Ghana	SBA	Aug. 3, 1983	Aug. 2, 1984	238.50	143.10	95.40
Kenya	SBA	Mar. 21, 1983	Sept 20, 1984	175.95	129.80	46.15
Liberia	SBA	Sept 14, 1983	Sept 13, 1984	55.00	28.00	27.00
Malawi	EFF	Sept 19, 1983	Sept 18, 1986	100.00	10.00	90.00
Mali	SBA	Dec. 9, 1983	May 31, 1985	40.50	10.00	30.50
Mauritius	SBA	May 18, 1983	Aug. 17, 1984	49.50	24.75	24.75
Morocco	SBA	Sept 16, 1983	Mar. 15, 1985	300.00	30.00	270.00
Niger	SBA	Oct. 5, 1983	Dec. 4, 1984	18.00	6.80	11.20
Senegal	SBA	Sept 19, 1983	Sept 18, 1984	63.00	31.50	31.50
Somalia	SBA	July 15, 1982	Jan. 14, 1984	60.00	51.25	8.75
Sudan	SBA	Feb. 23, 1983	Feb. 22, 1984	170.00	144.50	25.50
Togo	SBA	Mar. 4, 1983	April 3, 1984	21.40	19.41	1.99
Uganda	SBA	Sept 16, 1983	Sept 15, 1984	95.00	44.00	51.00
Zaire	SBA	Dec. 27, 1985	Mar. 26, 1985	228.00	. . .	228.00
Zambia	SBA	Apr. 18, 1983	Apr. 17, 1984	211.50	76.50	135.00
Zimbabwe	SBA	Mar. 23, 1983	Sept 22, 1984	300.00	97.50	202.50
Total				2,628.85	1,297.61	1,305.74
Total (excluding Sudan)				2,458.85	1,153.11	1,305.74

Stand-By Arrangements and Arrangements Under Extended Fund Facility at End of Year, 1980-84

	Stand-By or Extended Fund Facility	Date of Agreement	Expiration Date	Amount Agreed	Amount Purchased	Undrawn Balance
1984						
Central African Republic	SBA	July 6, 1984	July 5, 1985	15.00	5.00	10.00
Côte d'Ivoire	SBA	Aug. 3, 1984	Aug. 2, 1985	82.75	41.38	41.37
Gambia, The	SBA	Apr. 23, 1984	July 22, 1985	12.83	2.63	10.20
Ghana	SBA	Aug. 27, 1984	Dec. 31, 1985	180.00	66.00	120.00
Liberia	SBA	Dec. 7, 1984	June 6, 1986	42.78	8.50	34.28
Madagascar	SBA	Apr. 10, 1984	Mar. 31, 1985	33.00	27.00	6.00
Malawi	EFF	Sept 19, 1983	Sept 18, 1986	100.00	34.00	66.00
Mali	SBA	Dec. 9, 1983	May 31, 1985	40.50	34.00	6.50
Morocco	SBA	Sept 16, 1983	Mar. 15, 1985	300.00	210.00	90.00
Niger	SBA	Oct. 5, 1983	Dec. 4, 1984	18.00	35.20	12.80
Sierra Leone	SBA	Feb. 3, 1984	Feb. 2, 1985	50.20	19.00	31.20
Sudan	SBA	June 25, 1984	June 24, 1985	90.00	20.00	70.00
Togo	SBA	May 7, 1984	May 6, 1985	19.00	16.00	3.00
Zaïre	SBA	Dec. 27, 1983	Mar. 26, 1985	228.00	158.00	70.00
Zambia	SBA	July 26, 1984	Apr. 30, 1986	225.00	80.00	145.00
Total				1,435.06	718.71	716.35
Total (excluding Sudan)				1,345.06	698.71	646.35

An Evaluation of the IMF Policy Conditions in Africa

The International Monetary Fund was created for the purpose of providing loans to its member states facing balance of payments deficits. However, as we have seen many African countries have frequently relied upon the IMF, but they feel that IMF policies usually ignore economic and political realities and place unwarranted burden upon their economies. Thus, they rely upon the IMF only as a last resort.

In particular, African states object to strict limits on the size of loans they can obtain from the IMF. Countries are normally limited to borrow 125 per cent of their quota, with longer-term stand-by agreements negotiated with the Fund sometimes permitting states to double that figure. Since quotas are calculated upon states' overall economic size and capabilities, African states typically have relatively small quota - and, thus, small borrowing capacities in the IMF. Also, by linking stand-by agreement with economic assistance, most African states find it difficult to implement successfully, the IMF stabilization policies.

As we mentioned in our theoretical and conceptual framework, the difference between low conditionality and high conditionality is the level of IMF influence. The Fund's
conditions take into consideration the revolving nature of its resources and its basic objective to promote international payments and trade. Drawings by African states after 1979 have been overwhelmingly of the high- conditionality type.   High-conditionality drawings are subject to compliance with performance criteria and other conditions stated in the arrangement. These criteria and conditions, put together in a program of action, are related mainly to domestic credit, public sector financing, external debt, some key elements of the price system (including the exchange rate), interest rates, and prices of primary products.   The main characteristic of the conditionality imposed under arrangements relating to high-conditionality drawings is therefore the adoption of an adjustment program in which the implementation period is defined and limited.

The IMF has been inclined to impose severe economic austerity programs upon African countries with serious payments deficits.   These programs include stringent curtailment of public expenditures, restrictive fiscal and monetary policies, devaluation of the nation's currency, removal of state subsidies, removal of restriction on the free flow of trade and foreign investment and the like.

An examination of the International Monetary Fund policy prescriptions in specific African countries such as Zambia, Zaire, Sierra Leone and Sudan indicates the inadequacy of the Fund policies in Africa. Table 27 summarizes the economic indicators of the sustainability of adjustment for the sub-Sahara countries implementing World/IMF adjustments program.

The present economic crisis in developing African countries calls for urgen and concerted action at the international level to ameliorate the deteriorating situation. Attention has earlier been drawn to the determined efforts being made at both national and regional levels to deal with the crisis. There is no denying that during the last few years the terrifying scale of the crisis has elicited positive response from the international community. In realation to the magnitude of the problem, however, the response of the multilateral financial institutions, especially the Fund, the World Bank, bilateral and multilateral

Table 26

Table 26

FUND STAND-BY ARRANGEMENTS FOR MEMBERS, FINANCIAL YEAR ENDED APRIL 30, 1988
(In millions of SDRs)

Member	Total Number of Stand-by Arrangements Approved for Member Since 1953	Current Arrangement Date of Inception	Current Arrangement Date of expiration	Amount Approved in 1986/87 Total	Amount Approved in 1986/87 Of which borrowed resources	Amount Approved in 1987/88 Total	Amount Approved in 1987/88 Of which borrowed resources	Amount Not Purchased at Expiration or Cancellation	Amount Not Purchased as of April 30, 1988
Argentina	12	07/23/87	09/20/88	—	—	947.50	631.67	17.30	331.00
Bolivia	14	06/19/86	07/20/87	50.00	—	8.00	—	21.00	—
Burundi	6	08/09/86	07/31/88	21.00	—	—	—	—	—
Central African Republic	3	06/01/87	05/31/88	—	—	—	—	—	7.00
China	3	11/31/86	11/31/87	597.73	—	—	—	—	—
Congo	2	08/28/86	04/28/88	22.40	—	—	—	—	—
Costa Rica	10	10/23/87	03/21/89	—	74.31	40.00	—	12.90	40.00
Côte d'Ivoire	5	06/23/88	—	100.00	—	—	—	76.00	—
Ecuador	12	08/15/86	08/14/87	75.40	99.14	94.00	62.67	60.30	87.00
Egypt	3	05/15/87	11/14/88	—	—	75.35	—	—	60.28
Gabon	4	12/28/89	—	98.69	96.65	250.00	65.38	134.00	134.20
Gambia, The	3	11/23/86	12/31/88	5.13	—	—	—	—	51.16
Ghana	5	10/15/86	11/14/87	81.60	61.80	—	—	—	134.00
Guinea	3	07/29/87	08/28/88	85.00	—	11.60	—	11.60	15.00
Jamaica	5	03/02/87	05/28/88	—	56.67	85.00	—	15.00	89.25
Kenya	7	09/17/88	—	30.00	23.93	—	—	—	37.7
Madagascar	6	09/21/88	—	—	—	10.00	—	650.00	—
Malawi	8	05/04/87	—	—	—	—	—	—	—
Mauritania	9	05/20/88	—	1,400.00	1,037.19	—	—	—	—
Mexico	11	11/19/86	04/01/88	230.10	148.13	—	—	—	—
Morocco	8	08/30/88	—	10.11	9.13	—	—	—	70.00
Niger	7	12/04/87	—	650.00	131.17	—	—	—	27.62
Nigeria	1	01/30/87	12/31/88	198.00	20.75	—	—	18.73	8.60
Philippines	8	11/09/87	—	14.00	—	—	—	14.40	11.41
Senegal	9	10/20/87	10/25/88	—	—	—	—	—	—
Somalia	8	06/29/87	02/29/88	64.20	19.74	21.28	22.10	14.40	51.18
Tanzania	3	08/09/86	04/27/88	23.00	—	33.15	—	—	—
Togo	8	06/29/87	04/08/88	—	—	—	—	—	—
Tunisia	7	03/21/86	04/25/88	—	—	13.00	8.67	166.60	10.41
Zaire	7	05/31/86	05/31/88	103.65	171.76	—	—	—	13.85
Zambia	6	02/21/86	02/28/88	214.20	—	100.00	80.66	194.60	78.30
Total				4,117.51	1,870.63	1,701.90	871.15	1,247.19	1,014.94

Source: International Monetary Fund Annual Report (Washington, D.C. IMF 1988), p 89.

overseas development assistance, and the private international financial markets has been totally indequate.[17]

This Table indicates that sub-Saharan Africa experienced an increase in investment, annual growth rate and a decline in budget deficit before the implementation of the Fund stabilization programs. The Table also shows that the debt service to GDP was relatively low before the application of the Fund policies. The table finally shows an increase in private consumption per capita growth. This, we suggest, may occur as a result of the use of loaned money to finance consumption. This is not a positive success on the part of sub-Saharan Africa as it will further increase the debt-servicing ratio to GDP. In the overall analysis, the Fund stabilization program has not been effective in addressing African economic crisis. Thus, many African countries are now looking for alternative approaches to Fund stabilization in solving their economic problems.

The deflationary policies imposed by the IMF produce political upheavals in less developed countries including African states, referred to as "IMF riot". Domestic chaos has confronted regimes in Turkey, Peru, Portugal, Egypt and Chile during the 1970s in the wake of these governments' acceptance and implementation of austerity packages required for access to IMF loans.[18] Over 700 people died in Egyptian riots in 1976. Countries such as Tanzania, Zambia, and Jamaica have found the conditions attached to IMF lending so objectionable economically, politically, and ideologically that they have broken off negotiations for desperately needed foreign loans. While most less developed African nations have not gone this far, they all find the intrusion of the IMF upon their domestic and foreign policies unacceptable.

Our finding indicates that many African countries have had various aspects of their economic policies fundamentally altered as a result of IMF policy conditionality. All of these countries under study have been faced with repeated demands for substantial devaluation or flotation of the exchange rates, labor retrenchment policies, the abolition of subsidies, cuts and/or privatization of the parastatal sector. They have been obliged to adopt what the International Monetary Fund likes to think of as "financial discipline"

---

[17]Africa and the IMF, p. 63.

[18]Payer, The Debt Trap: The IMF and the Third World, pp.184-204.

Table 27

Indicators of the Sustainability of Adjustment for sub-Saharan Countries Implementing Bank/Fund Adjustment Programmes

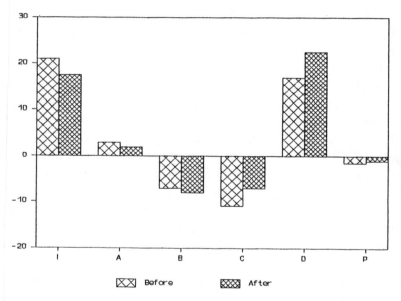

I = Investment/GDP
A = Annual GDP growth
B = Budget deficit/GDP
C = Current account/GDP
D = Debt service/Exports
P = Private consumption per capita growth

Source: World Bank Washington D.C., _Report on Adjustment_.
          8th August, 1988.

This financial discipline has had broadly similar implications in developing African economies, and with price inflation, shortages of essential commodities, unemployment rising due to government spending cuts, and intermediate inputs needed for development. The suggested benefits of this IMF policy (for example,increased agricultural production) remain fragmentary in their achievement at best. The IMF policy measures have resulted in increasing social unrest in Nigeria, Sierra Leone, Zaire, Zambia, Sudan to mention but a few.

The IMF blame lack of success of its policy in Africa on individual African leaders. According to Fund officials, many African countries have not been able to implement effectively a series of policy measures advocated by the IMF, including restrictions upon government expenditure, reducing the size of the cabinet, and an improvement in the efficiency of parastatal organizations.

Many African countries have been less leniently treated and have had to swallow the IMF medicine, whether appropriate or not. A major factor in forcing them to this decision has been the unwillingness of alternative donors to give support. African countries have found that acceptance of the IMF macroeconomic stabilization program has been the key to obtaining bilateral and multilateral aid that otherwise would not be given.

A criticism of balance of payments equilibrium as a main goal of the IMF programs is that imports may have to be suppressed in ways that deny essential intermediate and capital goods to those areas that needed to expand if the structural deformity is to be overcome. The nature of the beneficiaries of Fund assistance has changed dratically over time, and yet this change seems not to be taken into consideration in designing policy measures. For instance, with reference to Table 25, the majority of stand-by arrangement and extended Fund Facility Credits have recently gone to the poor and poorer developing countries including africa, yet in these countries the Fund's traditional policies are least suitable and successful in these areas. Also, the tightening conditionality of the Fund policies in the 1980s has contracted the economies of these poor African states. However, the current design of Fund programs reduces the Fund's ability to achieve its objectives, especially because of the nature of the economies of the recipients of this credit which the Fund fails to recognize.

Furthermore, the emphasis on internal factors as chiefly responsible for the current economic crisis for Africa seems to have resulted in   making adjustment into a prescription reserved for low income deficit countries of Africa. Many intellectual scholars such as, General Helleiner, shares the belief that some Fund programs are treated like mere intellectual exercises. According to him:

> The human element is not given the prominence it deserves. Political and social unrest have been constraints on the successful implementation of stabilization programs in most developing African countries and, as such, cannot be overlooked in our efforts to correct imbalances of our economies. Some programs have had to be abandoned in the past because of built in inflexibility on the part of the IMF regarding such unforeseen developments as deviations of official commodity prices from price assumptions. The IMF has normally been reluctant to change program targets in light of new developments, preferring to render the program inoperative. Canceling a program is costly to a country that finds itself in such a situation not of its own making.[19]

There is no doubt that the IMF has been of help to the supporting African countries. This help should have been even more, if the recent method to adjustment and adjustment had been changed in light of changing circumstances.

We do not advocate that the Fund turn into a development agency, but the structural reality of the problems in developing countries in general, and African states in particular, dictates that changes of approach take place if the IMF is to meet the primary objectives of economic policy. In this case, the question of conditionality is important if African states are to benefit from the IMF. The Fund should in particular try to avoid "overkill" in the application of severe demand-management policies.[20]

Having examined the causes of African economic crisis, we must ask what, if any, general conclusions can be drawn from the case studies. The answer is yes. African countries belong to the group of essentially mono-cultural primary commodity producers that are especially prone to balance of payments deficits. Their problems have been compounded by both endogenous and exogenous variable factors.

---

[19]Helleiner, IMF, p. 95.

[20]Ibid.

There are certain general similarities in the economic structure of African countries: small domestic markets because of low per capita incomes and quite small populations, predominantly agricultural activities, high dependence on some basic export commodities, and concentration of foreign trade on a few partners.   In addition, the education level is low, the reproduction rate is high, and the urban population is constantly increasing.

Over the last two decades, most African countries hae recorded slow economic development, with annual per capita income only rising by 1.3 percent in 1969-70 and by 0.8 percent in 1970-79, while food production grew by only 1.5 percent a year during the 1970s, against 2 percent a year during the previous decade.   In relation to size of population, food production fell by 0.9 percent in 1970-79 while cereal impports skyrocketed, thus increasing food dependency.   Export production, whihc had grown by 20 percent in the 1960s, shrank by about 20 percent during the 1970s, while percapita exports declined by 3.5 percent from one decade to the next.   During the present decade, production growth rates decelerated in African countries: from 3 percent in 1980 to 1.8 percent, 1.2 percent, and 0.1 percent in 1981, 1982, and 1983; while the inflation rate rose to 19.5 percent in 1983 from an average 7.5 percent in 1967-76.[21]

With respect to the response of these countries to their respective debt problems, they have sought further loans, from whatever source, to tide them over their immediate difficulties.   Unfortunately,, many of them have approached the IMF, although they have taken this course with varying degree of opposition.   For example, the Steven administration in Sierra Leone was reluctant to go to the IMF as it recognized that IMF policy direction would mean removal of subsidies on rice and petrol and a potentially discontented population.[22]   Whereas the new President Joseph Momoh, has been much more compliant as Sierra Leone's economic crises have increased.

As we see it in Ouattara's Paper a Fund designed adjustment program, whether for an Asian, African, Latin American, or European country includes a package of strategies oriented generally toward demand management,

---

[21]Helleiner, Africa and The International Monetary Fund, p. 105.

[22]Sierra Leone National News Bulletin, 25 December 1984, p. 5.

including variations in exchange and interest rates and reduction of both the fiscal deficit and the rate of expansion of domestic credit. Exchange rate devaluations and interest-rate changes in the African context are more of a demand-management than a supply-oriented measure. So are the various recommended pricing measures, including the elimination of subsidies. No one will generally question the use of these approaches to ensure prudent fiscal and monetary policies and realistic exchange rate. One is position to question whether these policies are adequate to meet the specific African reality. These are economic tools best designed to correct short-term departures from equilibrium caused by imbalances like temporary loss of budgetary control. However, the payments problems facing African states are due not only to temporary disequilibria but also to the problems originated in the very nature of African economies.

Also, stabilization or policy measures that do not put into consideration of these structural weaknesses in Africa stand little or no chance of success. Regretably, macro economic policies that could remedy these problems, including improvements in the quality of manpower through education, agriculture, and infrastructures, are issues which the IMF has not been able to address in African and other developing countries.

CHAPTER 10

The Buhari's Foreign Exchange Regulations: An Alternative To International Monetary Fund Policy Prescriptions

In this chapter we are concerned with the critical examination of the Buhari government economic policies, particularly the Foreign Exchange Control Act of 1984 implemented to address Nigeria's economic problems. To this end, we will find out whether these policies are likely to achieve the long-run objective of self-reliant development. What we are trying to do is arrive at a critical understanding of the nature of these government policies and their implications. Chapter 9 examines some specific IMF stabilization policies implemented by the Babangida administration to reach an agreement with Nigerian creditors, especially the Paris Club and Britain's Export Credit Guarantee Department.

We begin our analysis with a detailed examination of the provisions of the two military government policies. At the same time, we discuss the IMF forces which gave rise to and currently influence these government policies. In order to understand the nature of Buhari and Babangida's economic policies, we need to understand first, the perspectives from which Nigeria had the opportunity to choose and which shaped its development strategy. It is argued that a set of perspectives, drawn primarily from neoclassical and monetarist economic theory, influenced both policy making and the formulation and execution of the various National Development Plans in

Nigeria. The plans are analyzed in chapter four. This chapter examines the literature for a particular purpose: to lay out the development paradigm that Nigeria adopted since 1960.

While it does not fall within the scope of this research to go into detail about the origin and motives of these theories, it is nevertheless useful to analyze the difficulties involved with the application of such policies in a developing country like Nigeria.

The military coup d'etat which removed President Shagari's administration on New Year's Eve, 1983, took place against a background of corruption, enormous debts, high rate of inflation and unemployment, deteriorating terms of trade, and low rate of economic growth. Nigeria's global debt at the time of the military takeover had reached an estimated $17 billion. Trade deficits amount for nearly $4.8 billion of this debt.[1] Imports had increased from an average of about $300 million a month in mid-1979 to about $1.8 billion a month in 1983.[2]

However, the short-period military adminstration headed by General Mohammed Buhari sought to end the debt crisis, curtail corruption (especially in the acquisition and use of foreign exchange), and put Nigeria on the road of self-reliant economic development. In realize of the two short-term objectives and the long-term goal of self-reliant development,the Buhari administration implemented a number of economic policies. Many of these policies aimed in general to conserve foreign exchange. More narrowly, they aimed at bringing under government control literally any foreign exchange accruing to the citizen as a result of services rendered at home or as a result of activities, investments, or gifts overseas.[3]   The New administration directed attention to eliminating the loopholes through which abuses and corruption had hitherto occurred and as well banned products that had been smuggled into the nation.[4]

The policies implemented, include the 1984 foreign Exchange Control Regulations and Supplementary Regulations. These regulations restrict how

---

[1]Onaolapo Soleye, West Africa (2 March 1985) The Wall Street Journal (21 February 1984), p. 31.

[2]African Economic Digest March 1984.

[3]National Concord, Lagos, 2 March 1984, p. 5.

[4]Africa Today, 1986, p. 8.

much Nigerian currency a traveler may bring into or take out of the country; require immediate official exchange into naira of any foreign currencies or travelers checks brought into the country; demand that foreign visitors pay for hotel services in foreign exchange; reduce maximum salary remittance by expatriates from 50 to 25 percent; cut the basic travel allowance of Nigerian citizens to the equivalent of $130 a year.[5] Whether or not these policies were responsible for his overthrow will be seen in the later part of this chapter. The overthrow of the Buhari administration in 1985 had led to serious changes in Nigeria's monetary and economy policy.

However, the Buhari regime wanted the IMF loan but maintained a firm stand on most of the IMF policy prescriptions. During Nigeria's negotiation for a loan in 1984, some of the IMF's requirements were devaluation of the naira, cut in petroleum subsidies and trade liberalization. The consensus in Nigeria was that these conditions would be detrimental to the already ailing economy. Labor leaders, for instance, warned that the IMF conditionalities would lead to higher prices for many consumer goods and services such as gasoline, electricity, and transport, as well as the closing of more factories and greater foreign domination of the economy.[6] The feeling was that the poorest people were likely to be hit hardest by the IMF requirements.

In his interview with the editor of West Africa (1984), Major General Buhari challenged the logic of the IMF requirement:

The way the IMF sees it, if we devalue our exports would be cheap, imports would be dearer. If so, the effect on Nigeria is irrelevant because we hardly export anything other than oil which is price in dollars and which is subject to currency fluctuations, so devaluation doesn't make sense, because our industries hardly satisfy our needs up to 50 percent. so we are not exporting anything other than oil; finished goods are second, so that argument does not hold. On the cost of imports, we need cheap imports, because our essential raw materials for our industry are mostly imported from the united States and Europe so we don't want to make it expensive. If we make it expensive our end product would be more

---

[5]Ibid.

[6]Daily Times, Lagos, 2 March 1984, pp. 4-5.

expensive, and the inflation will go up again, so the argument against devaluation in Nigeria is real, and we hope the IMF will see it that way.[7]

The Buhari government refused to accept these three conditions because of the risk to political stability. President Buhari believed that he would achieve rescheduling of Nigeria's debts at the same time receive the IMF loan without necessarily reaching agreement with the IMF.   To accomplish these goals, Buhari put in place the Foreign Exchange Control Programs as alternative to IMF conditions. Whether the Buhari regime was able to achieve the above started goal will be seen later in this chapter. Nigeria's recent military regimes have been acutely aware of the dire economic and political implications which have accompanied this type of monetary and economic policy package elsewhere in the developing African states.[8]

However, the case of devaluation is particularly sticky. Instead of official and sudden devaluation, Nigerian governments have preferred to allow the value of the naira to slide. In 1980, the official rate for the naira came to $1.80. Over the next four years, the government quietly and gradually decreased its value to $1.12 by changing the mix in the basket of currencies to which the naira is pegged.[9] The Buhari administration further believed that foreign exchange controls are more likely than devaluation to accomplish the stated goal of revitalizing the economy, provided that the new loan would be forthcoming and existing debts rescheduled. The objectives of Nigeria's 1984 budget according to the Head of State Major-General Bunari, were "to arrest the decline in the economy, to put the economy on a proper course of recovery and solvency, to chart a future course for economic stability and prosperity, and to achieve in the long-run self-reliant economic

---

[7]New Nigeria, (4 April 1984), p. 16.

[8]See Ronald Libby "External Co-option of a Less Developed Country's Policy Making: The Case of Ghana 1969-1972", World Politics, (29 October 1976), pp. 6-9. In an interview conducted by Michael Holman, General Buhari predicted that Implementation of the Fund conditionalities would result in riots that seem to signify the arrival of the IMF inmost developing countries, Financial Times, (25 February 1985).

[9]New Nigeria, (10 June 1984), p.14.

development".[10]   To achieve these intended objectives, the Buhari's government introduced the foreign exchange control regulations along with other supplementary regulations as alternative to the IMF conditionalities.

The Scope of Buhari's Foreign Exchange Control

The 1984 foreign exchange control regulations cover a broad activity. They prevent payments overseas outside of official means, make it illegal for peoples to buy, sell, or lend foreign currency. The regulations further reduce imports and the national demand for foreign exchange. The 1984 Decree makes its an offense, punishable by five years imprisonment and a fine in the amount of foreign exchange involved, for a person to make any payments outside official means or place any sum to the credit of an individual outside Nigeria (or to an individual inside Nigeria on the order or on behalf of somebody outside the country)".[11] This provision is generally targeted at corrupt politicians, bureaucrats and top businessmen, the so called "ten percenters" who siphoned away thousands, or even million, in foreign accounts from kickbacks and inflated prices and other similar activities.

Another measure of the 1984 Decree makes it an offense to pay, without authority approved, money to an individual in Nigeria in consideration of any acquisition, property, services, right, or favor outside Nigeria or to make such payments overseas in consideration of similar benefits within country. However, aimed at the "ten percenters," this measure generally includes the academician whose friend in the United Kingdom, for instance, agrees to pay his subscription to Journal of Modern Africa in exchange for a subscription to The Nigerian Daily Times. Also, it captures a situation where a Nigerian goes overseas and a friend back home requests him or her to bring back a spare part for which the traveler is paid the naira equivalent.[12]

In addition, the Decree also makes it illegal for an individual, while resident in Nigeria, to buy, sell, borrow, or even lend any foreign currency to

---

[10]Onyema Ugochukwu, "Structural Adjustment Budget aiming for Self-Reliance", West Africa, (14 May 1984), p.1009.

[11]Olatunde Ojo and Peter Koehn "The Nigerian Economy: Critical Issues" Africa Today (October 1986).

[12]Ibid, p. 11.

any individual inside or outside Nigeria. Aimed at open black markets where the naira could be exchange for as low as 30 to 40 cents instead of the official $1.40 in 1982.[13] This policy measure further makes traveler's checks useless as a medium of exchange until converted to local currencies by authorized dealers, clearly banks. Following the passage of the 1984 Law, the amount of traveler's checks bought in Nigeria for travel overseas was limited to $130 per person a year and must be recorded in one's passport and the traveller has the responsibility of explaining any extras at currency control check points at the departure terminal.

Also, the Buhari government passed a number of policy measures that limit the opportunity for persons to receive foreign exchange vis-a-vis the black market or by other unofficial means. According to the Decree, Nigerians travelling abroad may take with them no more than N20 in Nigerian currency. They must declare and exchange within twenty-four hours all foreign currencies brought into the country. For example, visitors are also affected; they are now required by law to pay for their hotel services and other purchases in foreign exchange.[14]

Moreover, apart from it serious implication on would-be black-marketeers, kick-backers,and even petty users of foreign exchange outside officially sanctioned frameworks, Decree No. 7 (as the Exchange Control Decree is otherwise called) is meant to be punitive of the elected politicians and officials widely perceived to have profited from corruption and foreign exchange activities under the second public. Hence, the effective date of the Decree's coming into effect is retroactive to October 1, 1979, the day civilian government assumed power after thirteen years of military rule.[15]

Also, supplementary to Decree No. 7 are measures to control the outflow of foreign exchange.

> The basic strategy underpinning these regulations is to reduce both imports and the demand for foreign exchange. The regulations are three pronged: (1) a lower ceiling on the total amount of foreign exchange available to the public (that is the private sector); (2) end-use regulation of the reduced allocation;

---

[13]Ibid, p.11

[14]Ibid.

[15]Ibid p. 12.

and (3) restrictions on the availability of foreign exchange to private individuals.[16]

To this end, the Buhari government decreased the total allocation of foreign exchange to commercial and merchant banks for apportionment among their various customers to $4.85 billion in 1984. This amount comprised about 30 percent of the foreign exchange needed to keep the economy operating at the 1983 level.[17] The Federal government distributed the total sum to the banks according to their size. Each bank according to the federal government allocation, is required to allocate its share according to an end-use formula which reserves 58 percent for industrial raw materials, spare parts and equipment, 18 percent for food imports, 12 percent for other consumer goods, and 12 percent for invisible such as foreign travel, education, medical services, and repatriation of expatriate wages and salaries.[18]

As a result of these regulations, remittances for education, medical services, and expatriate salaries are severely curtailed. In this direction, the new regulations affected foreign students most. For instance, only students already pursuing courses of instruction abroad and those graduate students whose programs of study are not available in Nigeria are eligible to receive foreign exchange. While this measure is not new, it is being vigorously carried out and new emphases have been added to it. For example, the Federal Government withheld the transfer of foreign exchange to over 80 overseas private business colleges and GCE "A" level private tuition houses because these organizations provide educational programs readily available in Nigeria.[19] Moreover, many state governments also canceled scholarship awards to their students studying abroad and requested that they come back home.

In a similar fashion, patients requesting overseas medical services now face serious eligibility tests. As Africa Today put it:

---

[16]Ibid.

[17]Ibid, p. 13.

[18]National Concord, October 14, 1984, p.3., The Guardian, 18 October 1984, p.7., West Africa, (February 20, 1984), p.395.

[19]West Africa, (20 May 1985), p. 1017.

Only medical services not available in Nigeria and so certified by competent authorities qualify for foreign exchange for attention overseas. Foreign staff under this policy have faced much stricter regulations. The government slashed the proportion of their salaries which may be remitted abroad from 50 percent to 25 percent. Even Nigerian staff (eg. exchange scholars), who before could remit up to 50 percent of their salaries when on educational programs abroad, now are restricted to 25 percent. Under the new government policy, only 1 or 5 percent of the faculty at each educational institution may be allowed to spend their sabbatical leave abroad in a given year.[20]

Furthermore, the Buhari administration also implemented policies designed to discourage foreign travel by Nigerians as a means both of saving foreign exchange and curtailing imported luxuries and Eurocentric mentality. The government has taken such measures because of the growing concern that top-level Nigerians spent their vacations in Europe and North America at the expense of domestic tourism.

The deepening of the international debt problem has greatly increased the role played by the IMF in Nigeria. Due to the growing importance of the IMF for the Paris Club (and also for commercial bank) rescheduling, the Buhari government adopted a series of structural adjustment budget measures. The purpose of these economic measures according to President Buhari was to qualify Nigeria for rescheduling of her external debt as well as for the IMF loan.

To achieve these objectives, the government's budget measures cut government expenditures, reduced imports, broadened its revenue base and revived the country's productive capacity. A tight monetary policy and strict import and exchange control were already in place before the budget. These have been restated and reinforced, with interest rates raised by two percent, and all imports placed under license and made subject to the availability of foreign exchange.[21]

---

[20]Africa Today, p. 13.

[21]National Concord, 6 May 1985, p.12

While the Nigerian government under Buhari pursued conservative monetary and fiscal policies which the IMF would approve of, it draws the line at any massive devaluation, or direct interference by the IMF in domestic policy formulation or implementation.[22]

Also, commenting on an observation about the close similarity between the budget measures and the classic IMF programs, the former Minister of Finance, Dr. Onaslapo Soleye, pointed out that:

A country in economic difficulties has a responsibility to take corrective measures whether or not it is seeking a loan from the IMF. Soleye sees the long-term solution in a greater determination internally to achieve self-sufficiency. But it can hardly be denied, that determination, without the infusion of the necessary funds, such as the IMF can provide, will only produce results very slowly. The need to reach an agreement with the IMF seems still to be as important as it ever was.[23]

One can see that the attitude of creditor governments in the rescheduling negotiations is greatly influenced by their economic evaluation of the country and the likelihood of a successful implementation of the IMF programs. Although, the Buhari regime was able to reach negotiations for rescheduling of most of its debts with the officials in the creditor states by its own economic measures, the deadlock still existed with the IMF over the conditions for the $2.4 billion loan. Consequently, Nigeria did not receive the additional foreign exchange which the Buhari administration had been counting upon.[24]

The Buhari government had made considerable progress in balancing Nigeria's chaotic external payments, but only by pushing the economy into even deeper hardship. Failure to reach agreement with the IMF on a $2.4 billion program to restructure Nigeria's debt left the country desperately short of foreign exchange. This and other factors accounted for the military coup

---

[22]Peter Asimota, "The IMF-Nigeria Deadlock,"New Nigeria, April 1985, p.9.

[23]Soleye, West Africa, 19 February 1984, p.4.

[24]Baine Harden, "Nigeria See Debt Payment Ceiling", Africa Red Family, (5 January 1986), p.13.

that toppled the government of Major General Mohammed Buhari in August 27, 1985. As Larry Diamond put it:

> The grim economic performance would have been enough to bring down any government, but in fact, the Buhari government might have survived if it had reached agreement with the IMF, sought to involve the people in the decision-making process and to build a popular consensus around a long-term strategy for economic recovery. Instead, it governed with unprecedented arrogance and disdain for public opinion.[25]

The Implications of the Buhari's Foreign Exchange Control Measures

The regulations implemented here named the "1984 Foreign Exchange control Measures", are extreme in that they make normal day-to-day international transactions generally impossible for the ordinary citizens. Buhari's foreign exchange control measures had an immediate implication on its international balance of payments situation and on the domestic economy. They seriously affected Nigerian citizens, and involved essential economic and social consequences. Whether the macro policies were politically sustainable for long is an important question. We first examine and analyze the short-run implications for the individual, the economy, and the polity and then, assess the long-run impacts.

Short-term Socioeconomic Consequences

The 1984 foreign exchange policies caused problems for those individuals who need foreign exchange and shortages for society at large. For instance, stricter enforcement has prevented Nigerian students from going abroad for further studies. This entails particular deprivation for those who are not successful in gaining admission to Nigerian Colleges and Universities. Students already overseas who rely heavily on funds from relatives at home. such as the researcher, also have encountered hardships.

---

[25]Larry Diamond, "Nigeria High Stakes for Babangide", Africa Report, (November-December, 1985), pp. 54-55.

On March 1984, the federal ministry of Commerce and Industry had a backlog of more than 4,000 requests for import licenses. However, small and medium-scale businesses feared that they would be short-changed under the government policy of issuing no import licenses without foreign exchange backing.[26] Also, Nigerian businessmen and would-be tourists seeking their basic travel allowance (BTA) or approval of their form M (the basic import document which authorizes importers to make foreign exchange remittances abroad) felt discontented.

In addition, foreign employees threw up their arms in despair over the rigmarole surrounding remittance of the permissible portion of their salaries. Some even decided to depart their jobs and the country.[27] Moreover, tourists who had exchanged their currency into naira in obedience to the law discovered, on departing the country, that it is not an easy matter to re-convert the naira back to foreign currency.

Furthermore, if the concern of specific people is unenviable, that of the general urban populace is deplorable on account of the immediate effect of the foreign exchange controls on the economy.   Structural adjustment measures and closed line of credits on account of rising debts already had led to a reduction of imports from $17 billion in 1981 to $13.7 billion in 1983.[28] The Buhari's foreign exchange policies, together with changes in methods whereby all imported goods came under specific licenses, further decreased imports. Since the first year of the new policies (in spite of some carryover 1983 license), the import bill went down to $11.7 billion, a decrease of 10 percent from 1983. In 1985, the government imposed a $3.5 billion ceiling on imports.[29] The new ceiling, a 70 percent reduction from 1984, led to shortages of many products. Such consumable goods as rice, tea, sugar, coffee, and many others disappeared from local markets. Also, prices of other household commodities, such as cooking oil and soap, soared by as much as 400 percent.[30]

---

[26]Sunday Concord, (October 14,1984) Africa Economic Digest (London, March 23), p. 14.

[27]Sunday Triumph, (14 October 1984)

[28]Daily Times, 2 March 1984.

[29]Ibid.

[30]New Nigerian, 2 March 1985. U.S. Doc. Nigeria, p 3.

Moreover, the quick decrease in imports affected the economy and the people in many different ways. Many firms experienced shortage of raw materials and spare parts as a result of receiving only ten to fifteen percent of their requested imports after months of waiting for licenses. Some closed down; other operated at between 30 and 40 percent capacity.[31] This only exacerbated commodity shortages and the price inflation. Hoarding became the order of the day among middlemen and long queues and mob actions became a fact of life for thousands of people seeking to buy essential commodities. Also, increase in unemployment is one of the major short economic implications of the Buhari's foreign exchange control measures. As industries closed or operated at lower levels of production, thousands of workers found themselves laid off. When the indigenous electrical goods manufacturer, Adebowale Electrical Industries, shut down its Ilorin and Enugu factories, for instance more than 800 workers lost their jobs,. And when the Road construction Company of Nigeria (RCOON) sought to avoid imminent collapse, it retrenched 1000 employees.[32] In the public sector, the Buhari government, on its own initiative and accidental with one of the IMF conditions for the $2.4 billion loan under negotiation, also engaged on retrenchment.[33] Apart from in a few departments and parastatals the government mandated 15 percent across-the-board decrease in personnel in both the federal and state public services. The Bendel government dismissed some 5000 civil servants in a day. In all, about one million public employees had been laid off by the end of September 1984.[34] Many state agencies also engaged in workers retrenchment during Buhari's regime. Table 28 provides the summary of the workers' retrenched by the state government agencies between January 1 and September 30, 1984. This development meant increasing competition for work.

In addition, the problem in receiving import licenses for raw materials combined with two other considerations, scared away foreign private investment. For some period of time, Foreign firms have found that doing business in Nigeria can be extremely frustrating because of an obstructive

---

[31]Ibid., p. 4

[32]The Guardian, 21 August 1984.

[33]National Concord, 14 October 1984, p. 11.

[34]The Guardian, 21 August 1984, p. 12.

bureaucracy, ubiqous and brazen demands for bribes, unreliable power and water services, the threat of industrial unrest, and misadventures due to inadequate information and intercultural misunderstanding.[35] The coup d' etat of December, 1983, and the IMF's position on devaluation as a precondition for a loan created further uncertainties and, therefore, discourage private foreign investment and made it increasingly difficult to attract expatriates with technical skills. Indeed, many of those already in Nigeria resigned their appointments for reasons "not unconnected with the Federal Military Government's reduction of their home remittance".[36]

Table 28

SOME OF THE WORKERS RETRENCHED BY THE
STATE GOVERNMENT AGENCIES BETWEEN 1 JANUARY
AND 30 SEPTEMBER 1984

State/Government Agency	Number of workers sacked
Anambra State	4,177
Bauchi State	4,133
National Assembly	2,100
Kwara State	7,000
Federal Ministry of Finance	369
Niger State	2,144
Ogun State	900
Nigeria External Telecommunications	184
Sokoto State	2,545
Benue State	6,850
Bendel State	21,000

[35]Africa Research Bulletin, Economic Series, 15 October 1979, pp5298-5299.
[36]Sunday Triumph, 14 October 1984.

Nigeria Airports Authority	238
Federal Minstry of Works	255
Federal Ministry of Agriculture	220
Ondo State	1,176
Oyo State	3,000
Federal Minstry of Communications	1,029

Source: Bade Oninode, The IMF, The World Bank and African Debt: The Economic Impact (London: Zed Books, Ltd., 1989), p.230

Moreover, tourism dratically decreased. In 1984, the well known five-star Eko Holiday Inn and the Ikeja Palace Hotel in Lagos reported a drop in occupancy rates from around 98 percent to 70 percent and 60 percent, respectively. These hotels, which usually take care of foreign tourists, attributed their business declines to the "impossible regulations passed early 1984".[37]

Also, the short term economic and personnal hardships accompanied with introduction of the Buhari administration's foreign exchange measures resulted in unintended social effects. One result has been the increasing evidence of some specific types of crime in the economy. There are two cases in point to this phenomenon. According to Africa Today, the first is the making of criminals out of otherwise law-abiding citizens. The retroactive nature of the Exchange Control (anti-Sabotage) Decree can be viewed in this direction. The imprisonment of Fela Anikulapo Kuti is even more straight to the point. Fela, Nigeria's internationally acclaimed musician, possess talent which, if properly marketed, could be a source of foreign exchange for the nation. As Africa Today put it:

---

[37]The Guardian, 27 August 1984, p.10.

After a trip to Britain in 1984, Fela had legally imported some 1600 pounds sterling he had earned abroad. Given that his 40-member band soon would be travelling to the United States, Fela did not convert this money into naira. If he had, of course, he would only have been entitled to a $130 (BTA) upon departure. Indeed, he might not even have seen this amount because of bureaucratic red tape and shortages at banks. On travelling to the United States, Fela failed to declare the 1,600 pounds, knowing that if he did so he would be arrested for failure to convert to naira within 48 hours and/or failure to get the Minister's authority to take the money out again. The authorities arrested Fela anyway for failure to declare and for export without authority and sentenced him to a five-year term of imprisonment.[38]

The second result of crime goes above white lies of convenience to more brazen criminal efforts to secure foreign exchange outside the law. One such activity which is on the increase is drug trafficking to Europe and North America. In 1984, authorities arrested 42 men and 16 women on charges of smuggling narcotics, namely cocaine and heroin, with a total estimated value of $2.4 million.[39] Also, out of 608 Nigerians reported to be in Jail in 25 countries, the majority are serving terms for drug trafficking offenses.

Furthermore, another unintended short-term social implication of the foreign exchange measures pertains to labor unrest. This is best shown by the doctor's strike of February 1985. Due to foreign exchange squeeze and the placing under specific licenses of all goods (including medicines) previously imported under open general licenses, Nigeria faced a critical shortage of supplies in all hospitals, including teaching hospitals. The intransigence of the government on the foreign exchange issue provoked the doctors strike and led to a confrontation with the military regime. The Buhari administration reacted forcefully; it dismissed all doctors in public hospitals, dissolved their union, and imprisoned the strike leaders.[40]

---

[38]Africa Today, p. 17.

[39]Africa News, (4 February 1985), p.48.

[40]"Nigeria Doctor Association Banned,"West Africa, (4 March 1985), p. 437.

The Long-run Economic Implications of Buhari's Foreign Exchange Measures

In the first place, we recognize that the Buhari's foreign exchange measures involved short-run hardships and sacrifices, they also exerted a salutary effect on the economy that augured well for self-reliant economic growth and development. The light at the end of the tunnel is the production and processing of raw materials domestically and the installation of spare parts factories. The performance of certain major firms after the new foreign exchange measures came into effect provided cause for optimism in this endeavor.

Table 29

ECONOMIC PERFORMANCE INDEX OF REPRESENTATIVE FIRMS
(Figures in millions ₦)

Firm	Turnover A			Gross Profit B			Gross Profit Ratio B/A	
	1983	1984	% change	1983	1984	% change	1983	
1	2	3	4	5	6	7	8	
UAC	719.12	596.12	-17.10	30.74	65.94	+114.50	4.27	1
PZ	347.45	314.63	-10.45	17.72	29.25	+8.60	5.10	
Flour Mills	264.86	251.02	-5.23	19.96	15.09	-24.40	7.54	
Guinness	240.34	215.70	-10.66	54.72	50.35	-8.00	22.80	2
Nig. Bottl. Co.	210.77	266.70	+26.53	40.94	54.35	+27.86	19.42	2
Leventis Motors	202.61	136.08	-32.84	3.02	4.24	+40.40	1.49	
Cadbury	112.74	119.20	+5.80	9.82	11.57	+17.80	8.20	
Nig. Tobacco Co	71.04	79.71	+12.20	9.30	16.02	+71.00	13.10	2
Metal Box	36.47	30.62	-16.04	6.94	4.80	-30.84	19.03	1
AG. Leventis	13.34	97.42	+630.28	3.12	5.26	+68.59	23.39	

Source : The Guardian (Lagos), April 14, 1985.

Table 29 indicates the activity of ten representative businesses in 1983 and 1984. One major result is that, with the exception of Guinness, Metal Box, and Flour Mills, the gross profit of all firms dratically rised in 1984 (see Column 7). This resulted even though turnover generally decreased over 1983 (Column 4), or indicated only a modest rise (with the exception of A.G. Leventis). Further interesting is the fact that, with the exception of Flour Mills, AG. Leventis, and Metal Box, all the others reported greater gross profit ratio in 1984 than in 1983. From economic stand point, this figure involves the profit return over turnover, or the profit per unit of sale or production (See Column 8 and 9). The achievement of high profits in the face of stable or lower turnover and the raw materials crisis, indicates greater efficiency in production. This has been achieved by a combination of internal restructuring, waste reduction, retrenchment of redundant workers, use of local materials, fabrication of one's own spare parts, and higher domestic prices for products.[41]

Obviously, it is in the area of using local materials and fabricating one's own spare parts that a transformation toward self-reliant development must begin. Many businesses resorted to producing their own raw materials, or experimenting with locally available materials. Guinness, for example engaged on agricultural projects to produce sorghum, maize, and rice for its breweries. John Holt, one of Nigeria's oldest businesses, planned to increase agricultural development and agro-industries by the cultivation of maize and soya beans, the building of feed mills and piggeries, fishing, fishing-boat construction, and the production of commercial and industrial generators.[42] Lever Brothers started to re-activate the oil palm estates it left some years back when imported palm oil proved cheaper.[43] Cadbury created its own spare parts fabricating workshop that meet 70 percent of its needs. The Buhari administration also sponsored seminars and international conferences to encourage the use of local materials in industries, and promised financial and technical assistance to farmers and firms wishing to go into the production of raw materials.[44]

---

[41]African News, (February 4, 1985) p. 43, The Guardian, April 14, 1985.

[42]The Guardian, 30 August 1984, p.7.

[43]The Guardian, 21 August 1984, p.4.

[44]Africa Analysis, 4 April 1984, p.7.

In addition, the foreign exchange measures enabled to cushion Nigeria's debt crisis. The country's overseas debt at the beginning of 1984 included approximately $10 billion in medium and long-term loans held by the government and about $7 billion in overdue short-term credits (plus interest) for goods and services already supplied. Uninsured obligation to overseas export businesses constituted about $5 billion of the total foreign trade debt; the national government (mainly OECD countries) of the creditor companies guarantee the balance.[45] Nigeria hoped both to reschedule these loans and to secure and additional capital infusion of $2.4 billion from the IMF. Many people believed that without the IMF loan, Nigeria would be unable to meet rescheduled repayment terms on its short-term loans.

At the beginning, negotiations for rescheduling these debts bogged down largely because government officials in the creditor states (led by Britain's Export Credit Guarantee Department) insisted that Nigeria reach agreement with the IMF on pre-conditions labeled an "economic stabilization program." [46] They strongly believed that any terms of agreement reached apply mutatis mutandis to the uninsured creditors. Eventually, however, the principal uninsured creditors, among them the Mobil Oil Company and ITT gave in. This allowed Nigeria to reschedule about $3.5 billion in debts without the necessity of first reaching agreement with the IMF and opening the way for rescheduling the uninsured debt owned to other companies.

However, the deadlock further remained with the IMF over the conditions for the $2.4 billion loan. Eventually, Buhari government did not receive the additional foreign exchange which the Buhari administration had been hoping for.[47]

Eventually, at the rate of $300-$400 million per month, the government continued to repay both the rescheduled bona fide short-term obligations and its non-rescheduled medium and long term debt to Western financial organization.[48]

Finally, by the end of February 1985, the nation's external liabilities had reduced to about $15.1 billion from $16.4 billion in December, 1984 and

---

[45]Economist, Vol.299, No. 7444, (3 May 1986), pp.6-7.

[46]The Search for External Loan", West Africa, (February 30, 1984), pp. 373-375.

[47]Washington Post, (5 January 1986).

[48]West Africa, 23 April 1984, p. 866.

its non-rescheduled medium and long term debt to Western Financial Organizations. Also, foreign exchange reserves stood at $1385 million in February 1985, compared with $1265 million the previous December and less than $1000 million at the time of the military coup in December, 1983.[49]

Having examined the extent to which the Buhari administration had put in place most of its independent economic policies and the IMF forces that shape these policies, we now turn our attention to the critical examination of the IMF policies implemented by the Babangida government to address the country's economic crisis as well as to achieve economic recovery and self-reliant development. Our objective is to provide a clear picture of the economic and other related measures taken by the new military government to resolve the crisis.

---

[49]Africa Africa, May 6, 1985, p. 908 West Africa, May 13, 1985, p. 958.

CHAPTER 11

Babangida's Government And The Nature Of The International Monetary Fund Involvement In Nigeria

Major General Ibrahim Babangida, when he came into power, raised the issue to center stage by immediately launching a nation - wide debate on whether or not Nigeria should accept and implement the IMF's economic stabilization policies in order to secure its credits and obtain debt rescheduling. In the midst of the world oil glut and continuously declining foreign exchange reserves, majority of people in the debate overwhelmingly rejected both the loan and IMF conditionalities. Nevertheless, the Babangida government went forward to introduce the chief components of the IMF policies at the same time that it publicly rejected the most resented requirements and kept the Fund in the background by arranging for the World Bank to monitor compliance. The decisive step in this direction occurred on October 1, 1986, when the Second-tier Foreign Exchange Market (SFEM) took place and the value of the naira plunged seriously.

The Nature of the IMF Involvement in Nigeria

It is important to note that the starting point of the Fund analysis is the reflection of the distorted structure of the Nigerian economy as evidenced in the fundamental disequilibrium of the balance of payments. The IMF in studying Nigerian economic crisis concluded that the diagnosed imbalances include those between consumption and savings, investments and savings, exports and imports, public revenues and expenditures and physical and management capacity of the economy.[1] It is surprising that the balance of payments crisis is described as a result of "inadequate economic management in most IMF/World Bank documents in Nigeria. This technical point of view has significant implications for the policy recommendations.

Internal variables according to IMF study are regarded as the primary causes. These variables include:

1.   Increase in population growth rate;
2.   Dependence on imports for both consumer goods and raw materials for industries;
3.   A grossly unequal gap between the rich and poor;
4.   Inability to mobolize domestic resources;
5.   Inefficiency of parastatals;
6.   Expansionary public sector financial operations;
7.   Inflated money supply;
8.   Over involvement of the government and suppression of private sector activities;
9.   Lack of infrastructure;
10.   Distorted in the allocation of resources resulting from an overvalued currency (a disincentive for exports and a benefit for imports), restricted trade and payments regimes and inadequate governmental price policy; and
11.   Lack of skilled and unskilled labor.

Furthermore, very recent studies also mention the excessive rates of profit in trade which have negative impacts both in draining investments from productive sectors and in furthering luxury imports.

Although the IMF identified some external variables that are responsible for Nigerian economic crisis, these external variables are claimed to aggravate the situations. According to the Fund, these external factors include: (1) worldwide inflation; (2) fall in oil prices; (3) weak international demand for Nigeria's export commodities; and (4) falling terms of trade. With

---

[1]Onyema Ugochukwu, "The Political Economy of IMF", Newswatch (9 February 1987), pp. 14-15.

the above analysis, the recommended strategy of the Fund is deduced. The nature of the Fund's involvement in Nigeria has evolved from a purely informative to a leading role. In the beginning the Fund provided the official creditors with information on the Nigeria's economic outlook and debt prospects, it also helped Nigeria prepare its negotiations with other financial lenders.

The adoption of an IMF adjustment program has become a sine qua non for the consideration of a Paris Club rescheduling since 1966. For commercial bank rescheduling, this has been the case only since 1977. In Nigeria, the creditors insist on the IMF program, believing this to be the surest way for it to adopt policies leading to more financial stability. The IMF programs thus have an important psychological effect on banks whose confidence in countries implementing such programs is enhanced.[2]

Nigeria first started negotiations with the Fund for a loan of $2.4 billion in 1983 under Shagari's regime. Before the negotiations broke down in the same year, the IMF had already approached Nigeria with seventeen conditionalities as indicated in Chapter One. The objectives of these adjustment measures or conditionalities in Nigeria, according to the IMF officials are to ensure that the financial assistance provided by the Fund is used to support sound economic policies leading within a short time span to a more viable balance of payments position. The stand-by agreement policies proposed by the Fund envisage to establish sound demand management coupled with measures to improve supply conditions and to strengthen the productive base of the Nigerian economy. The main strategies followed by the Fund include a combination of a reduction of fiscal deficits, curbs on the expansion of domestic credit (reduction of inflation), a substantial devaluation of national currency to return to a more "normal" exchange rate and other policies to raise the output of export products and imports substitutes.[3]"

Our close examination of the IMF-Nigerian relations indicates that the Fund concept is characterized by some misconceptions and inconsistencies. Some of these cam be deducted from the ideological model of the Nigerian economy and society underlying the analysis. Its basic theoretical assumptions

---

[2]Onyema Ugochukwu,   "Nigeria Debt Rescheduling Brightens the Outlook, " West Africa,(21 February 1987).

[3]Ibid., p. 2460.

are (1) that the free play of market forces (demand and supply) will produce an acceptable pattern of investment, production and trade; (2) internal and external imbalances (inflation and balance of payments deficits) are caused by excessive internal demand; and (3) market forces will be able to produce a sustained growth in production and employment, if not disturbed by government intervention or inflation.[4]

These conditions are perhaps fulfilled to a greater extent in integrated Western industrial nations. However, this model does not account for the structural deformities of peripheral economies such as Nigeria. Therefore, some of the measures proposed will have different or even contrary effects. Most important, the IMF analysis confining itself to the economic sphere fails to appreciate the reasons for the apparent mismanagement of the Nigerian economy. It does
not take into account the different meaning of the term "state" in Nigerian reality. As we indicated in Chapter five, state policies do not represent the general interest of Nigeria, but the interests of a few social groups such as the national capitalists, the military, the state employees and intellectuals. Also, the state's dwindling economic and social basis restricts its real options severely. The overall policy aim of development has been replaced by the fight for survival of the government.

The IMF also recommended the approach to raise industrial and agricultural output by giving more incentives to primary producers. However, this recommendation does not account for the marketing structure which prevents producers from receiving a reasonable part of consumer export prices for most commodities. Instead, the profits accruing to the big traders far exceed the returns on the farmers.

However, the Nigerian government with the Fund advise have put in place these IMF policies for balance of payments and economic stability. Whether or not these policies will achieve the above stated objectives will be seen in this chapter.

---

[4]Ibid.

Recent Changes Under the Babangida Government

Nigeria was held strong to its position until the overthrow of the Buhari governments in 1985. However, the military government resisted global pressures to carry its experiment. It convinced the politically group strata that their suffering and inconveniences were temporary and necessary for a better future, and that the situation would be worse under the IMF's measure. In former finance Minister Soleye's words, "In fact, if you go for the Fund, you can even expect more and more stringent tightening of the economy."[5]

Also the wide support which the Buhari government's position enjoyed and the degree with which Nigerians resented the IMF's patronizing attitude and unsuitable condition for securing a loan surfaced early in the successor Babangida government. Nigeria's new President favored accepting the IMF conditionalities and loan."[6]

In early moves which manifested his inclination, the new head of state appointed a former official of the IMF, Dr. Kalu , as Finance Minister and stacked the newly established "Committee on the IMF conditionalities and loan with appointees who favored accepting the money". Judging that the key political actors in Nigeria would be unwilling to tolerate for long the hardship which the extent foreign exchange-based approach entailed, General Babangida concomitantly initiated a great National debate on the issue in various public fora and on the pages of the newspapers. However, Nigerians overwhelmingly (repudiated the IMF conditionalities and Loan).[7]

Citizens expressed their willingness to tolerate hardship for as long as necessary in order to restore the economy by self-reliance.

---

[5]West Africa, (October 15, 1984), p. 2069.

[6]The extent to which the Buhari regime's rejection of the IMF conditions in favor of its own foreign exchange control approach constituted a factor in its overthrow by coup d'etat in August, 1985, is not clear. In any event, General Babangida immediately promised to resume negotiations with the Fund over the promised loan, See Peter Blackhum "The Year of the IMF? Africa Report, No. 6 (1986), p. 18, New York Times, September 4, 1985, p. 6, National Concord, September 20, 1985, p.1.

[7]National Concord, 20 September 1985, p. 6 and 21 September 1985, p.1

Again, while supporting the public's opposition of an agreement that would accept the IMF conditions, the Babangida administration proceeded to implement most of the Fund's prescriptions for revamping the economy. It removed the subsidy for the domestic sale of petroleum and fertilizer a policy that was rejected by the Buhari regime. This action seriously doubled the pump price. The government further dismissed more public servants and trimmed wages and salaries by 2 1/2 and 20 percent. On top of existing duties, it imposed a new 30 percent levy on all imports, as well as increased interest rates by 12 percent. In addition, the Babangida regime allowed the official value of the naira to slide further.[8] By mid 1986, the naira was worth only 85 U.S. Cents. At present, the government has cut federal deficit drastically, established the Second-tier Foreign Exchange Market and reviewed on going projects. In summary, the Babangida's economic measures had cut the money supply, push up interest rates, slashed public spending, cut health welfare and educational programs, implemented a wage freeze, restricted both domestic and foreign credit, dismantled price control, removed subsidies on Petroleum and Fertilizer, liberalized trade and finally established the SFEM where the foreign exchange rates are determined by the forces of demand and supply conditions. The objectives of these economic measures were to achieve economic recovery and self-reliance development.

Furthermore, the unexpected reduction of petroleum prices to as low as under $10 per barrel during the first half of 1986 added more pressure on Nigeria to negotiate debt rescheduling. The country's western creditors continued to insist on IMF guarantee.[9] Thus,

> fate helped bring Nigeria back to the IMF's doorstep and to additional conditionalities. The IMF demanded the privatization of government-owned enterprises in conformity with its long-standing policy vis-a-vis debtor Third World countries and the Reagan administration's campaign to transform Africa into free market economies. The Nigerian government, broke as a result of events in the worldwide petroleum market, obliged by meeting the IMF conditions. However, instead of massive privatization, it dissolved some

---

[8]Babangida's Deal", The Guardian, 16 January 1986, p. 19

[9]David Ottaway, "Nigeria Promotes its Strategy for Foreign Debt Repayment", Washington Post, 14 January 1986.

companies, began a program of gradual disinvestment in others, and removed subsidies to monopoly (parastatals which, in turn, milked their captive customers.)[10]

The privatization decree had called for selling ninety-six state-owned companies including hotels, dairies, cattle ranches, chicken farms, pig farms, slaughter houses, timber companies, textile mills, breweries, flour mills, boat yards and insurance.[11]   Also, partial privatization includes the following items: steel rolling mills,paper mills, fertilizer companies, railroads, two steel mills, a national park and the national television (For detailed number of companies that were affected by privatization program, see Table 30).

In addition, Babangida unilaterally established a ceiling on the amount of foreign exchange earnings which would be devoted to servicing the country's external debt in 1986. Most estimates had shown that Nigeria's debt repayments would consume approximately 60 percent of total foreign exchange earning in each of the five years. The Babangida administration establish the ceiling on servicing medium and long-term loans at half, of this level (30 percent).[12]   In addition to the absence of other major exports, the low price of petroleum on the international market during most of 1986 dramatically reduce Nigeria's capability to repay its foreign debt in any event. Under such situations, rescheduling is necessary for both creditor and debtor also. Nigeria is far from powerless in this regard.[13]

Second-tier Foreign Exchange Market and Devaluation of Currency

It is important to note that the most far reaching IMF prescription is devaluation of the naira. Since the Nigerian public resoundingly rejected outright devaluation, the Babangida government could not openly accept this term. Instead, it attempted to achieve the same objective by creating a Second-tier Foreign Exchange Market (SFEM) in which local banks are free to buy and sell foreign currency at rates determined by market forces of

---

[10]Africa Today.

[11]James Brooke, Ailing Nigeria Opens Its Economy", The New York Times, 15 August 1988, p.30.

[12]The Guardian, 16 January 1986, pp. 13-15.

[13]Africa Analysis, No. 1, (11 July 1986), p. 3.

Table 30

PRIVATIZATION PROGRAM

Ninety-six companies that were affected by the privatization programme currently being undertaken by the federal government. To facilitate the scheme, public parastatals been divided into five categories.

Details of the privatization plans are as follows

Full Privatization

Nigeria Hotel Limited
Durbar Hotel Limited
Aba Textile Mills
Central Water Transportation Company Limited
National Cargo Handling Limited
Nigerian Dairies Company Limited
Nigerian National Fish Company
Grains Production Company Limited
Nigerian Poultry Production Company Limited
National Root Corps Company Limited and other such food production companies
Nigerian National Shrimps Company Limited
The Nigerian Salt Company Limited
National Fruit Company Limited
National Salt Company Limited, Ijoko
Specoomi Nigeria Limited
South-East Rumania Wood Industries Limited, Calabar
Nigerian-Rumanian Wood Industries Limited, Ondo
Nigerian Yeast and Alcohol Company Limited, Bacita
Nigerian Film Corporation
National Freight Company
Nigerian Transport Limited, Abeokuta
Opobo Boat Yard
National Animal Feed Company, Port Harcourt
Madara Dairy Company, Vom
Ore/Irele Oil Palm Company, Bendel
Guinea Insurance
Mercury Assurance
American International Insurance Company
Crusader Insurance
United Nigerian Insurance
Royal Exchange Company
NEM Insurance
Law Union and Rock
Prestige Assurance
British-American Insurance
West African Prudential Insurance
Sun Insurance
Niger Insurance and all insurance companies except National Insurance Co. and National Re-Insurance Company
Nigerian National Supply Company (to sell assets and let the bulk purchase unit of the Ministry of Trade be re-activated)
National Livestock Production Limited
Road Construction Company of Nigeria
Nigeria Ranches, Kaduna
Impresit Bakolori Nigeria Limited
North Breweries Limited, Kano
Nigerian Beverages Company Limited
West African Distilleries Limited

Partial Privatization

All commercial and merchant banks
The cement companies
Nigerian Agricultural Co-operative Bank and other development banks (eg. NIOB, NBCI, FMB, FSB)

All the oil marketing companies, which must be converted to public quoted companies
All the steel rolling mills operating outside the iron complex
All the paper mills
All truck assembly companies
All vehicle assembly companies
New Nigerian newspaper
Daily Times of Nigeria
News Agency of Nigeria
Bacita Sugar Company
Nigeria Airways
Nigerian Sugar Phosphate Fertilizer Company
Tourist Company of Nigeria Limited
Electricity Meter Company of Nigeria Limited, Zaria
Nigerian Fertilizer Company Limited
Savannah Sugar Company Limited
Nigerian Engineering Construction Company Limited
Nigerian National Shipping Line Company

Public Institute

National Water Resources Institute
Education and cultural institutions

Partial Commercialization

Nigerian Railway Corporation
National Electric Power Authority
Nigerian Institute for Oil Palm Research
The Project Development Agency
Nigerian Security and Minting Company Limited
All the river basin authorities
National Provident Fund
Ajaokuta Steel Company
Delta Steel Company
Nigerian Machine Tools Limited
Federal hospitals
Federal Housing Authority
Kainji Lake National Park
Federal Radio Corporation
Nigerian Ports Authority
Nigerian Television Authority

Full Commercialization

Nigerian National Petroleum Corporation
Nigerian Telecommunications
Associated Ores Mining Company
Nigeria Mining Corporation
Nigeria Coal Corporation
National Insurance Corporation of Nigeria
Nigeria Re-Insurance Corporation
National Properties Limited
Tafawa Balewa Square Management Committee

Sources: Central Bank of Nigeria, Africa Research Bulletin, March 31, 1988, p. 90

supply and demand. All private sector and all most public transactions are now channelled through this market. Only debt repayments and contributions to international organizations are pegged at the official rate of exchange and handled through the first-tier market (Central Bank). In addition, the government is allowing the official rate of naira to continue to decline in value in relation to U.S. dollar.

The new market was opened on September 26, 1986, with the naira exchanging for about 22 U.S. cents (4.62=$1). In one week, the naira had decreased in value by 70 percent against the dollar.[14] In mid-December 1986, one naira was worth about 20 U.S. cents on the Second-tier Foreign Exchange Market. As Africa Today stated:

> The Second-tier Foreign Exchange Market alternative to outright devaluation had been acceptable in principle to the IMF, to Nigeria's international creditors, and to most Nigerians. From the beginning, the Fund and the creditors viewed SFEM's existence as the functional equivalent of an outright devaluation which would deflate the value of the naira far in excess of what the IMF originally asked for. They, also saw this step as introducing freer trade in Nigeria since it would make the stringent import controls and the 30 percent generalized import levy. General Babangida's June 29, 1986 "State of the Nation" broadcast supported this interpretation. After announcing the proposed SFEM, he stated that the existing import levy and restrictions would give way to a new profile of import tariff and excise duties"[15].

However, Nigerians agreed on Second-tier Foreign Exchange Market, in principle, as the lesser of two evils. They foresaw an end to the import levy[16]; (2) import (1) licensing, direct foreign exchange allocation, and the (4) accompanying bureaucratic bottlenecks corruption. Also, Second-Tier Foreign Exchange Market further replaces the Exchange Control (Anti-Sabotage) Decree of 1984. The Buhari's approach to foreign exchange management had made it nearly impossible for individuals to remit small amounts abroad. On the one hand, the Nigerian business sector looked

---

[14]Christian Science Monitor, 7 October 1986, p. 13.

[15]Africa Today, p. 24.

[16]Godfrey Umesi, Goodbye to Import Levy, " Business Concord, Lagos, 8 July 1986, p. 14.

forward to benefiting from an end to what the Permanent Secretary who created SFEM described as "to all kinds of devices for siphoning foreign exchange away from Nigeria[17]. Again, SFEM was anticipated to knock a hole in Nigeria's notorious import-based consumption pattern by raising the exchange rate to such a high level as to discourage frivolous importation as well as force import-dependent industries to seek alternative domestic means[18]. Hence, the supporters of the new approach expect that a fundamental structural reorganization of the Nigerian economy will occur provided that the citizenry can accept the resulting harshness of life for long period.

In addition, other problems center around operational bottlenecks, the ubiquitous corruption that could easily undermine the makret, and the uneven effect of SFEM. Prominent among the operational bottlenecks is the amount of foreign exchange funding necessary to ensure hitch-free operation of the market. The Central Bank of Nigeria put the figure at $100 million a week if confidence in the market is to be ensured and speculative buying, hoarding, and growth of a parallel black market are to be avoided[19]. The Central Bank, the main source of supply, could only provide $50 million a week from official reserves. As Africa Today indicates:

> Among the other potential sources of supply, the domiciliary foreign exchange accounts of Nigerians in local banks are estimated to be valued no more than $5 million. The World Bank's one-time loan of about $450 million for the purpose of SFEM averages less than $9 million a week. The "25 percent of foreign currency proceeds" which private exporters are allowed to retain cannot amount to a sizeable sum since there are few exports other than officially handled petroleum and agricultural products. Other anticipated sources (such as the unspent surplus of foreign currency held by Nigerians or brought in by foreigners for tourism and direct purchases or investments) are too insignificant to be a major source of foreign exchange for SFEM. From all sources, the Central Bank

---

[17]C.O. Ibe, "How Not to Use Second-Tier Exchange Market", Business Concord, 8 July 1986, p.6.

[18]Eric Okeke and Nkem Ossai, "The Bumpy Journal To a Second Window", The Guardian, 13 July 1986, p. 9.

[19]Business Concord, Lagos, 4 July 1986, p. 2.

Managed to inject around $70 million per week into the market, varying the exact amount in its attempt to establish a stable rate of exchange.[20]

Furthermore, there is concern, also, that the foreign exchange market will be cornered by a few financially powerful institutions and individuals, including commercial banks, the officially designated dealers. Given that commercial banks are among the most corrupt organizations in country, their central role in SFEM is suspect to begin with.[21] In an attempt to reduce this fear, reduce speculative buying, and protect financially less powerfully institutions and individuals, Central Bank decided to sell foreign exchange to the commercial banks at the rate they individually bid, while permitting them to sell at a particular rate marginally above the buying rate.

However, the opening of SFEM opened the way for new financial arrangement dealing with Nigeria's external credit problems. In November 1986, the federal government reached a rescheduling accord with representatives of its commercial bank creditors that included a ten year postponement in complete repayment of the $1.5 billion in principal originally due between April 1, 1987, and December 31, 1988, and a four year grace period that only requires interest payments. This debt rescheduling accord had given Nigeria further opportunity to receive $320 million in new foreign trade loans from commercial banks and for disbursal of a $452 million foreign trade promotion and export development loan from the world bank.[22] Within two months, however, the World Bank had promised to grant Nigeria $4.3 billion in project loans over the next three years.[23]

In addition to the above economic measures, the present administration in July 1986 introduced its Structural Adjustment Program (SAP), to last for two years, during which time it hoped the Nigerian economy

---

[20]Ibid., The Guardian, 13 July 1986, p. 9, Africa Today, pp. 25-26.

[21]Oliver Ibekwe, "SFEM Alternative to Devaluation", The Guardian, 1 August 1986, p.9.

[22]K. Witcher, "World Bank Approves Loan to Nigeria to Aid Nations Bid to Liberalize Trade", Wall Street Journal, 16 October 1986. Also see The New York Times, 22 November 1986.

[23]West Africa, (January 12, 1987), p. 47, Cheryl Payer points out that the World Bank has begun to take over for the IMF as the latter becomes increasingly discredited in the Third World. See Payer "The World Bank: A New Role in the Debt Crisis", Third World Quarterly, (6 April 1986), pp. 659-676.

Table 31

THE YEAR OF SECOND-TIER FOREIGN EXCHANGE MARKET (SFEM)
The naira's value against the dollar in 1986.

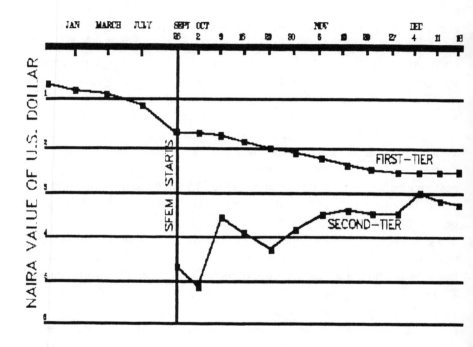

Sources: AED, Central Bank of Nigeria, 1987; Africa Resear
        Bulletin January 21, 1987, p. 8510.

would be substantially re-oriented towards productivity and self-reliance. The SAP's main component, the Second-tier Foreign Exchange Market, was spelt out in a decree in September 1986 budget. The main objectives of SAP were:

> the restructuring and diversification of the productive base of the economy in order to reduce dependency on importation and oil revenue; to lay the basis for a sustainable non-inflationary growth; to achieve fiscal and balance of payments viability; and to reduce non-productive investments in the public sector as well as encourage the growth of the private sector.[24]

Many intellectual Nigerians have quarrelled with these four broad aims of SAP. The controversy has been over these policies adopted by the government to attain its set objectives.

In the main, these policies have been to give the previously over-valued naira a realistic exchange rate by subjecting the currency to the forces of demand and supply through the Second-tier Foreign Exchange Market (SFEM); to take measures aimed at de-regulating business activities and minimizing bureaucratic intervention in the economy; the reduction or removal of government subsidies to the state parastatals; the privatization and commercialization of state-owned enterprises; and finally, the encouragement of foreign investment.

In June 1988, the Structural Adjustment Program came to the end of its two-year life span. At this point, however, it becomes necessary for us to assess and evaluate the successes and failures of these policies along with their socio-economic implications.

Socio-Economic Implications of SFEM and IMF Economics

Without doubt, the verdict of ordinary Nigerians, particularly the urban dwellers, has centered on the economic hardships associated with the Babangida's economic programs. Prices of basic commodities have risen while incomes remained unchanged. However, President Babangida never promised that it would be easy living under SAP. On the contrary, he told Nigerians in 1986 that life would get tougher. The real question must be:

---

[24]Ibid., P. 670.

has SAP taken the economy towards the road of recovery and internally-generated growth?.

Inevitably, the government's answer is yes. Whilst acknowledging that SAP has not proved an unqualified success, government officials insist that it remains the only realistic path that can take the country out of the doldrums. In April 1988, President Babangida included among the achievements of SAP:

> The restoration of the country's credit worthiness, that enabled it to reschedule over $14 billion debts and uninsured trade arrears; improvement in the balance of payments from 796.4 million deficit in 1986 to a surplus of 60.1 million in 1987; a marginal boast in external reserves from 4.5 billion at the end of 1987 to 4.75 billion at the beginning of 1988; a 1.2 percent increase in the gross domestic product (GDP last year against a 3.3 percent decline in 1986.[25]

In July of the same year, the President further highlighted the gains of SAP. The new price incentive, he said, had resulted in at least a five-fold increase in the production of cotton over the past three years, cocoa production has increased by 50 percent in the past two years and wheat output has increased several fold. "Never before in our history" he said, "have we witnessed such an upsurge in the production and prices of agricultural commodities"[26].

But what has been the price paid for the relative successes and their effect on the general economy? In agricultural production, for instance, there has not been a general increase in agricultural output. As Professor Dalton Philips, director general of the Nigerian Institute of Social and Economic Research (NISER) indicated recently.

> The apparent increase in agriculture's share have been due to an intra-sector shift away from the production of food crops to export crops in order to take advantage of the depreciation of the naira. This is a shift which combines with other factors to produce shortages of staple foods such as rice and garri.[27]

---

[25]Tunde Obadina, Sapping An Illusion" Newswatch Nigeria's Weekly News Magazine (20 February 1986), Vol. 9, no. 8, p. 31.

[26]Ibid., p. 32.

[27]Ibid.

In the case of improved credit worthiness, we also find out that in terms of the long-term development prospects, this gain is an illusion. The country's success at rescheduling much of the external debt service obligations which accrued in 1986 and 1987 may give temporary relief, but it has also led to an increase in the country's outstanding stock of external debt. According to the Federal Office of Statistics' 1986 figures, external debt has increased from about $15.1 billion in February 1985 to about $29 billion and $37 billion in 1987 and 1988 respectively (See Nigeria's debt servicing estimates to 1990 in Appendix 9).[28] Observers have noted that, by its debt rescheduling and quest for more borrowing, the government is accumulating an unbearable debt burden for future governments, a situation that could form the basis for future economic and political crisis.

Besides oil revenue, the country earns very little foreign exchange from non-oil exports. Between March and June 1988, non-oil exports earnings have declined from $44 million to $42 million.[29] Basically, Nigeria's non-oil export potential does not go much beyond primary products. In this, Nigeria has to compete with other Third World countries struggling desperately to acquire hard currencies. As far as export earnings were concerned, Nigeria had been led to believe by the World Bank that it would increase its foreign exchange earnings by expanding output. Yet, increased quantities of goods failed to yield increased revenues. World commodity prices have fallen across the board, with cocoa alone registering a 40 percent fall in price in 1987 as compared to the previous year.   Moreover, the outlook is no better; predictions are that prices will continue to fall, perhaps for the rest of the decade.[30] The main beneficiaries of devaluation of Naira are the advanced capitalist states that import these commodities.   Nor was Babangida's agricultural price liberalization uniformly successful. Nigeria is a huge country (more than four times the size of France) with only limited miles of paved roads; this means that certain farmers are too isolated to take advantage of the new incentives to market their surplus.   It has been calculated that

---

[28]Federal Republic of Nigeria: Federal Office of Statistics Annual Abstract of Statistics, (Lagos, 1986), p. 30.

[29]Africa Research Bulletin Economic Series (March 20 1988).Ibid., p. 34.

[30]The Guardian, 2 August 1986, p. 4.

farmers receive only 25 to 45 percent of the retail price of their goods due to high transport cost resulting from the removal of Petroleum subsidy.

In some areas farmers are at the mercy of some few operators in the region who own trucks. Even where the price rises have succeeded in raising production, there are doubts as to whether the benefits will be lasting. For instance, increased cocoa production was brought about by small holders who have no access to credit or training in improved farming method.

Also, the second tier foreign exchange market introduce in September 1986, primarily designed to stabilize the naira and reduce black market dealings, has resulted in a fall in the value of the naira from N3.30 = $1 at the beginning of September 1986 to N7.20 by December 1988. "It has led immediately to a 60 percent devaluation of the naira; but more important, it has come to dominate the national consciousness to such an extent that it is affecting every aspect of living".[31] The generally low exchange value of the naira has meant that industries have been unable to import necessary raw material to boost industrial output. Many factories are still operating at less than 10 percent capacity. Industries that could not afford to import at higher prices of raw materials inputs went out of business.   While those that managed to operate at less than full capacity engaged in retrenchment. For instance, in oil industry more than 50,000 workers were retrenched.

In addition, the introduction of the second tier Foreign Market Program in Nigeria has had adverse effect on lower and middle income Nigerians. Over the last three years, employers have laid off large numbers of workers due largely to raw materials shortages that resulted from devaluation of the naira.   Although, there is no official data for unemployment rate in Nigeria, the number so laid-off is now estimated to run in the millions[32].   The number of civil servants and teachers employed by the State fell from 2.0 million to 1.5 million.[33]   Unemployment not only reduces the income of the poor in the short-run but also reduces their long-term potential for employment.

---

[31]Onyema Ugochukwu, "Charting A new Cause" West Africa (5 January 1987), p. 18.

[32]Editorial, "Second-tier Foreign Exchange Market and the Future of Nigerian Economy, " New Nigeria 8 October 1986, p. 6.

[33]Ibid.

As a result of high cost of import of raw materials and spare parts, the cost of manufactured goods (both domestic and foreign) increased several fold. And this is eventually passed to the final consumers. For instance, the large packet of OMO detergent which had sold for N3, went as high as N 20 before stabilizing at N12. Electronic products and refrigerators more than quadrupled in price. Volkswagen cars previously selling at around N6,000 shot up to over N26,000 and Peugeots increased to N80,000 from N10,000 before SFEM.[34] As of March 1989, the cost of flight ticket (round trip) from Lagos to New York was N8,000. One can contrast this charge with the pre-SFEM cost of N950. The high cost of air fares has led to a sharp decline in international travel in spite of an increase in the BTA to N500. This, in turn, has resulted in reduced smuggling of consumer items which previously supplemented official imports and domestic production, and has further fueled inflation. Table 32 shows the market survey of some food items in ten major states in Nigeria.

Table 32

MARKET SURVEY

Item or Commodity	Quantity	Jan.-1988 N	May-1989 N
Bread	500 gram	5.00	10.00
Beans	50 kg bag	300.00	400.00
Eggs	Crate	25.00	35.00
Omo	Gaint	12.00	18.00
Matches	Packet	1.00	2.50
Garri	Tin	25.00	45.00
Bournvita	Medium Tin	6.50	15.50
Groundnut	50 kg bag	100.00	240.00

[34]News Ripples, Laos, (March Edition, 1989), p. 35.

Rice (Abakaliki)	50 kg bag	100.00	240.00
Rice (Aroso)	50 kg bag	180.00	600.00
Mackeabs toothpaste	Small size	2.00	3.00
Palm Oil	Tin	70.00	140.00
Corn	50 kg bag	120.00	200.00
Peak Milk	A Tin	80 k	3.00

Source: News Ripples, Lagos, March Edition, 1989

The states under market survey include Lagos, Sokoto, Kwara, Kano, Kaduna, Anambra, Imo, Plateau Bendel and River State. This table indicates that almost prices of every food items increased. some items such as bread, matches, groundnut, Abakaliki rice and palm oil even more than double in price. While Aroso rice and Peak milk more than quadrupled in price. News Ripples market investigation shows that an average family of five spends about 70 percent of their income on feeding, and the rest on accommodation, with virtually nothing left to save. According to this study, inflation rate in Nigeria is between 300 to 400 percent.[35] In response to this problem, President Babangida had recently indicated that governments answer to the rising food prices would be to continue to provide infrastructural facilities to farmers to enhance massive production of food. He made it clear that government will not introduce any price control measures but will rather allow market forces of demand and supply to determine the prices of commodities.

Also, in table 33 we present the principal indicators of ascending prices. In general, The composite price index numbers for food rise faster than the index number of all items. Also index numbers for food rise faster in 1986-1988 than in 1981-1985. One can now see the effect of devaluation of currency on consumer goods.

Devaluation, which has always been a prescription package of deflationary macroeconomic measures suggested by the IMF, have not helped to accomplish the desired objective, especially in terms of establishing a

---

[35]Ibid., p. 36.

realistic and sustainable real exchange rate, transferring resources to specific sectors of the economy, particularly to the export sector, and restraining aggregate demand in Nigeria. Instead, the economic situation of the masses has worsened following devaluation. To check the demand for foreign exchange, Babangida regime adopted import restriction measures which resulted to severe shortages of both consumer and investment goods. Scarcity of consumer goods aggravated domestic inflation, while scarcity of investment goods further contributed to the slowing down of domestic economic activity in Nigeria.

Table 33

CONSUMER PRICE INDICES IN NIGERIA 1981-1988 (1980 = 100

	1981	1982	1983	1984	1985	1986	1987	1988
COMPOSITE URBAN-RURAL								
All Items	143	167	186	205	248	268	330	401
Food Items	146	177	186	200	250	272	342	428
URBAN								
All Items	142	178	196	218	264	283	360	466
Food Items	155	198	210	234	304	328	410	502
RURAL								
All Items	143	165	185	203	245	264	327	372
Food Items	145	169	182	196	243	265	326	370

Source: Central Bank of Nigeria, Annual Report and Statement of Account 1984, 1986 and 1987. Federal Office of Statistics, Lagos 1986.

Also very problematic is the economic policy of currency devaluation typically imposed by the International Monetary Fund upon Nigeria as a precondition for access to substantial International Monetary Fund Loan package. Devaluation of national currency as we see it in the case of Nigeria has led to further increase in inflation and worsened Nigerias balance of payments as it is to reduce its payments deficits. A large proportion of its imports, such as, inter immediate and heavy industrial goods are vital to the effective functioning of the domestic economy, so the volume of Nigeria's imports cannot be reduced without undermining her economy. Devaluation, rather than reducing imports, merely increases the size of Nigeria's import bill by raising the cost of all foreign goods. Again, most primary products (the chief exports of Nigeria) exhibit a price inelasticity of demand-that is, lower prices made available to foreign consumers by devaluation did not lead to a proportionate increase in the volume of purchases. The demand for cocoa or coffee, for example, did not increase much when the price dropped in 1986.[36]   The dilemma is that currency devaluation in Nigeria neither increases export revenues nor reduces import expenditures in the manner expected by the International Monetary Fund and Liberal economic theory.

Nigeria's enormous debt burden (together with depreciation of the naira, which has increased the local currency commitment) has severely impaired the state's ability to budget for development. The investment budget for 1986 was set at a low $97.5 million only to be cut further to $70 million. Such low budgeting has directly impaired the Nigerian development effort. The World Bank has been able to disburse less than 50 percent of its commitment to Nigerian projects during the three years up to 1988 due to low government counterpart funding for agreed programs.[37]

As far as policies designed to reduce the current account deficit are concerned, the IMF's prescriptions put strong emphasis on regular debt-service payments which at present absorb a large share of external means of payments of Nigerian economy. This excessive emphasis has led, in some instances, to a large decrease in the import of goods required for recovery and adjustment and has created further overall economic problem.

Table 35 provides the figures for Nigeria's balances of trade, of goods and services, of capital and current accounts from 1970-1987. This table indicates that Nigeria had favorable balance of trade from 1970-1977, 1979-1980, 1984-1987 and unfavorable balance of trade in 1978, 1982 and 1983

---

[36]Paul Obi, "Economic Recovery The Problem of the Future" Africa Research Bulletin, (3 December 1986), p. 18.

[37]Paul Obi, "Loan and Project Financing" Africa Research Bulletin, (30 March 1987), p. 26.

Table 34

NIGERIA'S DEBTS: DEBT SERVICING ESTIMATES TO 1990

Figures for Nigeria's total debt repayments.
All figures in billions of dollars

	Federal government of Nigeria	IMF	World Bank	Financial Times	Economist AED
1986					
Medium/Long term repayments		3.2	3.4		
Short term repayments	3.3	1.3			
TOTAL	4.4	6.5	4.7		4.3
1987					
Medium/Long term repayments		3.2	3.0		
Short term repayments		3.3	1.5		
TOTAL	5.4	6.5	4.5		4.4
1988					
Medium/Long term repayments		2.7	2.7		
Short term repayments		2.8	1.3		
TOTAL	6.0	5.7	4.1		4.2
1989					
Medium/Long term repayments		2.0	2.2		
Short term repayments		2.8	1.3		
TOTAL	4.4	4.8	3.5		3.6
1990					
Medium/Long term repayments		1.2	1.5		
Short term repayments		0	0.3		
TOTAL		1.2	1.8		2.7

NIGERIA'S DEBTS: TOTAL DEBT ESTIMATES

Figures for debt outstanding and
disbursed on 1 January 1986.

Medium/Long term debt					
Official creditors	1.8	2.0			
Private creditors	12.6	10.0*			
Total	14.4	12.0	11.3	14	11(10.7)⁺ 12.0⁺
Short term debt					
Uninsured trade arrears	3.6	6.0	4.0	3.0	
Insured trade arrears		3.0	2.0	2.0	
Total		9.0	6.0	5.0	4(9.4)⁺ 5.5
TOTAL DEBT	18	22.9	17.3	19	15(20.1)⁺ 17.5⁺

Nigerian government figures converted from dollars into naira at exchange rate as of 1/1/86.
*Does not include $1.9bn (included in total) which was converted from short-term trade arrears into medium-term debt under a 1983 refinancing agreement.
⁺Figures in brackets from The Economist Intelligence Unit publications.

Sources: African Business, August, 1986, p. 48., Federal Office of Statistics Lagos.

respectively. From 1970 to 1973, the favorable balance of trade was as a result of increased in the production and price of oil. The sharp increase in oil prices in 1973-1974 and again in 1979 to 1980 resulted in a marked rise in the favorable balance of trade. Nigeria as a net exporter of oil, of course benefitted from the increases in oil prices, but had been adversely affected by the recent decline in these prices. The favorable balance of trade from 1984-1987 was a result of reduction in the importation of essential goods and services which include food by the military government.

This table also shows a corresponding decline of non-oil exports as the volume of oil export increases. Devaluation is urged to increase exports and to encourage domestic production of goods to replace imports. The IMF failed to remember or refused to accept the fact that Nigeria is only a producer of primary commodities for exports. The devaluation effects are considered to take longer to affect imports. There are also limited domestic alternatives to imported machinery spares and raw materials for manufacturing. Since local production is heavily dependent on imported inputs, capacity utilization and value added are seriously affected. Nigeria's exports of minerals require lengthy investment programs and most agricultural exports such as cocoa, palm oil, rubber, groundnut, wheat and the like require several years before plantings yield crops. Furthermore, the IMF stabilization policies have not resulted in any significant rise in gross national product (output) or exports that might protend economic recovery in Nigeria (See Table 36).

As can be seen the annual real growth of the GNP was uneven; it was not all upward, but yo-yo-like up and down. After the bitter Civil War that ended in 1970, reconstruction needs boosted the real GNP in 1971-1974 by more than 30 percent. During the nine year period (1971-1980), the arithmetic average growth rate came to 8.44 percent, even though during 1975 the country recorded a negative growth rate of two percent. The rapid growth of GNP per capita was due largely to petroleum discovery. It is important to note that the phenomenal growth recorded during the 1970s stopped in 1981 with the decline in petroleum demand. The table also indicates that Nigeria's economic performance was better off before the implementation of the Fund-supported Adjustment Program. From 1985-1987, per capita income had dropped in almost half from 770 to 393. This more than any thing,

Table 35

NIGERIA: BALANCES OF TRADE, OF GOODS AND SERVICES, OF CAPITAL AND CURRENT ACCOUNTS 1970-1987

	1	2	3	4	5	6	7	8	9	10	11	12	13	14	15
Year	Total Exports	Petroleum Major Exports	Petroleum as % of Total Exports	Non-Oil Exports	Non-Oil as % of Total Export	Total Imports	Food Imports	Food as % of Total Imports	Balance of Trade	Invisible Exports	Invisible Imports	Overall Balance of Goods and Services	Current Account	Capital Account	Balance on Capital and Current Account
1970	885.4	510.0	65.3	375.4	24.7	756.4	57.8	-	129.0	196	NA	NA	- 250	201	- 49
1971	1204.5	953.0	79.1	251.5	20.9	1076.4	88.2	7.6	128.1	225	NA	NA	- 102	- 127	- 229
1972	1327.6	1157.0	87.1	170.6	12.9	990.0	95.0	9.6	337.6	310	555	- 92.4	- 435	155	- 280
1973	2277.5	1893.5	83.1	384.0	16.9	1224.8	126.3	10.3	1052.7	394	1550	- 103.5	950	- 897	53
1974	5794.8	5334.7	92.1	1185.2	7.9	1737.3	154.8	8.9	4057.5	435	4618	- 135.8	2005	1060	3065
1975	4829.4	4629.6	93.9	199.8	4.1	3721.5	298.8	8.0	1107.9	490	3585	- 1987.3	- 355	50	- 405
1976	6751.1	6321.7	93.6	429.4	6.4	5134.7	441.7	8.6	1616.4	503	2285	- 165.6	- 224	42	- 66
1977	7630.7	7072.8	92.7	557.9	7.3	7368.0	780.7	10.6	262.7	581	2660	- 2016.3	- 650	154	- 496
1978	6064.4	5401.6	89.1	662.8	10.9	8136.4	1027.6	12.6	- 2072.0	741	2214	- 3545.0	- 2390	959	- 1431
1979	10836.8	10186.8	93.8	670.0	6.2	7472.5	766.5	10.3	3364.3	781	2508	1637.3	1006	744	1750
1980	14077.0	13523.0	96.1	554.0	3.9	9458.1	1091.0	11.3	4618.9	994	3985	1695.9	2804	- 29	2775
1981	11023.3	10680.5	96.9	342.8	3.1	12919.8	2113.1	16.4	- 1896.5	998	3717	- 4635.3	- 3668	1083	- 2585
1982	8722.6	8601.6	98.6	131.0	1.4	12565.5	2048.2	16.3	- 3842.9	574	2783	- 6051.9	- 5215	3970	- 1245
1983	7612.3	7337.4	96.4	274.9	3.6	9723.0	1477.9	15.2	- 2110.7	354	2373	- 4129.7	- 3438	3014	- 424
1984	8700.0	8425.1	96.3	74.9	1.7	7200.0	960.3		1500.0	410	2010	- 100.0	- 500	900	400
1985	8240.0	8050.0	97.6	190.0	2.4	3250.0	864.0	-	4990.0	313	2095	3208.0	3900	1250	5150
1986	5620.0	5560.4	98.2	59.6	1.8	3150.0	720.0	5.0	2470.0	396	2101	765.0	- 1350	NA	NA
1987	4410.0	5900.0	94.5	810.0	2.5	2007.4	510.4	4.0	2492.6	410	2341	581.0	NA	NA	NA

Sources: Central Bank of Nigeria, Annual Report and Statement of Accounts, 1980, 1983, 1984, 1986, 1987. Central Bank of Nigeria, Economic and Financial Review, Several Issues Compiled in 1985 Central Bank of Nigeria's Principal Economic Financial Indicators, 1970-1987; Lagos, 1979, 1988. Federal Office of Statistics and Federal Budget 1988.

Table 36

LEVEL OF OUTPUT

Year	GNP at Current Market Prices Naira million	Real GNP Growth (%)	Per Capita GNP (Naira)
1970	5621	NA	0
1971	7098	18.0	0
1972	7703	13.0	357.6
1973	10779.8	10.0	488.8
1974	18962.0	18.0	345.6
1975	21554.1	- 2.0	649.8
1976	27449.0	11.0	770.4
1977	32359.6	19.0	785.0
1978	33759.0	7.0	623.7
1979	39939	7.0	715.4
1980	43280	10.0	730.2
1981	43450	4.0	732.6
1982	40884	- 3.4	700.4
1983	28500	- 4.5	535
1984	30371	- 6.5	515
1985	37773	3.8	401
1986	30910	- 3.3	365.0
1987	32416	- 4.3	373.0
1988	35900	-2.7	397

Sources: National Planning Office, Lagos, 1984, Central Bank of Nigeria, Annual Report and Statement of Accounts, 1984, 1987. United National Account Statistics, 1988. World Bank, Nigeria: Country Economic Memo, Washington, DC, June 1986.

affected the standard of living of the people. A fall in per capita income was as a result of population increase and a fall in export earnings without a corresponding increase in output. In 1985-1987, the average growth rate was 1.3 percent while the population growth rate was 3.4 percent.

Not only has Nigeria shown little economic progress since the implementation of the IMF programs, but its social development has been quite slow in several dimensions. Table 37 summarizes selected social indicators from 1963 to 1988. During this period, the (estimated) population grew from 60 million to 105 million and the urban population as a percent of total population increased from 14.7 to 36. Life expectancy showed some improvement in the 1970s than in the 1980s; it increased from 39.9 to 48.0 and then declined to 42.9. Access to health care, as measured by population per physician, population per nursing person and population per hospital bed, showed remarkable improvement in the 1970s than the 1980s. However, what these statistics fail to disclose is the decline in the quality of health care delivery, such as frequent shortages of drugs, hospital equipment and supplies, and the deteriorating level of morale among hospital employees. Also, access to education, as measured by primary school enrollment ratio, improved dramatically from 39.0 percent in 1963 to 96 percent in 1979 and declined to 77 percent in 1984. Although there is no available data on the primary school enrollment for 1985-1988, but one could expect a further decline because of the removal of subsidies on education by the military government as a pre-condition for reaching agreement with the IMF. Even the labor force participation rate both in agriculture and industry showed a relative decline in the 1980s.

Furthermore, devaluation which has been a major concern for the IMF, has not helped to achieve the intended goal, especially in terms of providing enough foreign reserves through the expansion of non-oil exports (See Table 38). This table presents the foreign reserves from 1970-1987. By 1970, at end of the civil war, reserves stood at $202 million. Three years later, reserves had more than doubled to $559 million. In 1974, reserves grew to $5,602 million. The increased in reserves was due to increases in the prices of petroleum. The rapid increase in petroleum prices in 1973-1974 and again in 1979-1980 resulted in the increase of total reserves. Also, the recent decline in the oil prices affected Nigeria's foreign reserves seriously.

Table 37

NIGERIA'S SOCIAL INDICATORS

Indicators	1963-1967	1968-1971	1972-1975	1976-1979	1980-1984	1985-1988
*POPULATION (Total in Million)	60	74.0	80	88	93	105
Urban Population % of Total	14.7	16.8	19.8	23.7	30.2	36
Demographic Characteristics Life Expectancy (years)	39.9	43.2	45.8	48.0	44.0	42.9
HEALTH AND NUTRITION						
Population per Physician	78800	40328	22670	17684	32509	39770
Population per Nursing Person	4143	6558	5200	3013	3410	4003
Population per Hospital Bed	3201	2222	1641	1384	1702	2050
Calorie Supply per (% Requirements)	84	82	79	93	-	-
Infant Mortality Rate (per thousand)	180	171.4	142.0	147	160	-
EDUCATION						
Primary School Enrollment Ratio	39.0	35.0	40.0	96.0	77.0	-
Secondary School Enrollment Ratio	6.0	8.0	-	8.0	17.0	-
Adult Literacy Rate	17.4	-	-	34	36	-
EMPLOYMENT (%)						
Labor Force Participation Rate	11.2	42.4	38.7	33.6	28.7	-
Labor Force in Agriculture	11	66.0	60.9	54.0	52.4	51.0
Labor Force in Industry	12	14.9	19.0	23.5	31.3	23.4

Sources: Federal Office of Statistics, National Accounts for Nigeria, 1988.

Central Bank of Nigeria's Principal Social Indicators, 1988.

*World Bank Annual Reports (estimate of Nigerian Population based on 1963 Census), 1988.

Although Nigeria has experienced a decline in both GNP and per capita income before the implementation of the IMF macroeconomic stabilization policies, however, these policies aggravated further decline in these economic indicators. Devaluation which aimed at stimulating export production, balance of payments, and discourage black market, did not achieve these goals in Nigeria.   Despite serious devaluation through Second-tier Foreign Exchange Market established in 1986, the balance of payments, inflation, and the budget were not affected as projected by the Fund. In reality, Nigeria witnessed the expansion and acceleration of black market or parallels market as IMF called it more in 1986-1988 than ever before in history. From 1986 to the present $1.00 = 9.00$ or more in the black market.

Furthermore, Nigerians are paying a painful price for reform. Average per capita income for the country's 105 million people is 35 percent less now than in 1974. From 1985 to 1987, per capita income of Nigeria has dropped in more than half from $800 to $380.[38] In formal recognition of this new poverty, the World Bank plans to reclassify Nigeria from a "middle-income" country to a "low income" country (See Appendix 4).

Another example of the IMF Policy that needs to be examined in Nigerian context is the demand for internal suspension of all subsidies including fertilizer and petroleum. Insistence in the IMF programs that the government cut subsidized credits to farmers has led to severe shortages of pesticides, fertilizers, and other essential agricultural inputs for small scale farmers. In Nigeria, for example, a 1986 IMF- advised cutback in rural credits led to a precipitous drop in rice, maize and garri production and an increase in malnutrition. Today, in Nigeria, such measures have combined with the worst drought in the last few years to dispossess thousands of agricultural producers. The IMF officials are often quick to point out that one of their favored policy recommendations can benefit the rural sector, namely lifting government controls that have kept urban prices of agricultural products quite low. While partially true, the Fund ignores the fact that such resulting price increases are seldom passed on to agricultural workers on fixed salaries, and are devastating to the urban poor.

The urban poor, including unemployed and marginally employed populations, are especially vulnerable to such pricing policy changes. Many have incomes that are unstable or fixed at very low levels. Overnight doubling or tripling of prices of essential commodities following the IMF austerity measures have resulted in food riots in Nigeria. As The Atlanta Journal and Constitution puts it: The austerity measures instituted recently by the military government were demanded by Western creditors and have led to sharp price increases for some basic goods and services. Those price rises touched off a violent students' demonstration at a University in the midwestern city of Benin on May 24, and rioting spread to most of Nigerian

---

[38] James Brooke, "Ailing Nigeria Opens Its Economy" The New York Times 15 August 1988, p. 30

states in which many people were killed".[39]   A Lagos newspaper, Punch reported Sunday, June 4, that more than 50 people had died nationwide in six days of clashes between police and demonstrators".[40]

Furthermore, the IMF's policy prescription in other policy areas have been far more politically sensitive. The cost of fertilizer subsidies was argued seriously, but in addition, the IMF has pressed for a reduction in the subsidy for petroleum and other oil products. Babangida agreed in 1986 that the state subsidy for petroleum resulted in the lowest consumer price in Africa. He subsequently raised petroleum prices by 45 percent in the 1986 budget. Petroleum prices were again raised in February 1987 and in April 1988, the government finally hope to remove all subsidies on petroleum by 1990s. As the majority of food and raw materials are distributed amongst Nigerias 105 million population by road, the increase in fuel prices that the IMF has demanded for has led to further increase in inflation. Increase in the cost of transporting commodities from rural to urban centers, though sometimes, marginal, has contributed more than marginally to the general price increases. Price inflation further reduces workers' real income. Also, the education and health budgets have been reduced to a level whereby they have virtually no significant effect on Nigeria's population of about 105 million. The cut in subsidies to educational has led to the re-introduction of fees as well as educational levies in many states, while university students whose maintenance costs are due to rise substantially, are shaping up for a confrontation with the government. In one academic year, more than ten universities have been temporarily suspended because of some disagreement between the government and student unions.[41]   Even, the Academic Staff Union of Universities was banned in July 1988 following a university teachers' strike over low pay and poor working condition. The Universal Free Primary Education enjoyed in the 1970s is no longer in service. All for the purpose of satisfying the IMF policy conditions.   With these austerity measures and cutback of government expenditure in other areas, including employment, social and public services life becomes extremely difficult for poor people.

---

[39]The Associated Press, "Nigerian President Sticks with Austerity Policies," The Atlanta Journal and Constitution, June 6,1989.

[40]Punch, Lagos Newspaper, Sunday, 4 June 1989, P.1.

[41]African News December 1988, p.4.

Table 38

FOREIGN RESERVES (1970 - 1988)

Year	U.S. $Millions
1970	202
1971	408
1972	355
1973	559
1974	5602
1975	5586
1976	5186
1977	4232
1978	1887
1979	5548
1980	10235
1981	3895
1982	1613
1983	990
1984	1285
1985	1365
1986	1145
1987	1074

Sources: Federal Republic of Nigeria, Federal Office of Statistics Annual Abstract of Statistics 1986 Lagos 1986 p.105, Central Bank of Nigeria, Economic and Financial Review 1987. Peter Olayiwola, Petroleum and Structural Changes in a Developing Country: The Case of Nigeria (New York: Opraeger, 1987), p. 109.

Moreover, women make up the majority of Nigerian rural (and particularly rural poor) population. They produce the bulk of food in Nigeria and , for example, make up 50-60 percent of the agricultural work force in the society. Hence labor-displacing that shifts from food to export crops hit women the hardest. Furthermore, sex discrimination has left women with few economic resources to weather still austerity plans. Fewer opportunities for wage employment are open to women, who also suffer lower wage level and more layoffs. Likewise, women usually have less access to basic education, health care, clean water and agricultural services, and are therefore especially hard hit by susterity measures that cut government spending in these areas in Nigeria.

Despite the weight of the crisis that is shouldered by rural and urban poor in Nigeria, they play only a minimal role in decision-making in the institutions that advocate and administer susterity both nationally and internationally. Urban workers are affected by most of the same factors that erode the economic sustenance of the urban poor. In addition, the IMF stabilization programs generally involve a freeze in workers' real wages. However, wage controls without price controls erode the already marginal living standard of the working poor. An average middle income family cannot afford two square meals a day. African Economic Digest, November 2, argued that Babangida deliberately targeted the austerity program on the lower levels of Nigerian society in order to leave the perquisites of his elite intact as far as possible.

Also, affected by current policies of the Fund implemented by the present military government is domestic entrepreneurs. Many entrepreneurs producing for domestic markets have gone bankrupt as policy incentives are shifted to favor exporters. The elimination of protective tariffs and the difficulty in obtaining foreign exchange for vital raw materials and machinery imports have accelerated the liquidation of small and medium-sized enterprises. In the process, tens of thousands are thrown out of work.[42] Small scale local industries are further being killed by import liberalization because foreign manufacturers are deliberately selling at uneconomic prices,

---

[42]David Nwake, "Nigeria Gets to Grips with the Economy," Anambra State Daily Star 14 June, 1988, p. 8.

with imported goods costing less than the price local manufacturers pay for their raw materials.

The liberalization of prices is one of the Fund-supported adjustment program in Nigeria. These measures aim at transmitting exchange rate movements throughout the economy, improving incentives, and encouraging a more efficient resource allocation. Administered prices benefitted both traders in illicit markets and bureaucrats who administer the controls at the expense of low-income producers.

Also, Fund-supported adjustment program generally seek to limit aggregate credit expansion. Within this overall constraint, they limit the access of the public sector to credit from the banking system in order to ensure that an adequate share of total credit is available to the private sector. In a repressed financial system like Nigeria, credit controls and the associated credit rationing have strengthened the position of larger firms and farms relative to their smaller counterparts,with the latter being forced to turn to curb markets in which higher interest rates are
charged. This process prevented the poor engaged in either small-scale enterprises in the informal sector or small farms in the rural sector from expanding their productive capacity, thus limiting their participation in the process of economic development and structural adjustment program.

However, international capital did secure substantial advantage: the dollar value of Nigerian currency was slashed four fold, import restrictions were lifted, import licenses abolished, privatization initiated, subsidies removed, wages frozen, price controls lifted, jobs cut, the minimum wage was eliminated and profitability of foreign investment (especially in oil) enhanced. In return for this structural adjustment program (June 1986 to December 1988), the government received a new debt repayment timetable along with the new loans from the World Bank and commercial sources. Currently, economists from Washington, D.C. virtually run Nigeria's Central Bank and finance ministry. In short, IMF conditions were imposed through the back door and under different names. The military regime is being bolstered by outside advisors in order to impose the IMF package. While private foreign capital gains, ordinary Nigerians are pushed further into more or less desperate strategies to avoid destitution and death.

The quandary of the Babangida administration reflects a situation common to many LDCS in sub-Saharan Africa and elsewhere. Any regime experiencing Nigeria's problems is only likely to gain external financing under severe IMF-dictated, terms implying huge reduction in public expenditure, rises in the costs of essential items and a decline in the purchasing power of wages and local money.   However, such a government is likely to gain or maintain popular support if living standards improve.   Yet, the decline of economic condition of many vocal urban elements in Nigeria (including the unemployed and industrial workers) has led to increasingly vociferous public protests and riots directed against the administration and the Fund.   The regime has lost much of its popularity and is perceived as having "sold out" to the West without any benefits accruing to most Nigerians.[43]

To Western industrial nations and the IMF and World Bank, Nigeria is the success story of West Africa. The paradox is that the government is doing all the "right " things at immense political cost, yet failing conspicuously to succeed. .At this point, however, if the donors cannot settle Nigeria's financial needs, it is inevitable that internal discontent or a coup will bring the regime crashing down.   Nigeria remains the example of how tenuous "recovery" can be within the confines of a primary product dependent economy, utilizing monetarist economic policies and the larges of the West to develop.

---

[43]Africa Analysis No. 1 (11 July 1986) p.8.

CHAPTER 12

As We See It: Concluding Assessments And Recommendation

Research Findings on the IMF Policies in Nigeria

The results of our study suggest that adjustment programs in general have important distributional implications. The study discovers that the least skilled were the first to be laid off during the programs under studies. They, therefore, suffer most from unemployment, which not only reduces their incomes in the short-run but also adversely affects their human capital. The poor are often the hardest hit by the high prices prevailing on black markets, since they lack access to goods at official prices.

Also, the Structural Adjustment Program which the Babangida government has been implementing with the help of the International Monetary Fund and the World Bank has caused tremendous suffering on Nigeria's working population. The program has had the implication of further polarizing the country by increasing the gap between rich and poor. Yet, demand management and market-oriented in Nigeria show no evidence of pushing the country into the road to economic recovery and self-reliance development. These macroeconomic stabilization policies do not assure that the economy will not be beset by additional crises of accumulation. In reality, what the working population of Nigeria needs at this time is not a Structured Adjustment Program that undermines their living conditions at the expense of foreign and local exploitative enterprises, but a strong program of structural change in which the working population will have the power to control their own fortune.[1]

Devaluation in a country like Nigeria with large urban poverty groups imposed immediate costs on the urban poor who were locked into the production of non-tradable. Devaluation was inefficient in improving the short-run position of those poor farmers whose short-run supply elasticities were small relative to those of rich farmers. Low elasticities of supply could reflect supply bottlenecks (such as inadequate or insufficiently maintained infrastructure), production of non-tradable food stuffs for the domestic market, or concentration on subsistence agriculture.[2]

Furthermore, sudden cuts in capital expenditures have hurt the poor both in the short run and the long run. In the short run, such cutbacks decreased real wages and employment opportunities for the poor. In the long run, they have seriously affected those social and economic services provided to the poor by the government. For instance, cuts in health and education expenditures accruing to the poor seriously affected poverty groups. Economically, in the short run, the cuts reduced consumption benefits available to the poor. In the overall analysis, restrictive monetary policies adversely affected both employment opportunities and earnings for urban poverty groups in Nigeria.

Also, conditionality shows a means of ensuring that the international adjustment process operates properly and benefits all member nations of the IMF. By linking stabilization to the supply of financial resources, the IMF endeavors to assist member nations accomplish a viable payment equilibrium condition in the medium term, that is, a position of sustainable current transactions, with considerable price and exchange rate stability, an acceptable and sustainable level and rate of growth of economic activity, and a liberal international payment regime. However, the Fund's policies in this area do not efficiently put into consideration the structural realities of Nigerian economy.

Eventually, the IMF has been criticized in Nigeria for its conditionality. In Nigeria, social tension has been created and economic growth has been

---

[1]Onimode, The IMF, The World Bank and the African Debt, p. 233.

[2]International Monetary Fund, (May 1988).

checked because of the unnecessary policies taken with regard to major economic factors, specificly domestic credit, external debt, and public sector financing, as well as some components of the price system, including commodity prices, exchange rates, and interest rates.

As a result of lack of diversified economy based largely on a few export commodities, Nigeria becomes a victim to external shocks. Because of this structural peculiarity, the type of stabilization sometimes required by the Fund/Bank for the use of its financial resources entails loss of output and public revenues, with costs that, while possibly negligible in industrialized and more diversified economies, are considerable in Nigeria.

Price liberalization that, in normal situations, is anticipated to lead to increased competitiveness and hence, to lower prices through market forces of demand and supply has provoked social tension in Nigeria. Liberalization of commercial transactions, according to Hellenier suspected to lead to harmonious world trade relations, does not seem to bring valid medium term solutions for Nigerian economy. Its weak structure does not permit it to quickly measure up to the fierce competition of manufactured goods from industrialized economies.

Moreover, the Nigerian industrial nucleus receives very little encouragement since public revenues are so dependent on foreign trade. Restructuring requires far more time and more fundamental change than is implied in the Fund's conditionality. There obviously remains conflicting points of view about ultimate structural objectives. Instead of granting financial assistance consistent with the magnitude of the required recovery and economic revival, the Fund offers a short term regressive care, followed by high conditionality.

As a matter of fact, many African countries which implemented the Fund stabilization policies have results similar to that of Nigeria. For instance, the brain behind currency devaluation as part of structural adjustment programs are of three kinds; to curtail import demand, discourage the black market operation, and stimulate export production. However, in spite of the major devaluations that have taken place in these countries, the balance of payments, inflation and budget did not improve as expected. The economic indicators such as GNP, per capita income, inflation, unemployment, debt servicing ratio to mention but a few of these countries even worsened following the application of the Fund supported adjustment programs. The IMF policy prescriptions in Zambia, Sudan, Sierra Leone, and Zaire have resulted in increasing social unrest; a situation similar to that of Nigeria. The suggested benefits of the Fund programs (especially increased agricultural productivity in these countries) remain illusive in their achievement at best. With the sort of competitive devaluation the IMF seems to encourage among them, these countries including Nigeria have witnessed persistent increases in output and export volumes, but reduced foreign exchange earnings. The net beneficiaries are the industrialized countries importing these commodities at the cheapest possible rates. The Fund macroecomonic stabilization programs, in effect result in economic underdevelopment of the less developed countries of Africa. For one thing, the Fund knows that the major export commodities produced by African states are priced in U.S. dollars. What then is the usefulness of domestic currency devaluations of these nations? Although, it derives from a concern for enhancing efficiency in the use of resources, the idea of devaluation which has been advocated by the Fund, seems to reflect a preconceived notion of economic organization. The point to make here is that the Fund has an objective role of constructing and maintaining an international economic system based upon capitalist forms of production and exchange. The negative impact of this role on the less developed countries' economy is not the primary concern of the IMF. The Fund's conceptual framework and policy conditionalities ignore the structural realities and inevitable nature of payments imbalances that result from the development process over which leaders of African states do not have control.

Concluding Assessments

We have indicated many useful advantages of Nigeria's short-period tight foreign exchange control approach over the IMF's prescription for economic growth. The major benefits of foreign exchange restrictions over second-tier foreign exchange market in terms of a policy of economic self-reliance are (1) the foreign exchange regulation approach can be selectively employed to control access to available foreign exchange, while the IMF conditionality distributes foreign currency primarily according to individual or corporate purchasing power on the open market operation; (2) the first strategy is predicated upon domestic resourcefulness, whereas SFEM encourages and supports foreign penetration vis a vis corporate investment and new loans; and (3) the Buhari's foreign exchange control approach involves no obligations to adopt the other policy conditions contained in the typical IMF package. Under SFEM, in general, there is little progress of rectifying the entrenched structural problem of external economic dependency and underdevelopment which afflicts Nigeria's economy. Nigerian experience also indicates that the Western financial concern will firmly resist radical strategies to currency devaluation and the other IMF conditionalities. This simply indicates that any nation which engages on an independent strict foreign exchange control measure must be ready to forego debt rescheduling and additional loans - an outcome which could prove to be in its long-run benefit.

However, some early positive proofs could be discerned, we are not able to evaluate the long-run economic implication of the foreign exchange control measure given the nature of the particular case under study in this research. The overthrow of the Buhari administration in 1985 indicated that the forced Nigerian experiment outside the IMF framework would not be given a chance to survive. Also, the strategy is problematic in political, economic and social terms. The Buhari foreign exchange control policies led to economic hardship and suffering, specificly for well to do Nigerians. It is not certain that any administration could maintain such restrictive policies without incurring significant political unrest and/or inviting a military coup.

However, Second-tier Foreign Exchange Market has been sold as a milder, market-imposed rather than government-imposed "alternative" to official devaluation, the main IMF conditionality, and the 1984 foreign exchange strategies.[3] Nigeria's recent experience with IMF stabilization program has been influenced by external pressure, internal debate, and the drastic reduction in the price of a barrel of crude oil. For the past four years, citizens and policy makers have unquestionably gained greater awareness of the negative domestic implications accompanied with the IMF "remedies". Meanwhile, the Babangida regime had set mainly all of the IMF's policy prescriptions in operation within Nigeria by the end of 1986.

In our evaluation, the recent policy measures implemented the Babangida military government are more accurately described as capitulation

---

[3]Africa Today October 1986.

to IMF and creditor demands than as independent economic policy initiative. They result to a reversal of the previous government's endeavors to replace IMF conditionalities with strict foreign exchange regulations. This study shows that the international financial concern will mobilize its forces to resist fundamental challenges to its authority and objectives. Acting alone, and confronting low prices for crude oil in the global market and a receptive new military government, the Nigerian public proved to be no match for the unified counter attack mounted by the country's lenders.[4]

In the first chapter, we suggested that Nigeria would not progress toward national economic recovery and self-reliant development if the government accepted and implemented the IMF conditionalities and secured new loan.

To start with, the new loans saddle Nigeria with an additional debt burden. Rescheduling buys time, but at the cost of more onerous repayment term. In addition, regeneration of the Nigeria economy would be impeded by some of the IMF policies. Let us examine the devaluation national currency, for example. This policy is protected on the grounds that devaluation makes local products cheaper, leads to increased exports, and thus prompts higher production. At least one prominent spokesman for the Nigerian business community, Dr. Michael Omolayola, Chairman of Lever Brothers, supported devaluation on the grounds that it would make locally manufactured goods more competitive on the global market.[5] As we indicated in our theoretical foundation, the major problem with this argument is that it only works for an industrialized, export-oriented society. Nigeria, however is hardly an industrialized nation and it exports no manufactured products. Its chief export, petroleum, already is priced in dollars. Devaluation of the naira brings no benefits to Nigeria in terms of increased sales of crude oil. Also, most of the Nigeria's majoragricultural exports products such as rubber, palm oil, and palm kernels, take years to cultivate and, therefore, are not likely to show a substantial response immediately to reduction in the naira's value, or even to the abolition of the country's exploitative marketing boards.

---

[4]See Chandra S. Hardy "Africa's Debt Structural Adjustment with Stability", New Nigeria, 12 April 1985, p. 19.

[5]The Guardian, 21 August 1984, p. 3.

In Nigeria industrial machinery and spare parts will have to be imported at far greater expense if the country is to develop its export and import substitution capacity and break out of its dependent economic position. In order to prevent starvation and feed the country's rapidly growing population at required nutritional standards, Nigeria will be forced to continue to import a major proportion of its food needs regardless of cost. Sustained self-sufficiency in food production is not on the Nigerian horizon.[6]

The actual effect of devaluation is higher inflationary expectations and spiraling domestic prices, particularly for food. The fact that Nigeria provides a seller's market for imports owing to dependency and oligopoly, cost is rarely the major determinant of prices. For example, a sack of rice cost N21 in early 1983 upon arrival at the port. After passing through many middlemen, the same sack of rice sold for as much as N80 to the final consumer. In the words of one economist, "a 400 percent increase from offshore cost to consumer price can only represent a frightful and unjustified tax."[7]

Devaluation, therefore provides more numerous and often even more lucrative opportunities for "taxing" the urban poor. Hence, Nigeria's working class and its 5 million unemployed job seekers must assume the heaviest burdens imposed by devaluation and rising food prices.[8]

The Fund request that Nigeria liberalize its external trade policy has been aptly described by a former finance minister, Soleye as "an invitation to commit suicide.[9] The nation's marginal propensity to import may be the highest in Africa. Relaxation of import restrictions allows the renewed importation of luxury products such VCRs, automobiles, refrigerators, television and stereo sets, lace and polished cotton cloth, fashionable shoes, etc., in place of industrial machinery. Domestic import substitution industries, whose products Nigerians shun in favor of "the original" (identical, but

---

[6]Peter Koehn, "African Approach to Environmental Stress: A Focus on Ethiopia and Nigeria, "Economic Digest, (March 23, 1984), p. 17. Timothy Shaw and Orobola Fasehum, "Nigeria in the World System: Alternative Approaches, Explanations and Projections, "Journal of Modern African Studies, (December 18, 1980), p. 561; Africa Analysis, (11 July 1986), Africa Today, p. 29.

[7]The New York Times, 20 January 1984, p. 9.

[8]Blackburn, "The Year of the IMF? New Ripple, (7 June 1986), p. 20.

[9]West Africa, (22 October 1984), p. 2113.

foreign-made), would suffer further decline and produce even higher rates of unemployment.[10]   The Buhari foreign exchange measures, coupled with restrictive controls on imports, ensured that essential raw materials, equipment, spare parts, and food consumed scare foreign exchange. This strategy showed a more rational and effective method of restraining imports in comparison to the IMF's preferred drastic devaluation of the currency.

In reality, the approach to stabilization and recovery adopted by the Buhari administration makes more economic and political sense for Nigeria than the IMF's package does. The cornerstone of this macro economic policy is stringent foreign exchange regulation; the emphasis of the IMF and the successor Babangida is on substantial devaluation of the national currency.[11]

However, if the foreign exchange regulation/import restriction approach holds out greater economic promise and is politically more acceptable, why does the Fund insist on the adoption of packages which only lead to the further deterioration of conditions in Third World countries? As we mentioned earlier in our theoretical considerations, one answer to this question can be found in the Fund's raison d'etre. The IMF is created and designed to maintain the restructured international trade system and to stabilize the international monetary system. This dual purpose is ostensibly economic, but in essence political. Since 1945, the industrial powers which dominated the international economic relations have viewed the IMF as a political instrument for the propagation of capitalism. External capital is to be stimulated to flow into "developing" countries through trade liberalization and the creation of a favorable climate for direct foreign investment. The Fund encourages the flow of private foreign capital by insisting on specific types of internal reform measures and policy conditions that depend largely on free market economic principles. The main adjustment measure involves both economic and political requirements designed to curtail anti-capitalist propensities and economic independence. The economic elements mainly include favored treatment and devaluation of the national currency as well as liberalization of trade, are geared at "denationalizing" the recipient economy and making it dependent, vis a vis transnational corporations, on Western capitalist institutions. Also, the political elements, usually including cutbacks

---

[10]Africa Today.

[11]The Economist, (3 May 1986), pp. Survey 8, 12.

in government expenditure, elimination of state subsidies, reorganization of public enterprises, trimming of bureaucracy, and termination of counter trade (frequently with the socialist countries), are designed to de-socialize the economy.[12]

Also, its major political ends to be accomplished by economic means create dilemmas for the Fund. It must insist upon policies that it knows are dangerous to the domestic economy of Less Developed Countries (LDCs) that have accumulated vast outstanding debts to Western financial establishments. One of the Fund officials believed that Nigeria's devaluation dicotomy can raise a lot of problems for the government and that "it is a dilemma, but there is no more alternative".[13]   In reality, our evaluation and assessment of the two economic measures indicate that there is at least one viable alternative: the Buhari foreign exchange control-based measure.   Nevertheless, this alternative route undermine the Fund's power to control a nation's economic policies in the short run and, in the long run, threatens to enhance self-reliant development and independence from Western multinational and transnational corporations.

The progress of successful economic stabilization policy outside the Fund framework clearly is not in the interest of the IMF and the Western nations.[14]   Such a result in Nigeria would impose a major threat to the Fund's authority anywhere in the less developed countries and reduce the leverage of western organizations anxious with enforcing a dependent "answer" for debt crisis. This shows the economic pressure which Nigeria and other LDCs experience to accept a package which would exacerbate a serious economic situation and perpetuate external dependence and underdevelopment.

Also viewed in a more positive economic light, the foreign exchange control regulations are intended to guarantee that no international transaction involving money can take place outside official agencies and without official

---

[12]Editorial, "Nigeria and the IMF Loan" New Nigeria, Lagos, Friday, 20 September 1986, p. 13.

[13]Washington Post, 9 March 1984, Also see "Agonies of Adjustment," West Africa, (1 October 1984), pp. 1981-1982.

[14]See IMF/Africa Applying Pressure on Nigeria," West Africa, (22 October 1984), pp. 2113-2114. For a more recent case in point, see Eric N. Berg, "IMF-Style Pact Seen for Brazil," New York Times, 25 February 1987, p. 25.

approval. That way, not only would governmental control over the acquisition and use of foreign exchange be assured, but its access to more invisible sources of foreign exchange would be enhanced.

In summary, our examination of the Buhari government's foreign exchange control measure indicates that this approach contained some of the components required to set Nigeria on a more self-reliant economic development. It is very difficult to see such opportunity in current policy measure. Second-tier foreign exchange market encourages increased direct foreign investment. New loans and rescheduling, established in part to finance food and other essential imports, indicate little promise of leading Nigeria away from a state of perpetual debt crisis and external dependency.

Recommendation of Alternative Approaches to Fund Stabilization in Africa

As we indicated in the early stage of this research that alternative approaches to stabilization will be recommended in Africa and other LDCs based on our evaluation, and assessment of the Fund stabilization Programs in Nigeria. At this point, however, the case for recommending an alternative approach to stabilization to that espoused by the Fund rests on both practical and theoretical grounds. The strongest practical argument is that the Fund's record in Nigeria is relatively poor. There is no evidence that the performance in the mid 1980s of Nigeria in terms of balance of payments, gross national product, per capita income, inflation, savings and investment was any better with Fund programs than without. What is more, in a study of adjustment experience in 1986-1988, the Fund itself admits that in only a minority of cases were its targets met by Nigerian government. Growth targets in gross domestic product were only improved from 3.3 decline in 1986 to 1.2 percent increase in 1987. The Fund also shows a marginal boast in external reserves from N4.5 billion at the end of 1987 to N4.75 billion at the beginning of 1988.

There are in addition, sound theoretical reasons why Fund programs fail to accomplish its objectives in Nigeria. Nigerian economy has a low capacity to adjust because its problems are structural. This means that it is not particularly susceptible to treatment by an approach which is heavily oriented toward demand restraint and short-term adjustments.

To start with, the most serious restraint on adjustment endeavors in Nigeria is foreign exchange availability, but this is unlikely to be eased significantly by standard IMF macro economic stabilization programs. Domestic demand constraint can be expected to have little implications either by way of reducing import transaction or by freeing up local goods for expanded export earnings because the substitutability of traded for non-traded goods is generally quite low in Nigeria; imports do not compete with goods produced locally, while exports are not generally consumed locally to any significant degree. The possibilities of improving the balance of trade through expenditure switching are, therefore, quite low.[15]

We also tend to be less certain about the capacity of substantial devaluation to stimulate improvement in the balance of payments. Individual Africa countries including Nigeria fit the "small economy" assumptions and can therefore generally export as much as they can produce at the going world price. In this case, the Marshall-Lerner principle for a devaluation to improve the balance of trade in foreign exchange terms is quite simply that the sum of the elasticity of supply of exports and the elasticity of demand for imports exceeds zero.[16] With these conditions, it is certain that a devaluation cannot cause a decline in the trade balance in Nigeria; but we argue that there are evidences for agreeing that improvements may, at best, be minimal and may take time. Exports do not respond much to price incentives partly because non-price factors are often the essential constraint on their expansion. Therefore, if intermediate and capital goods are in short supply, an increase in local prices paid to exporters may achieve little other than the worsening of inflationary pressures. This is exactly the problem Nigeria is experiencing since 1985.

Furthermore, increasing the capacity of tree crop or mineral exports also takes a long period of time so that output may respond only four to five years after the initial price incentive. Expanding nontraditional exports, such as manufactured goods, needs much more than correct pricing presumes. It presupposes a considerably well developed manufacturing sector and an ability

---

[15]Crock Andrew, Stabilization Policies in Developing Countries, Staff paper, International Monetary Fund (Washington, Vol 28, March 1981).

[16]John Williamson, The Open Economy and The World Economy (New York: Basic Books, 1983).

to enter foreign markets that implies overseas contracts, product quality, and appropriate credit system. Only few African countries, if any, could meet these requirements and certainly not within the one-year time frame of most IMF measures.

Again, devaluation issue has been especially controversial in Nigeria, and on this issue we have disagreed seriously with the IMF macroeconomic policies. The IMF's preference for relatively large adjustments in advance of quite small amounts of balance of payments assistance is seen by many Nigerian economists as a prescription for inflation and political instability. It is assumed that supply elasticities are such that price increases would rapidly erode attempts to depreciate the real effective exchange rate and that this raises the questions about the validity of this approach.[17]

We also question the preference of the IMF for the introduction of positive real rates of interest. Our argument is based on the fact that this too can contribute to both inflation and recession when interest costs are a significant proportion of total cost of production.[18]

The distributional implications of Fund stabilization programs have also been the subject of controversial in Nigeria. Fund conditionalities make no effort to guarantee employment levels nor to preserve or extend the provision of basic need.[19] Thesometimes have their serious implications on low-income urban dwellers by raising unemployment, by cutting subsidies and government spending, and by raising inflation while restraining wage adjustments. The rural poor were affected adversely by cuts in spending and benefit little if any from changes in the internal terms of trade.[20]

Our argument further centered around the analytical, some would call ideological, preference of the Fund, for greater reliance on market forces in economic decision making. Allowing domestic prices to move into line with global prices is one endeavor of this preference, but it also goes beyond

---

[17]Ibrahim Dogo, "The Political Economy of The IMF: Instability and Crisis" Economist, 3 May 1986, p.

[18]Lance Taylor, IS/LM in the Tropies: Diagrammatics of the New Structuralist Macro Critique, in Economic Stabilization in Developing countries, ed by William and Sidney (Washington: The Brookings Institution, 1981) p. 463-506.

[19]Brandt Commission, North-South: A Program For Survival: Report of the Independent Commission on International Development Issues, (Cambridge: Massachusetts Institute of Technology, 1980), p. 215-217.

[20]UNICEF, The Impact of World Recession on Children (New York: UNICEF, 1984)

liberalizing domestic markets in general. On efficiency evaluations, therefore the IMF demands for reduction in state intervention in the form of price, exchange and import controls, and of market-distorting tariffs and subsidies. However, the case against this emphasis is that market prices are suspect as guides to effective resource allocation or optimal investment in a context in which social costs and benefits deviate from private ones, which is especially likely to be the case when far-reaching structural changes are taking place in the society.[21]   Considering the structure and narrowness of the Nigerian market, the decisions based on market prices are not appropriate. Also, Olu Akaraogun argues that there is a case for the use of controls or direct state intervention in Nigeria and that prices are so "profoundly important that markets cannot in general be trusted to set them.[22]

Therefore, even if in the present situations it might make sense to move some prices in the same direction that the market is moving them, it does not follow that complete Laisser-Faire is the solution to Nigeria's economic problems.

The policy initiative of IMF adjustment strategies is toward integrating its members more fully into the world capitalist economic system through trade and payments liberalization. In this regard, Fund prescription is entirely consistent with the purposes of the IMF as laid down in Article I of its Articles of Agreement. For example, on the trade side, the emphasis is very much on export expansion, while on the payments side Fund strategies serve to improve the internationalization of capital in the form both of bank debt and of direct foreign investment. In fact, the IMF goes so far as to argue that "expanded flows of direct investment to the less developed countries are in everybody's interest-hence the IMF is encouraging Third World countries to remove obstacles to such flows and to place greater emphasis on policies designed to attract foreign private investment as part of their development strategy.[23]

A real point can be made that this underlying strategic thrust to Fund conditionality is not line with that prescribed by the Lagos Plan of Action

---

[21]Africa Today, 1986.

[22]Akaraogun Olu, "Politics of IMF Loan to Nigeria" Daily Times, Lagos, 25 February 1987, p. 6.

[23]J. de Larosiere, "Does The Fund Impose Austerity?" (Washington: IMF 1984).

(LPA) to which more than 50 African governments are signatories. The Lagos Plan of Action takes the decline in African agriculture as an indication that current development strategies are not working and that new directions are necessary. The Lagos Plan of Action further states:

> The effect of unfulfilled promises of global development strategies has been more sharply felt in Africa than in the other continents of the world.   Indeed, rather than result in an improvement in the economic situation of the continent, successive strategies have made it stagnate.. faced with this situation, and determined to undertake measures for the basic restructuring of the economic base of our continent, we resolved to adopt a far-reaching regional approach based primarily on collective self-reliance.[24]

The objective of self-reliance provides the cornerstone of the LPA and distinguishes it, in an essential way, from many of the alternative development strategies that have been proposed for Africa. It seeks to restructure Africa's links with countries outside the continent. As Lagos Plan of Action indicates:

> Africa must cultivate the virtue of self-reliance. This is not to say that the continent should totally cut itself off from outside contributions. However, these outside contributions should only supplement our own effort: they should not be mainstay of our development.[25]

The LPA focuses on national efforts for greater self-reliance but it also emphasizes the need for regional and sub-regional cooperation. What it envisages as self-reliance is development that incorporates the following attributes:

1   it relies on national and regional resources and therefore reduces the dependence of Africa on inputs and technical know-how imported from outside the region;

2   it responds to internally-formulated priorities and needs;

---

[24]OAU, "Lagos Plan of Action for the Economic Development of Africa, 1980-2000," (Geneva: International Institute for Labor studies, 1981).

[25]Ibid., p. 25.

3   at the regional level, it coordinates and integrates the economic activities of African state and

4   at the international level, it attempts to change the economic and technical relationships between African states and industrialized countries "from one of dependence to one of true interdependence", that is, to strengthen the position of African states within the context of economic, technical, and other forms of negotiation and exchange <u>vis-a-vis</u> the position of the industrialized countries.[26]

The LPA called for the design and pursuit of a uniquely African strategy based on "internally generated, self-sustained processes of development," and on "national and collective self-reliance". Central to this strategy is an explicit drive towards self-sufficiency on food production, greater regional integration, and less reliance on traditional exports and markets.[27] These strategic emphases are for the most part quite at odds with those of the Fund, and it is instructive that in the review of its own performance in Africa, the Fund apparently made no mention of the LPA. This is perhaps not surprising since the literature on stabilization is remarkably silent on the issue of economic strategy, even when it is proposing alternatives to the orthodoxy.

For these reasons, the justification for alternative programs to stabilization lies, therefore, in the weak theoretical consideration of the IMF's current approach as well as in its indifferent track record in practice. In outlining the nature of possible alternative adjustment programs one can be guided by the perceived shortcomings of Fund programs outlined in Chapter 11. To start with, and in contrary to the IMF approach, we do not provide a blueprint for adjustment to be applied in all circumstance. Rather, we suggest that alternative approaches should be tailored to the structural characteristics of the country in question, to deal with the specific economic crisis being experienced at any specific time. Hence, alternative approaches could be expected to vary greatly between and among nations depending upon their economic structure and the precise cause of their disequilibrium. At the sam time, the mix between finance and adjustment would also vary according to these factors to a much greater degree than it does now with relatively more

---

[26]Ibid.
[27]The Lagos Plan of Action vs. The Berg Report," 1984.

finance being made available where exogenous shocks are clearly the main source of disequilbrium.

Also member states would be much more strongly involved in the design and implementation of alternative programs than they appear to be at present. This would be justified on the ground that "conditionality --must reflect the sovereign right of states to choose their own social and economic approaches and development paths."[28]

Furthermore, without this serious involvement, the effectiveness of programs is likely to continue to be severely limited simply because programs that are imposed do not stand. Members would be free, of course, to call on assistance from outside agencies and individuals; the important point is that nations would enter into negotiations with the IMF with their own clearly articulated, internally consistent, and feasible set of proposals to deal with economic disequilibrium.

Most importantly, alternative strategies should provide for stabilization with economic development. They should realized, further that the import restraint is the single most essential factor variable prohibiting both domestic and export growth in LDCs. Precisely,, alternative approaches should provide for external help to as far as possible precede or, at worst, accompany major policy initiative.   Our argument for this is that unless consumer and intermediate goods are in supply, increased prices and other incentives will accomplish little by mean of promoting exports or production in general and will tend, simply to be inflationary. Alternative measures would hence take a very different phasing of both assistance and adjustment measures from those of the normal Fund policies.

Increased imports resulting from an agreement according to Murray would be allocated in a very selective manner to priority areas and commodities using both market and non-market mechanism, with the three principal goals being restoring the output of crucial, locally produced basic needs or incentives goods, promoting exports, and raising production of important tax-revenue generating goods.[29]

---

[28]The Arusha Initiative, Development Dialogue (Uppsala) No. 2, (1980).

[29]Colin Murray, "Latin American Experiment in Neo Conservative Economic," Journal of Development Studies, Vol. 20., (August 1983), p. 71.

Furthermore, supply expansion would be the essence of alternative programs and adjustment would focus on a limited number of important areas and on selective, as opposed to economy wide, policy initiatives.[30] Increased food sufficiency in terms of basic foodstuffs (as opposed to luxury goods), such as cocoa or cotton would undoubtedly be a major preoccupation of Third World stabilization measures given the catastrophic condition in most of their continents.   In reality, it could be argued that this should be the main objective of stabilization endeavors at this time, since success in this area would accomplish several objectives; it would clearly contribute to the meeting of basic needs; would seriously be progressive in its distributional impplication, given the structure of land ownership in most of the LDCs; it would minimize the import bill of many countries by between 5 and 30% and heighten self-reliance and national economic integration; it would contribute to growth and, in the medium term, would help to minimize both inflationary pressures and the need for government subsidization of urban food consumption.   Furthermore, reliability of food surpluses might also create a strong foundation for the growth of manufacturing sector.[31] No other area is likely to offer such attractions to most developing nations.   These are, therefore, compelling reasons for a food-security stabilization strategy in Africa and other LDCs, a strategy which would be entirely consistent with the LPA.

Also, in reality a food-security measure would involve not only correcting the bias against the rural area in domestic terms of trade, but also developing an adequate structure of relative prices between food production and export crop production.   In general term stabilization programs adjustment measures both the IMF and World Bank structural have been much more concerned with the former than the latter.   Little emphasis has been paid to the cross-elasticity of supply between food and exports and truely no explicit weight seems to have been made to the desirability per se of food self-sufficiency in Fund and Bank adjustment policies. Both these weaknesses would require correction.

---

[30]Alejandro Foxley, Latin American Experiment in Neo Conservative Economics (Berkeley: University of Californai Press, 1983).

[31]Inn Adelman, "Beyond Export-Led Growth", World Development, (Oxford, Vol. 12, No. 9, September 1984), pp. 937-954.

Additionally, alternative strategies would explicitly outline their likely distributional implications. Clearly, they would be followed by a clearly spelled-out income policy,[32] which would contain the government's perspective of how the burden of stabilization would be shared. Certainly, the IMF policy should make provision for incentive programs so that urban workers could be encouraged to minimize cuts in real income through increases in their productivity. However, those nations committed to ensuring greater equity according to Helleiner might wish to safeguard a portion of the government budget committed to such basic expenditures as health, education, and water supply and to monitor the implication of adjustment programs on the receipt of such services by those groups considered specificly vulnerable. The well-being of children should, of course, be first concern in this endeavor, and concrete policies should be taken to prevent increases in the incidence of infant mortality, malnutrition and deprivation of food, water, health care, and education. Attempts to reduce budget deficits would, as far as possible, therefore protect these expenditures and focus on restraining spending in other areas or on raising revenue. The less well-off groups of society might also be given a degree of protection against structural adjustment programs through the maintenance of limited subsidies on basic food stocks, through price control on, or rationing of items essentials in their budgets or through increases in the minimum wage.   Each of these recommendation is open to objections on efficiency grounds, but may be justified in terms of equity where it can be proved that their benefits accrue predominantly to the low-income target units. The severity of the economic crisis in the LDCs is such that it would be impossible to protect all low-income groups fully from the implication of adjustment programs. The best that can be accomplished for is a more equitable sharing of the burden and a concerned effort to prevent basic needs from being out of reach completely. In this respect, the restoration of positive per capita growth rates, and an unambiguous focus on expanded food production would greatly facilitate more equitable macro economic stabilization policies. In addition, this approach suggests the removal of price control on all but essential goods

---

[32]Alejandro Foxley, Latin American Experiment in Neo Conservative Economic (Berkeley: University of California Press, 1983).

and the focusing of limited subsidies on goods and services consumed largely by the poor group.

Finally, alternative programs to IMF stabilization would, therefore, be more supply oriented than are traditional Fund measures, would avoid shock treatment and provide for more gradual, longer-term adjustment with more sensitivity to distributional implications. Strategic effects of stabilization policies would be put much more to the fore and an across-the-board commitment to export production would be avoided. Food sufficiency would be given first priority, and provision would be made for the pursuit of other measures in line with the LPA. In reality, increased exports would be encouraged since additional foreign exchange earnings would be needed to finance this eclectic strategic approach, to assist pay off debt-servicing obligations and to help reduce external economic dependency.

This approach emphasis less reliance on market forces than would the IMF and envisages a blend of direct controls and state intervention together with enhanced use of the price mechanism in some sectors. The precise mix would again vary from country to country depending on the structure and level of their economic problems.

In conclusion, therefore, we share the same view with Helleiner, Cavangh, and others that the International Monetary Fund should seriously consider the following points in its future endeavor:

1.   As in the political arena, so it is true in the economic: power derives its ultimate legitimacy from the consent of the governed. The International Financial system, so long dominated by private organizations, needs to be democratized. Increased public authority and democratic controls are necessary if the present inequitable system is to be replaced with a fairer one.

2.   Because of the shortage of available external resources for supporting economic adjustment measures necessary for a durable economic recovery, the IMF should rapidly approve a new allocation of SDRs, the main part of which should be reserved for less developed countries to finance their balance of payments deficits and particularly to settle their external debts. Such a decision by the IMF, whose major member states are official creditors of deficit developing countries, would allow the international community to

move toward a lasting solution to the thorny problem of external debt in the poor nations.

3.   The international monetary system includes policies which need to be adapted to recent developments in the global economy. Since the reform initiated many years ago fell far short of meeting the needs of an important category of member countries, we emphasize that efforts at reform should be resumed and taken into consideration the changes that have occurred since Bretton Woods. Doing so will help the IMF fully to perform the function expected by all its members, particularly in resource mobilization, economic adjustment and supervision, with the aim of creating an equitable sharing of the austerity burden between the rich and the poor nations.

4.   Currently, representation and voting in international financial organizations such as the International Monetary Fund are based on economic power: "one dollar, one vote". Thus, the United States and other industrial states exercise dominant influence over these institutions' decisions, while the vast majority of poorer countries have no real power at all. In accord with democratic principles, voting power in these institutions should reflect the basic United Nations principle of "one nation, one vote".

5.   The structural nature of the balance of payments deficits of most developing nations, particularly African countries demands large financial resources over many years. The present limitation on the use of the IMF's resources is not an answer to the needs and expectations of many, particularly African, member nations. The IMF should review its access policy, a lasting solution would be to enlarge the recurrent resources of this institution through increases in quotas and to reserve a large part of this increase for countries with low quotas to allow them more access to resources needed to adjust their economies.

6.   The role played by the IMF in the renegotiation of the external debt of some of its member states has become very significant that creditors systematically demand that these nations conclude stand-by arrangement with the IMF before starting any discussion. The IMF should use this opportunity to request that creditors set conditions that would encourage economic recovery in developing countries and, more importantly to persist that they provide new financial facilities to those nations that successfully apply substantial adjustment measures. Such financial support is necessary to

ensuring the smooth functioning of the economy and would allow recipient countries to continue to meet their external responsibilities.

7.   Given the growing economic interdependence among nations, all countries should be members of major international financial organizations.   Universality also requires ending discrimination within the organizations against nations whose social and economic systems and macroeconomic objectives differ from those of the dominant western societies.[33]

---

[33]   Helleiner, Africa and the IMF Cavanagh, From Debt To Development.

APPENDIX

Appendix 1

EXPENDITURE ON THE GROSS DOMESTIC PRODUCT (1981-1984)
₦ Million

	1981/82	1982/83	1983/84
Government final consumption expenditure	5,503.5	5,50.0	5,560.7
Private final consumption expenditure	33,853.3	36,834.8	33,843.0
Increase in stocks	673.5	450.0	391.5
Gross fixed capital formation	13,318.2	10,870.4	8,925.1
Total domestic expenditure	53,348.5	53,659.2	48,720.3
Exports of goods and services	11,375.8	9,650.2	7,806.7
Less Imports of goods and services	16,081.9	12,119.3	7,875.3
GDP in purchasers' values	48,642.5	51,190.1	48,651.7
GDP at constant 1977/78 prices	30,366.2	29,860.1	27,861.3

Source: U.N., *National Accounts Statistics*, 1986.

Appendix 2

GROSS DOMESTIC PRODUCT BY ECONOMIC ACTIVITY
₦ million at factor cost
1981-1984

	1981/82	1982/83	1983/84
Agriculture and hunting	7,952.4	10,092.8	9,369.5
Forestry and logging	321.7	329.7	337.7
Fishing	1,589.0	1,987.8	2,458.5
Mining and quarrying	12,400.2	11,555.4	9,923.0
Manufacturing	2,647.5	2,726.3	2,372.5
Electricity, gas and water	309.7	386.0	460.3
Construction	4,001.6	3,603.0	3,268.3
Wholesale and retail trade	10,449.7	10,463.6	10,344.6
Restaurants and hotels	115.1	130.1	145.3
Transport, storage and communications	2,129.0	2,396.5	2,187.7
Finance, insurance, real estate and business services	1,161.7	1,298.1	1,494.3
Government services	2,569.9	2,809.1	2,911.5
Other community, social and personal services	1,398.1	1,492.0	1,498.9
Total	47,045,4	49,370.4	46,772.6

Source: U.N., National Accounts Statistics, 1985.

Appendix 3

FOURTH NATIONAL DEVELOPMENT PLAN
January 1981-December 1985 Investment Programme - ₦ million

Sector	Allocation
Agriculture	5,588.9
Power	3,278.7
Electricity Distribution	271.0
Rural electrification	1,345.4
Transport	10,504.1
Roads	8,863.0
Railways	1.630.0
Air transport	653.1
Water transport	988.0
Communications	2,000.0
Telecommunications	1,700.0
Postal services	300.0
Education	7,533.5
Teacher training institutions	782.7
Secondary education	1.908.6
Technical education	1,077.3
Scholarships	752.7
Health	3,066.6
Labour and social welfare	178.5
Information	624.1
Regional development	4,869.9
Housing	2,661.7
Water supply	2,940.4
Defence and security	3,940.0
General administration	2,247.0
Public sector investment	70,500.0
State governments	28,000.0
Private sector investment	11,500.0

Under the Plan, GDP at constant 1973/74 factor cost is
projected to rise from about ₦18,740 million in 1979/80 to
₦27,941.1 million in 1984/85, implying an average annual
growth rate of 8.3%.

Source: Central Planning Office, Lagos, 1986.

Appendix 4

GROSS DOMESTIC PRODUCT
(Constant prices)

Year	GDP, Nbn	GDP per head
1975	27.2	360
1976	30.0	385
1977	32.1	405
1978	30.2	370
1979	32.2	380
1980	30.8	355
1981	29.9	335
1982	29.9	325
1983	27.4	290
1984	25.9	365
1985	26.2	260
1986	25.3	245
1987	25.6	240
1988	26.8	230

Sources: Federal Government and various independent
      estimates. Also see Africa Research Bulletin,
      March 31, 1988, p. 9032.

Appendix 5

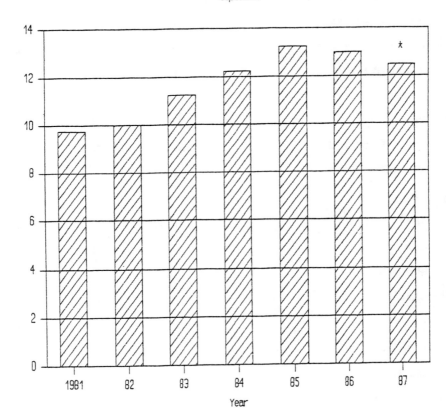

MONEY SUPPLY

* September

Source: Central Bank of Nigeria, 1989.

Appendix 6

PRINCIPAL TRADING PARTNERS (₦ million)

Imports*	1982†	1983†	1985
Belgium and Luxembourg	271.3	364.9	108.1
China, People's Republic	197.3	38.3	37.3
Czechoslovakia	24.7	19.2	2.7
Denmark	111.0	68.0	41.4
France	888.0	1,197.9	458.0
Germany, Federal Republic	1,973.3	1,274.5	650.6
Hong Kong	222.0	296.8	36.8
India	24.7	19.1	24.8
Italy	838.6	422.3	211.5
Japan	1,356.6	890.5	408.3
Netherlands	518.0	451.0	202.6
Norway	49.3	87.2	18.6
Poland	86.3	19.2	18.8
Switzerland	98.7	210.8	115.0
U.S.S.R.	37.0	38.8	68.1
United Kingdom	2,750.2	2,010.8	1,098.7
U.S.A.	1,381.3	1,359.7	741.6
Total (including others)	12,332.9	9,575.1	5,536.9

*Figures for 1984 are not available.

†Estimates.

Source (all external trade statistics): Central Bank of
    Nigeria, 1986.

Appendix 7

PRINCIPAL TRADING PARTNERS (₦ million)

Exports	1983*	1984†	1985
Belgium and Luxembourg	49.4	-	6.1
Denmark	86.1	51.3	9.3
France	1,507.2	1,924.2	1,902.7
Germany, Federal Republic	888.4	915.1	863.5
Ghana	43.6	140.2	171.4
Italy	826.4	1,457.1	1,921.0
Netherlands	637.2	1,135.6	1,434.2
United Kingdom	197.4	298.8	538.6
U.S.A.	1,645.9	1,210.9	2,116.3
Total (including others)	7,201.2	8,840.6	11,720.8

Note: 1983-84 figures based on oil exports alone.

*Provisional.

†Estimates.

Source (all external trade statistics): Central Bank of
    Nigeria, 1986.

Appendix 8

NIGERIA'S FISCAL CHANGES UNDER BABANGIDA'S REGIME

(i) Downward adjustment of import tariffs:

(a) New rates for commercial vehicle tyres 5% and for tractor tyres 5%

(b) New rates for copper and aluminum sections and wire 10%

(c) New rate on R20 batteries 25%

(d) New rate on vehicle parts and accessories 5%

(e) New rate on lorries, trucks, vans and four-wheel drive vehicles 20%

(f) New rate on buses 10%

(g) New rates on completely knocked down (CKD) components between 5-10%, depending on location of assembly plant

(h) New rate for outboard engines and boats 10%

(i) New rate for outboard engines and boats 10%

(ii) Advance payment of import duty has been reduced to 25%, with the remaining 75% payable when goods arrive in Nigeria

(iii) Import duty surcharge of 6% has been re-introduced, following the abrogation of the 30% import levy which applied from january 1st - September 26th, 1986.

(iv) Raw materials and components for manufactured goods for export can not be imported duty free

(v) Reduction in corporation tax rate from 45% to 40%

(vi) The highest rate of income tx is now 55%, down from 70% previously, and chargeable on incomes above N40,000 a year

(vii) Tax free dividends on new investments between January 1st, 1987 - December 31st, 1992. The tax free period is three years — or five years if the company is engaged in agricultural production or processing or production of petrochemicals or liquefied natural gas

(viii) Expatriate home remittance increased from 50% to 75% of net salary

(ix) The air travel levy of N100 a ticket abolished

(x) Growth in money supply restricted to 11.8% in 1987

(xi) Growth in aggregate bank credit restricted to 4.4%

(xii) Bank interest rates fixed at a maximum of 15% on lending and a minimum of 12% on time deposits

Source: Africa Research Bulletin, January 31, 1984, p. 8513.

Appendix 9

EXECUTIVE DIRECTORS AND VOTING POWER ON APRIL, 30, 1989

Director Alternate	Casting Votes of	Votes by Country	Total Votes[1]	Percent of Fund Total[2]
APPOINTED				
Charles H. Dallara *Charles S. Warner*	United States	179,433	179,433	19.14
Frank Cassell *Carles Enoch* Guenter Grosche	United Kingdom	62,190	62,190	6.63
	Germany, Federal Republic of	54,287	54,287	5.79
Hélène Ploix *Dominique Marcel* Koji Yamazake	France	45,078	45,078	4,81
	Japan	42,483	42,483	4.53
Yusuf A. Nimatallah *Ibrahim A. AlAssaf*	Saudi Arabia	32,274	32,274	3.44
ELECTED				
Renato Filosa (Italy) *Nikos Kyriazidis (Greece)*	Greece Italy Malta Poland Portugal	4,249 29,341 701 7,050 4,016	45,357	4.84
Leonor Filardo (Venezuela) *Miguel A. Fernández Ordóñez (Spain)*	Costa Rica El Salvador Guatemala Honduras Mexico Nicaragua Spain Venezuela	1,091 1,140 1,330 928 11,905 932 13,110 13,965	44,401	4.74
G.A. Posthumus (Netherlands) *G.P.J. Hogeweg (Netherlands)*	Cyprus Israel Netherlands Romania Yugoslavia	947 4,716 22,898 5,484 6,380	40,425	4.31
Jacques de Groote (Belgium) *Johann Prader (Austria)*	Austria Belgium Hungary Luxembourg Turkey	8,006 21,054 5,557 1,020 4,541	40,178	4.29
Mohamed Finaish (Libya) *Abdul Moneim Othman (Iraq)*	Bahrain Egypt Iraq Jordan Kuwait Lebanon Libya Maldives Oman Pakistan Qatar Somalia Syrian Arab Republic United Arab Emirates Yemen Arab Republic Yemen, People's Democratic Republic of	739 4,884 5,290 989 6,603 1,037 5,407 270 881 5,713 1,399 692 1,641 2,276 683 1,022	39,526	4.22
Marcel Massé (Canada) *Dara McCormack (Ireland)*	Antigua and Barbuda The Bahamas Barbados Belize Canada Dominica Grenada Ireland Jamaica St. Kitts and Nevis St. Lucia St. Vincent	300 914 591 345 29,660 290 310 3,684 1,705 295 325 290	38,709	4.13
E.A. Evans (Australia) *Chang-Yuel Lim (Korea)*	Australia Kiribati Korea New Zealand Papua New Guinea Philippines Seychelles Solomon Islands Vanuatu Western Samoa	16,442 275 4,878 4,866 909 4,654 280 300 340 310	33,254	3.55

Director Alternate	Casting Votes of	Votes by Country	Total Votes[1]	Percent of Fund Total[2]
ELECTED (continued)				
Jorgen Ovi (Denmark) Markus Fogelholm (Finland)	Denmark Finland Iceland Norway Sweden	7,360 5,999 846 7,240 10,893	32,338	3.45
Bimal Jalan (India) L.Eustace N. Fernando (Sri Lanka)	Bangladesh Bhutan India Sri Lanka	3,125 275 22,327 2,481	28,208	3.01
Alexandre Kafka (Brazil) Luis Manuel Piantini (Dominican Republic)	Brazil Colombia Dominican Republic Ecuador Guyana Haiti Panama Suriname Trinidad and Tobago	14,863 4,192 1,371 1,757 742 691 1,272 743 1,951	27,582	2.94
J.E. Ismael (Indonesia) Skamol Kiriwat (Thailand)	Fiji Indonesia Lao People's Democratic Republic Malaysia Myanmar Nepal Singapore Thailand Tonga Viet Nam	615 10,347 543 5,756 1,620 623 1,174 4,116 282 2,018	27,094	2,89
El Tayeb El Kogali (Sudan) L.B. Monyake (Lesotho)	Botswana Burundi Ethiopia The Gambia Kenya Lesotho Liberia Malawi Mozambique Nigeria Sierra Leone Sudan Swaziland Tanzania Uganda Zambia Zimbabwe	471 677 956 421 1,670 401 963 622 860 8,745 829 1,947 497 1,320 1,246 2,953 2,160	26,738	2.85
DAI Qianding (China) ZHANG Zhixiang (China)	China	24,159	24,159	2.58
Ernesto V. Feldman (Argentina) Ricardo J. Lombardo (Uruguay)	Argentina Bolivia Chile Paraguay Peru Uruguay	11,380 1,157 4,655 734 3,559 1,888	23,373	2.49
Mohammad Reza Ghasimi (Islamic Republic of Iran) Omar Kabbaj (Morocco)	Afghanistan Algeria Ghana Iran, Islamic Republic of Morocco Tunisia	1,117 6,481 2,295 6,850 3,316 1,632	21,691	2.31
MAWAKANI Samba (Zaire) Corentino V. Santos (Cape Verde)	Benin Burkina Faso Cameroon Cape Verde Central African Republic Chad Comoros Congo Côte d'Ivoire Djibouti Equatorial Guinea Gabon Guinea Guinea-Bissau Madagascar Mali Mauritania Mauritius Niger	563 566 1,177 295 554 556 295 623 1,905 330 434 981 829 325 914 758 589 786 587		

Director Alternate	Casting Votes of	Votes by Country	Total Votes[1]	Percent of Fund Total[2]
ted (concluded)				
	Rwanda	688		
	Sao Tome and Principe	290		
	Senegal	1,101		
	Togo	634		
	Zaire	3,160	18,940 927,718[3]	2.02 98.94[2,4]

[1]Voting power varies on certain matters pertaining to the General Department with use of the Fund's resources
that Department.

[2]Percentages of total votes in the General Department and the SDR Department (937,625).

[3]This total does not include the votes of Democratic Kampuchea and South Africa, which did not participate
the 1988 Regular Election of Executive Directors. The combined votes of those members total 9,907 — 1.06 percent of
e in the General Department and SDR Department.

[4]This figure may differ from the sum of the percentages shown for individual Directors because of rounding.

urce: IMF Annual Report, Washington, D.C., 1989,
pp. 104-106.

Appendix 10

INTERNATIONAL MONETARY FUND
GENERAL DEPARTMENT
STATUS OF ARRANGEMENTS

As of April 30, 1989
(In thousands of SDRs)

Member	Date of Arrangement	Expiration	Total Amount Agreed	Undrawn Balance
GENERAL RESOURCES ACCOUNT				
STAND-BY ARRANGEMENTS				
Brazil	August 23, 1988	February 28, 1990	1,096,000	730,700
Cameroon	September 19, 1988	March 31, 1990	69,525	46,350
Guatemala	October 26, 1988	February 28, 1990	54,000	30,840
Hungary	May 16, 1988	May 15, 1989	265,350	50,000
Jamaica	September 19, 1988	May 31, 1990	82,000	68,300
Kenya	February 1, 1988	July 31, 1989	85,000	22,400
Madagascar	September 2, 1988	July 1, 1989	13,300	10,500
Malawi	March 2, 1988	May 30, 1989	13,020	3,770
Mali	August 5, 1988	October 4, 1989	12,700	10,160
Morocco	August 30, 1988	December 31, 1989	210,000	140,000
Nigeria	February 3, 1989	April 30, 1990	475,000	475,000
Pakistan	December 28, 1988	March 27, 1990	273,150	104,890
Trinidad and Tobago	January 13, 1989	February 28, 1990	99,000	56,500
Yugoslavia	June 28, 1988	June 27, 1989	306,000	183,600
			3,054,045	1,933,010
EXTENDED ARRANGEMENTS				
Chile	August 15, 1985	August 14, 1989	825,000	37,500
Tunisia	July 25, 1988	July 24, 1991	207,300	207,300
			1,032,300	244,800
			4,086,345	2,177,810
TOTAL GENERAL RESOURCES ACCOUNT				

Source: International   Monetary   Fund   Annual   Report,
Washington, D.C., 1989, p. 126.

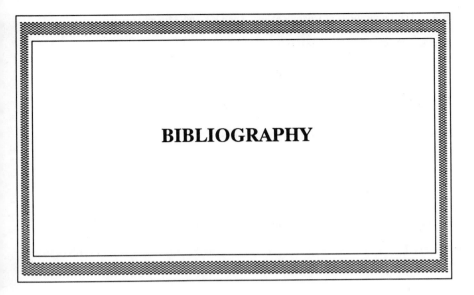

BIBLIOGRAPHY

Abadalla, Ismail-Sabri. "The Inadequacy and Loss of Legitimacy of the IMF," Development Dialogue. 1980.

Adedeji, Adebayo. Economic Commission for Africa and Africa's Development, 1983-2008: A Preliminary Persepective Study. (Addis baba ECA, 1983).

Adelman, Inn. "Beyond Export Led Growth." World Development, Oxford, Vol. 12, No. 9 (September 1984).

Africa, No. 49 (September, 1975).

Africa Analysis No. 1 (11 July 1986).

African Continental Bank of Nigeria. "Balance of Payment Report From Second Tier Foreign Exchange Market." Lagos News December 1987.

African Development Vol. 10, No. 3 (March 1976).

African Economic Digest, London, 23 March 1984.

African Market. "Nigerian's Shh! Devaluation. " New Africa (September 1986).

African Review. 3 December 1980.

African News (4 February 1985).

Africa Red Family, Vol. 2, No. 3 (1975).

Africa Research Bulletin, (31 March 1985).

Africa Research Bulletin, Economic Series, (October 15, 1979).

_____. (14 October 1987).

Africa South of the Sahara. London: Eruope Publication, 1983.

Ainley, E. M. The IMF: Past, Present and Future. Cardiff: University of Wales Press, 1979.

Akaradgun, Olu C. "Politics of IMF Loan to Nigeria." Nigerian Daily Times, 15 February 1985.

Ake, Claude. A Political Economy of Africa. Nigeria: Longman Nigeria Limited, 1981.

Akin, Mabogurije. The Development Process: A Spatial Perspective. New York: Holmes & Meier, 1981.

Akinsanya, Adeoye. Economic Interdependence and Indigenization of Private Foreign Investments: The experience of Nigeria and Ghana. New York: Praeger, 1983.

Alfred, Helen, ed. The Bretton Woods Agreement and Why It Is Necessary. Citizens Conference on International Union, 1944.

Ali Abdel, Gadier. "Everything You Already Know About the IMF." African Business October 1986.

Aliber, Robert. Monetary Reform and World Inflation. California: Sage Publication, 1973.

Almed, Abdelkair. "Nigeria: The Agonies of Adjustment." West Africa October 1984.

Aluko. "Nigeria Will Survive Without IMF Loan." New Nigeria 20 September 1985.

Aluko, S.A. and Ijere, M.O. "The Economics of Mineral Oil," Nigerian Journal of Economic and Social Studies, Vol. 7 (1965).

Amin, Samir. Imperialism and Unequal Development New York: Monthly Review Press, 1976.

_____ Self-Reliance and the New International Economic Order Monthly Review, (July-August 1977).

Arodnson, Jonathan D. The Impact of American Commercial Banks on the International Money. New Jersey: Princeton University Press, 1980.

Arnold, Guy. Modern Nigeria. London: Longman Group, 1977.

Ascher, William. "New Development Approach and the Adaptability of International Agencies: The Case of the World Bank." International Organization 37 (Summer 1983).

Asimota, Peter, "The IMF-Nigeria Deadlock, "New Nigeria". April 1985.

Associated Press, "Nigerian President Sticks with Austerity Policies" The Atlanta Journal and Consititution, 6 June 1989.

_____ "Oil Boom's End Leaves Nigeria Over a Barrel", Sunday News Journal 8 January 1984.

Atlantic Council of the United States. The International Monetary System, Progress and Prospects. Westview Press, 1977.

Awolowo, Obafemi. The People's Republic. Ibadan: Oxford Universtiy Press, 1968.

_____. The Autobiography of Chief Obafemi. Ibadan: Cambridge: Cambridge University Press, 1960.

Ayagi, I.A. "Consequences of Accepting IMF Loan." New Nigeria 21 September 1985.

Ayida, A.A., and Onitri, H.M.A., ed. Reconstruction and Development In Nigeria. Ibadan: Oxford University Press, 1971.

"Babangida's Challenge Nigerian Economy." Imo State Statesman 6 March 1986.

Babangida, Ibrahim.   "Nigerian At Twenty-Six Year."   New Nigeria 6 November 1986.

Babangida, Ibrahim.   "Nigerian Budget Aims to Reflate Economy." Newswatch, February 1987.

"Background Notes on the International Monetary Fund." Debelopment Dialogue. 1980.

Balabkins, Nicholas.   Indigenization and Economic Development: The Nigerian Experience. Longon, England: JalPRess, 1982.

Belassa, Bela. Trade Liberalization Among Industrial Countries. New York: McGraw-Hill, 1967.

Bello, V.I.   "The Intentions, Implementation Process and Problems of the Nigerian Enterprises Promotion Decree (No. 4) 1972" In Nigeria's Indigenisation Policy, Proceedings of the 1974 Symposium Organized by the Nigerian Economic Society. Ibadan: The Caxton Press, 1975.

Berger, Manfred. Industrialization Policies in Nigeria. Munich: Weltforun Verlag, 1975.

Bhatia, J.B. and Tahari, Amor.   "External Debt Management and Macroeconomic Variables: Problems of African Countries in the 980s." Presented at a seminar on External Debt Problems of African Countries Organized by the African Center for Monetary Studies, Tunis, Tunisia, September 1983. Newswatch. March 1984.

Bienen, Henry, and V.P. Diejomaoh (eds.) The Political Economy of Income Distribution in Nigeria New York: Holmes and Meier, 1981.

Birnbaum, Eugene A. Gold and the Internationaal Monetary System: An Orderly Reform. Princeton, New Jersey: Princeton University Press, 1968.

_____. Changing the U.S. Commitment to Gold. Princeton, New Jersey: Princeton University Press, 1967.

Black, C. E. The Dynamic of Modernization. New York: Harper Row, 1966.

Black, Stanley W.   Exchange Policiesfor Less Developed Countries. Princeton, New Jersey: Princeton University Press, 1976.

Blackhum, Peter. "The Year of the IMF?" Africa Reprot No. 6 (1986).
Blaine, Harden. "Nigeria: Welcome to Hard Times." Washington Post (23 March 1987).

Blake, David H. and Walters, Robert S. The Politics of Global Economic Relations. Nw Jersey: Prentice Halls, Inc., Englewood Cliffs, Third Edition, 1987.

Block, Fred. The Origins of International Economic Disorder. Los Angeles: University of California Press, 1977.

Boddie Michael. "Africa, the IMF and the World, New Nigeria, March-April, 1983.

Bolin, William H. and Decanto, Joge. "LDC Debt: Beyond Crisis Management." Foreign Affairs Fall 1981.

Botswana Daily News. 6 March 1985.

Brandt, Willy. Independent Commission on International Issues North-South: A Program for Survival. Cambridge, Massachusetts: MIT Press, 1980.

Brooke, James. "Ailing Nigeria Opens Its Economy," The New York Times, August 15, 1988.

Brown, Welt M. World Without National Policies Ruling the Waves. Princeton, New Jersy: Princeton University Press, 1976.

Browne, Robert and cummings, Robert J. The Lagos Plan of Action vs The Berg Report. Washington, D.C.: Howard University Press, 1984.

Brunner, Allan H. Politics for Employment, Prices and Exchange Rates. Amsterdam/New York: North-Holland Publishing Company, 1979.

Buhari, Muhammadu. "Budgeting for Recovery." West African Magazine (April 1984).

Burns, S. A. History of Nigeria London: University of London Press, 1969.

Business Concord, 6 July 1986.

_____. 4 July 1986.

Business International. Nigeria: Africa's Economic Giant, Geneva: Business International, 1979.

Camps, Murian. Collective Management: The Program of Global Economic Organizations. New York: McGraw-Hill, 1981.

Carbaugh, Robert J. The International Monetary System: History, Institutions Analysis. Lawrence, Kansas: University of Kansas Press, 1976.

Cavangh, John and Obadia, Cynthia. From Debt to Development. Washington, D.C.: Institute for Policy Studies, 1985.

Caves, Rhichard E. and Jones, Ronald W. World Trade and Payments. Boston: Little Brown and Company, 1981.

Central Bank of Nigeria Annual Reports and Economic and Financial Review, Various Issues posted Prices from United Nations Monthly Bulletin of Statistics, Novemver, 1976.

Central Bank of Nigeria. Annual Report: Logas, 1972 and 1974.

Central Bank of Nigeria. Annual Report: Various Issues Complied in 1980, Lagos: 1981.

Cervenka, Zkenek. The Nigerian Civil War, 1967-1970 Frankfurt; Bernard and Graefe Inc., 1971.

Chimeka, Uchem I. The Evolution of Nigerian Exchange Rate. Ibadan: Ibadan University Press, 1984.

Chisholm, Derek. The International Monetary System in Retrospect and Prospect: An Overview. Ottawa, Ontario: Conference Board of Canada, 1983.

Christian Science Monitor, 7 October 1986.

"Clarify Nigerian Fate Without IMF Loan." Nigerian Sunday Newspaper 22 September 1986.

Clark, Paul G. American Aid for Development. New York: Praeger Publisher, 1972.

Cline, W. and Weiintraub, S. Economic Stabilization in Developing Countries (Washington, D.C.: Brookings Instittue), 1981.

Cockcroft, James; Frank, A. G.; and Johnson, Dale. Dependence and Underdevelopment: Latin American Political Economy. New York: Doubleday & Company, INc., 1972.

Codhem, Benjamin J. The European Monetary System: An Outsider's View. Princeton, Ne wJersey: Princeton University Press, 1981.

Cohen, Benjamin. Balance of Payment. Baltimore: Penguin Books, 1972.

Coleman, J.S. Nigeria: Background to Nationalism, Berkley and Los Angeles: University of California Press, 1963.

Committee for Economic Development. Strengthening the World Monetary System. New York, 1973.

Cooper, Richard N. The International Monetary System Essays in World Economics. Cambridge, Massachusetts: MIT Press, 1982.

_____. The International Monetary System Under Flexible Exchange Rates. Cambridge, Massachusetts: MIT Press, 1982.

Daly, D. J. Globerman, S. Tariff and Science Policies: Application of a Model of Nationalism, Toronto: University of Toronto Press, 1976.

Damanchi, Ukandi G. Nigerian Modernization: The Colonial Legacy. New York: The Third Press, 1972.

Dan, Kenneth. The Rules of the Game: Reform and Evolution in the International Monetary System. Chicago: Chicago University Press, 1982.

Dangogo, Kabir. "Reject IMF Loan." Sunday News 22 September 1986.

Danny, Leipziger. The International Monetary System and the Developing Countries. Washington, D.C.: Agency for IDA, 1976.

De Larosiere, J. Does the Fund Impos Austerity? Washington, D.C.: International Monetary Fund, 1984.

De Vries, Margaret G. The International Monetary Fund, 1966-1971: The System Stress. Washington, D.C.: International Monetary Fund, 1976.

Dean, Edwin. Plan Implementation in Nigeria 1962-1968. Ibadan: Oxford University Press, 1972.

Diamond, Larry. "Nigeria High Stakes for Babangida," Africa Report November-December 1985.

Dike, Oji F. The Political Economy of the IMF. Ife: University of Ife Press, 1987.

Dudley, Billy. Instability and Political Order: Politics and Crisis in Nigeria, Ibadan: Ibadan University Press, 1973.

Eckes, Jr. A Search For Solvency Texas: Austin University Press, 1982.

Economic and Financial Review. Lagos, 1976.

Economic Commission for Latin American and the Caribbean (ECLAC). Debt, Adjust ment, and Renegotiation in Latin America: Orthodox and Alternative Approach. Boulder, Colorado: L. Rienner Publishers, 1986.

Economist 16 April 1983.

_____. 26 May 1983.

_____. 4 June 1984.

_____. 16 May 1985.

_____. Fall 1983.

_____. Vol 299. No. 7444 (3 May 1986).

Economist Intelligence Unit. Quarterly Economic Review of Zaire, Kwanda, Burundi, Vol. 1, No. 3 (1985).

Economic Journal Vol. 87 (Fall 1979).

Edelson, Rick, International Monetary Fund, New York: Praeger, 1980.

Editorial. "Nigeria and IMF Loan." New Nigeria 20 September 1985.

Editorial. "Nigeria's Outlook in the World Economy" Nigerian Observer Lagos 24 November 1984.

Eicher, Carl. Growth and Development of the Nigeria Economy. East Lansing: Michigan State University, 1970.

Eisenstadt, S. N. Protest and Change. Englewood Cliffs, New Jersy: Prentice-Hall, 1966.

Ejofor, Pita N.O. "Multinational Corporations As Agents of Imperialism" In B.O. Oribonoje, and O.A. Lawal (eds.), The Indigence for National Development, Ibadan: Oribonoje Publishers, 1976.

Eleazu, Uma. Federation and National Building, Elms Court, Devon: Arthur Stockwell, 1977.

Emeka, Eluem. "Nigeria vs. IMF>" New Africa December 1985.

Emminger, Otmiar. Inflation and the International Monetary System. Washington, D.C.: Jacobson Foundation, 1973.

Erb, Guy F. and Kallab, Valerianna, eds. Beyond Dependency: The Developing World Speaks Out. New York: Praeger, 1975.

Ezera, K. Constitutional Developments In Nigeria. London: Cambridge University Press, 1960.

Federal Reserve Bank. The International Monetary System, Forty Years after Bretton Woods. Boston: Federal Reserve Bank, 1984.

Federal Republic of Nigeria. Annual Abstract of Statistics. Lagos Federal Office of Statistics (Various Volumes), 1985 and 1987.

_____. "Annual Abstract of Statistics". Lagos Federal Office of Statistics (Various Volumes), 1982 and 1986.

_____. "National Development Plan: Progress Report." Federal Ministry of Development, March 1964.

_____. "Guide Posts for Second National Development Plan". Lagos: Ministry of Economic Development, June 1964.

_____. "Background Notes on the Nigerian Crisis". Lagos: Ministry of Information, 1968.

_____. "Second National Development Plan, 1970-74. Programme of Post-War Reconstruction and Development". Lagos: Ministry of Information, 1970.

_____. "Nigerian Enterprises Promotion Decree 1972". In supplement to Official Gazette Extraordinary 59, no. 10 (February), 1972.

_____. "Guidelines for the Third National Development Plan 1975-80". Lagos: Central Planning Office, 1973.

_____. "Second National Development Plan, 1970-74. First Progress Report", Lagos: Central Planning Office, 1973.

_____. "Second National Development Plan, 1970-74. Second Progress Report", Lagos: Central Planning Office, 1974.

_____. "Third National Development Plan, 1975-80. Special Launching Edition", Lagos: Central Planning Office, 1975.

_____. Economic and Statistical Review. Lagos 1976.

_____. Economic and Statistical Review. Lagos 1983.

_____. First Progress Report on Third National Development Plan, 1975-1980. Lagos: Central Planning Office, 1975.

_____. "Federal Military Government's View on the Report of the Industrial Enterprises Panel". Lagos: Federal Ministry of Information, 1976.

_____. "Economic and Statistical Review, 1978", Lagos: Federal Government Press, 1976.

_____. "An Address to the Nation on the 1984 Budget by Major-General Muhammadu Buhari, C.F.R., Head of the Federal Military Government, Commander-in-Chief of the Armed Forces on 7th May, 1984". Washington, D.C.: Nigeria Information Service, 1984.

_____. "Statement on the 1984 Budget by Dr. O. O. Loleye, Minister of Finance". Special news release. New York: Consulate General of Nigeria, May 9, 1984.

_____. "National Development Plan, 1962-68". Lagos: Federal Ministry of Economic Development, 1961.

Federal Republic of Nigeria. Economic and Statistical Review. Government Press, Lagos: 1980.

Federal Office of Statistics. Second National Development Plan: A Review of First National Development Plan, Lagos, 1975.

Federal Ministry of Economic Development. First National Development Plan (1962-1968): Sectoral Distribution, Lagos, 1965.

Federal Ministry of Economic Development. Third National Development Plan: 1975-1980, Vol. 1 Lagos: The Central Planning Office, 1979.

Feinberg, Richard and Kallab, Valeriana. Adjustment Crisis in the Third World, Washington, D.C.: Overseas Development Council, 1984.

Financial Times Survey. 18 February 1985.

Foxley, Alejandro. Latin American Experience in Neo-Conservative Economics. Berkeley: University of California Press, 1983.

Frank, A. G. Capitalist and Underdevelopment in Latin America. New York: Monthly Review Press, 1969.

Galbraith, J. K. "The Need for Foreign Investment" Newswatch Fall 1975.

Gardner, L.C. Economic Aspects of New Deal Diplomacy, Madison: University of Wisconsin, 1964.

Gardner, Richard and M.L. Kan, M. In the Global Partnership, New York: Praeger, 1968.

Gardner, Richard. Sterling Dollar Diplomacy rev. ed. New York: McGraw-Hill Book Co., 1969.

Gee, Wilson. Social Science Research Methods. New York: Appleton Century Crofts, 1950.

George, Edward. "Nigeria's Economy Faces New Burden," The New York Times 27 January 1986.

Girman, Norman. Corporate Imperialism: Conflict and Expropriation. New York: Monthly Review Press, 1980.

Girvan, Norman. "Harsh Correctives that made the Patient Worse." World Bank Review (March 1980).

_____. "Swallowing the IMF Medicine in the Seventies." Development Dialogue (1980).

Girvan, Norman, Bernal, Richard, and Hughes, Wesley. "The IMF and the Third World: The Case of Jamaica, 1974-1980." Development Dialogue (1980).

Gold, Joseph. The Fund and Nonmember States: Some Legal Effects. Washington, D.C.: International Monetary Fund, 1966.

_____. Financial Assistance by the International Monetary Fund: Law and Practice. Washington, D.C.: International Monetary Fund, 1980.

_____. International Capital Movements Under the Law of the IMF. Washington, D.C.: IMF, 1977.

_____. The IMF and International Law: An Introduction. Washington, D.C.: IMF, 1977.

_____. Floating Currencies, SDRs, and Gold: Further Legal Development. Washington, D.C.: IMF, 1977.

Goldstein, Morris. Effects of Slowdown in Industrial Countries on Growth in Non-Oil Developing Countries. Washington, D.C.: IMF, 1982.

Goode, Richard. Economic Assistance to Developing Countries Through the IMF. Washington, D.C.: Brookings Institute, 1985.

Goulet, Dennis. Economic Development in the Third World. New York: Longmans, Inc., 1981.

Green, Reginald and Seidman, Ann. Unity or Poverty? Economic of Pan Africanism. Baltimore: Penguin, 1969.

Gruhn, Isebill V. "The Recolonialization of Africa: International Organization on the March." Africa Today, Vol. 30, No. 4 (1983).

Grundy, Kennedy V. "To Some Poor Nations, IMF Cure is Worse than the Disease." The Atlanta Journal and Constitution, 4 October 1987.

Guitian, Manuel. Fund Conditionality: Evolution of Principles and Practices. Washington, D.C.: IMF, 1981.

Gutkind, P. and Waterman, P. African Social Studies: A Radical Reader. New York: Monthly Review Press, 1969.

Haberler, Gotfried and Willett, Thomas. A Strategy for U.S. Balance of Payment. Washington, D.C.: American Institute, 1971.

Halm, George. A Guide to International Monetary Fund Reform. New York: Lexington Press, 1975.

_____. The International Monetary Fund and Flexibility of Exchange Rates. Princeton, New Jersey: Princeton University Press, 1971.

Hansohm, Dirk. "The Success of the IMF/World Bank Policies in Sudan." Journal of Modern Africa 34 (June 1985).

Harden, Baine. "Nigeria See Debt Payment Ceiling," Newswatch, 5 January 1986.

Hardy, Chandras. "African Debt Structural Adjustment With Stability" New Nigeria April 1985.

Harris, Richard. The Political Economy of Africa. London: Halstead Press (Schenkman Publishing Company), 1975.

Hausman, W. M. Managing Economic Development in Africa. Cambridge, Massachusetts: M.I.T. Press, 1963.

Haynes, Jeff. "Debt in Sub-Saharan Africa: The Local Politics of Stabilization." African Affairs 86 (July 1987).

Hayter, Teresa. Aid as Imperlialism. England: Pengui, 1972.

_____. Aid: Rhetoric and Realty. London: Plato Press, 1985.

Helleiner, Gerald. The IMF and Africa in the 1980s. Princeton, New Jersey: Princeton University Press, 1983.

Helleiner, Gerald. Presant Agriculture, Government and Growth in Nigeria. Homewood, Illinois: Irwin, 1966.

Herbert, Obudozie. Nigeria: From Dependency to Development. Ibadan: University of Ibadan Press, 1986.

Hobson, J.A. Imperialism: A Study. Michigan: Ann Arbor, 1965.

Holman, Michael. FinancialTimes, 25 February 1985.

Hopkins, A.G. The Creation of a Colonial Monetary System: The Origins of the West African Currency Board. Ibadan: University of Ibadan Press, 1975.

_____. The Currency Revolution in South-West Nigeria. Ibadan: University of Ibadan Press, 1983.

Hooke, A.W. The International Monetary Fund, Its Evolution, Organization, and Activities. Washington, D.C.: IMF, 1983.

Horsefield, Keith. The International Monetary Fund, 1945-1965. Washington, D.C.: International Monetary Fund, 1967.

Ibekwe, Oliver. "SFEM Alternative to Devaluation," The Guardian, 1 August 1986.

Ibrahim, Abajah. "The Political Economy of the IMF." Nigerian Daily Times 16 August 1986.

Ibrahim, Abubakar O. "Laugh #3.b Economic Revival Fund in Place of IMF Loan." New Nigeria, 10 September 1985.

Igbozurike, Martin. Problem Generating Structure In Nigerian's Rural Development. New Haven: Yale University Press, 1976.

Ikoku, Samuel G. Nigeria for Nigerians. Takoradi, Ghana: A.I. Press, 1962.

Ikpong, I.M. "IMF? Yest or No." Nigerian Concord 21 March 1985.

International Bank for Reconstruction and Development. The Economic Development of Nigeria. Baltimore: The John Hopkins Press, 1955.

"IMF Deal for Tanzania." New Africa September 1986.

IMF, World Economic Outlook Occasional Paper, No. 27, Washington, D.C., IMF (1984).

IMF Annual Report, 1950-1978. Washington, D.C.: IMF, 1989.

International Monetary Fund, Annual Report, Washington, D.C., IMF, 1988.

International Monetary Fund, Annual Report, Washington, D.C., IMF, 1989.

International Monetary Fund, Beurea of Statistics, Washington, D.C., 1985.

International Monetary Fund. International Financial Statistics Yearbook. Washington, D.C.: 1984.

International Monetary Fund. World Economic Outlook, Washington, D.C., April 1985.

Jacob, Dreyer S. The International Monetary System: A Time of Turbulence. Washington, D.C.: American Enterprise Institute for Public Policy Research, 1982.

Johnson, Harry G. Economic Nationalism in Old and New States. Chicago: University of Chicago Press, 1967.

Kamarck, Andrew. The Economics of African Development. New York: Praeger Publishers, 1972.

Kaufman, H.M. Germany's International Monetary Policy and the European Monetary System. New York: Brooklyn College Press, 1985.

Kaunda. "IMF Slaves Africans." The New Federalist National Newspaper 13 June 1987.

Kegley, Charles W. and Wittkopf, Eugene. World Politics: Trend and Transformation. New York: St. Martin's Press, 1985.

Keynes, John M. The General Theory of Employment, Interest and Money. New York: Harcourt, 1936.

Kilby, Peter. Industrialization in an Open Economy: Nigeria 1945-1966. London: Cambridge University Press, 1967.

Killick, Tony. The IMF Stabilization: Developing Country Experiences. New York: St. Martin's Press, 1984.

_____. "The IMF Case For a Change in Emphasis, in Adjustment Crisis in the Third World" Finance and Development 20 April 1983.

Koehn, Peter. "African Approach to Environmental Stress: A Focus on Ethiopia and Nigeria" Economic Digest 2 March 1984.

Korany, Bahgat. How Foreign Policy Decisions are Made in the Third World: A Comparative Analysis. Colorado, Boulder: Westview Press, 1984.

Kuczynski, Pedro-Pablo. "The Outlook for Latin American Debt" Foreign Affairs, (Fall 1987).

Lagos, Nigeria, Federal Office of Statistics. "Balance of Payment." Annual Abstract of Statistics, 1985.

_____. "Money Supply and Currency in Circulation." Digest of Statistics 29 (December 1984).

_____. Economic and Social Statistics Bulletin (January 1984/85).

_____. Distribution Survey, 1978-1981.

_____. Nigeria Trade Summary, June 1980.

_____. Review of External Trade, 1979.

Lagos, Nigeria, Chamber of Commerce and Industry. Nigerian Business Review (December 1981).

Lagos Report November-December 1985.

Lancaster, Carol. "Africa's Economic Crisis." Foreign Policy Vol. 52 (Fall 1983).

Landell-Hills, Joslin. The Fund's International Banking Statistics. Washington, D.C.: IMF, 1986.

Landes, David S. "The Nature of Economic Imperialism, Journal of Economic History, (December 1961).

Latin American Bureau. The Poverty Brokers: The IMF and Latin America. London: Latin American Bureau Research and Action, Ltd., 1983.

Lenin V.I Imperalism: The Highest Stage of Capitalism New York: International Publishers, 1970.

Lewis, A.O. Nigerians Exports: Problems, Prospects and Implications for Economic Growth. Budapest: Center For Afro-Asian Research of the Hungarian Academy of Sciences, 1973.

Lewis, Arthur W. The Evolution of the International Economic Order. Princeton, New Jersey: Princeton University Press, 1978.

Libby, Ronald. "External Co-option of a Less Developed Country's Policy Making: The Case of Ghana 1969-1972," World Politics, 29 October 1976.

Liedholm, C., ed. Growth and Development of Nigerian Economy. East Lansing, 1970.

Lieftinick, Peter. Recent Trends in International Monetary Policies. Princeton, New Jersy: Princeton University Press, 1982.

Long, Dianne. The Other World: Issues and Politics in the Third World, eds. New York: MacMillan Publishing Company, 1987.

Loxley, John. "IMF and World Bank conditionality and Sub-Saharan Africa." African Affairs 63 (January 1985).

Luckham, Robin. The Nigerian Military: A sociological Analysis of Authority and Revolt 1960-1967. Cambridge: University Press, 1971.

Maboqunije, Akin L. Urbanization in Nigeria. London: University of London Press, 1969.

Macessiah, George. The International Political Economy and the Third World. New York: Praeger, 1981.

Madeley, John. "The IMF in Africa: Now an Object of Resentment, African Experts Seek Alternative Care." African World News (January 1988).

Magdoff, Harry. "Third World Debt." Monthly Review 37 (February 1986).

Magdoff, Harry. The Age of Imperialism. New York: Monthly Review Press, 1969.

Malthus, T.R. An Essay on the Principle of Poulation or A View of Its Past and Present Effects on Human Happiness with an Inquiry into Our Prospects Respecting the Future Removal or Mitigation of the Evils Which it Occasions. Homewood, Illinois: Richard D. Irwin, 1963.

Martin, Clara. "Home and Foreign Investments." This Week July 1975.

Meier, Gerald M., ed. Leading Issues in Economic Development. New York: Oxford University Press, 1972.

Mikesell, Raymond F. "IMF and Industrialization Strategies in Less Developed Countries: Some Lessons of Historical Experience" Concord International Vol. 20, No. 2 (August 1983).

Miller, Morris. Coping is Not Enough: The International Debt Crisis and the Rules of the World Bank and IMF. Homewood: Bon Jons Irain, 1986.

Miller, Norman. International Reserves, Exchange Rates and Developing Countries. Lexington, Massachusetts: Lexington Books, 1962.

Momoh, Joseph E. "Sierra Leon Agreeing With the IMF." West Africa March 1986.

_____. "Sierra Leon Enter the IMF." West Africa February 1986.

Monroe, Wilbur. International Monetary Reconstruction. Lexington, Massachusetts: Lexing Books, 1974.

Morgan, Carlyle. Bretton Woods: Clues to a Monetary System. Boston: World Peace Foundation, 1945.

Mortime, Robert A. The Third World Coalition in International Politics. Boulder, Colorado: Westview Press, 1984.

Murray, Colin. "Latin America Experiment in Neoconservative Economics" Journal of Development Studies. Vol. 20 (August 1983).

National Concord, Lagos, 29 December 1983.

National Concord, Lagos, 2 March 1984.

National Concord, Lagos, 23 March 1984.

National Concord, Lagos, 11, 15 and 26 September 1984.

National Concord, Lagos, 14 October 1984.

National Concord, Lagos, 20 December 1984.

National Management Conference. Indigenisation and Economic Development. Nigerian Institute of Management, Lagos, 1974.

New Nigeria, 2 March 1974.

New Nigeria, 6 June 1977

New Nigeria, 10 April 1982.

New Nigerian, 4 April 1984.

New Nigeria, 10 June 1984.

New Nigeria, 2 March 1985.

New Nigeria, 12 April 1985.

New Nigeria, 6 May 1985.

New Nigeria, 19, 20, 27 September 1986.

New Nigeria, 8 October 1986.

New Nigeria, 10 October 1987.

New Nigeria, Lagos, 6, 8 October 1988.

New Nigeria, Lagos, 13 March 1989.

Newswatch, Lagos, 5 February 1975.

Newswatch, Lagos, 9 September 1980.

Newswatch, Lagos, 13 June 1983.

Newswatch, Lagos, 3 December 1986.

Newswatch, Lagos, 1 September 1987.

Newswatch, Lagos, 20 February 1989.

News Ripples. March Edition 1989.

News Ripples. 7 June 1986.

Nigeria. "Agriculture and Trade Policies Asia, Africa, and Eastern Europe Division." International Trade Policy (September 1981).

"Nigeria: Debt Rescheduling Brightens the Outlook." African Business (February 1987).

"Nigeria Gets to Grips With the Economy." African Business (August 1987).

"Nigeria Survey." New Africa (April 1985, December 1985, and May 1986).

Nigerian Daily Times, 14 April 1980.

Nigerian Daily Times, 12 March 1982.

Nigerian Daily Times, 2 March 1984.

Nigerian Daily Times, 9 April 1984.

Nigerian Daily Times, 18 June 1984.

Nigerian Daily Times, 2 November 1988.

Nkrumah, Kwame. Neo-Colonialism: The Last Stage of Imperialism. New York: New York Publishers, 1966.

Nkrumah, Kame. Towards Colonial Freedom: Africa in the Struggle Against World Imperialism. London: Panaf, 1962.

Nnadozie, Chima. "Investment in Nigeria: The Political Climate." New Nigeria August 1981.

Norman, Gemmell. "The IMF Stabilization Policies in the Third World." The Journal of Development Studies 18 (October 1982).

Nowzad, Bahran. The IMF and Its Critics. Princeton: Princeton University, Press, 1981.

Nurkse, Ragnar. International Currency Experience: Lessons of the Inter-War Period. Geneva: League of Nations: Princeton University Press, 1944.

Nwake, David. "Nigeria Gets to Grips With The Economy," Anambra State Daily Star, June 14, 1988.

Nwankwo, Emeka. "Indirect Rule and Nigerian Development." 19 July 1980.

Nyerere, Julius K. Ujamaa Essays on Socialism "The Arusha Declaration", The Section on What of External Aid? New York: Oxford University Press, 1971.

OAU, Lagos Plan of Action for the Economic Development of Africa, 1980 - 2000. Geneva: International Institute for Labor Studies for OAU, 1982.

Obadina, Junde. "Sapping An Illusion," Newswatch Nigeria's Weekly News Magazine, 20 February 1986.

Obi, Paul. "Economic Recovery The Problem of the Future," Newswatch, 3 December 1986.

_____. "Loan and Project Financing." Newswatch, 30 March 1987.

O'Connel, James, "Political Integration: The Nigerian Case." In A. Hazzlewood, (ed.), African Integration and Disintegration: Case Studies in Economic and Political Union. London: Oxford University Press, 1967.

Odetola, Theophilus O. Military Politics in Nigeria. New Brunswick, N.J.: Transaction Books, 1978.

Oddy, Chukwu. The Theory and Experience of Nigerian Economic Development. Ife: University of Ife Press, 1984.

Odumosu, O.I. The Nigerian Constitution. London: Sweet and Maxwell, 1963.

Ogunsheye, A. "Experience and Problems of Indigenous Exterprises." In The Proceedings of the Tenth Annual Conference of the Nigerian Institute of Management: Indigenisation and Economic Development. Lagos NIM., 1972.

Okarar, F.O. "The Nigerian Capital Market." in J.K. Onoh (ed.) The Foundation of Nigeria's Financial Infrastructure.

Okafor, S.O. Indirect Rule: The Development of Central Legislature in Nigeria. Ikeja, Lagos: Thomas Nelson Nigeria LTD., 1981.

Okpaku, Joseph. ed. Nigeria: Dilemma of Nationhood. New York: The Third Press, 1971.

Okubadejo, N.A.A. "Economic Development and Planning in Nigeria 1945-68." in T.M. Yesufu (ed.), Manpower Problems and Economic Development in Nigeria. Ibadon: Oxford University Press, 1970.

Olaloki, F.A., et al Structures of the Nigerian Economy.   New York: St. Martin's Press, 1979.

Olannyiwola, Peter. Peter Petroleum and Structural Change in a Developing Country: The Case of Nigeria, (New York: Praeger Publishers, 1987).

Olayide, S.O. Economic Survey of Nigeria, 1960-1975. Ibadan: Armolaran Publishing Co., 1976.

Olu, Akaraogun. "Politics of IMF Loan to Nigeria." Daily Times, Lagos 25 February 1987.

Oni, O., and B. Onimode. Economic Development of Nigeria: The Socialist Alternative. Ibadan: The Nigerian Academy of Arts, Sciences and Technology, 1975.

Onimode, Bade. The IMF, The World Bank and The African Debt: The Economic Impact. London: Zed Books Ltd., 1989.

_____. Imperialism and Underdevelopment in Nigeria. London: 2ed Press, 1985.

Onuoha, Stephens. "Future Problems of SFEM," Business Concord, Lagos, 4 July 1986.

Oridota, I.A. "IMF and Integration of Modern Societies." Nigeria Sunday Times 19 July 1985.

Othman, Shehu. "Classes, Crisis and Coup: The Demise of Shagari's Regime," Business Concord April 1986.

Ottaway, David. "Nigeria Promotes its Strategy for Foreign Debt Repayment," Washington Post, 14 January 1986.

Otuyelu, Sam. "How Save it Bottle Feeding," Nigerian Daily Times, October 22, 1975.

Oyebode, A. "National Participation and Control of Nigerian Economic Activities", Paper presented at the 15th Annual Conference of the Nigerian Association of Law Teachers, Lagos, University of lagos, April 1977.

Oyejidi, T.A. Tariff Policy and Industrialization in Nigeria. Ibadan: Ibadan University Press, 1964.

Payer, Cheryl. The Debt Trap: The IMF and the Third World. New York: Monthly Review Press, 1971.

_____. "The Perpetuation of Dependence: The IMF and The Third World," New York Monthly Review, Vol. 23, No. 4 (September 1971).

_____. "The World Bank: A New Role in the Debt Crisis." Third World Quarterly, 6 April 1986.

Peter, Lawrence. World Recession and the Food Crisis in Africa. London: James Curry, 1986.

Peterson, J.C. "Second-tier Foreign Exchange Market and Nigeria Dependency," Business Concord, Lagos, 6 July 1986.

Pollin, Robert and Zepeda, Eduardo. "Latin America Debt." Monthly Review 38 (February 1987).

Prebisch, R. The Economic Development of Latin America and Its Principal Problems, New York: Lake Success, 1950.

Punch, Lagos Newspaper, Sunday, 4 June 1989.

Rimmer, Douglas. "Development In Nigeria: An overview In H. Bienen and V.P. Diejomaoh, eds. The Political Economy of Income Distribution in Nigeria. New York: Holmes and Meier, 1981.

Robison, Joan. "The International Currency Proposals." Ecnomic Journal Vol. 53 (1943).

Rhodes, Robert. Imperialism and Underdevelopment: A Reader. New York/London: Monthly Review Press, 1970.

Rodney, Walter. The States of Economic Growth: Non-Communist Manifesto. Cambridge, Massachusetts: University of Cambridge Press, 1967.

Sathyamuirthy, T.V. Nationalism in the Comtemporary World: Political and Sociological Perspectives. London: Frances Printer, 1983.

Schatzl, L.H. Petroleum in Nigerian Economy. Ibadan: Ibadan University Press, 1973.

Selltiz, Claire et al. Research Method in Social Science Relation. New York: Rhinehart and Winston, 1959.

Shaacladin, E. and Umbadda, S. International Monetary Fund Stabilization Policies: The Experience of Sudan, 1972-1982. Hamburg, 1983.

Shallandra, J.A. Development in International Trade Policy. Washington, D.C.: IMF, 1983.

Shaw, Timothy and Fasehum, Orobola. "Nigeria in the World System: Alternative Approaches, Explanations and Projects" Journal of Modern African Studies 18 December 1980.

Shen, T.Y. "Marco Development Planning in Tropical Africa: Technocratic and Non-Technocratic Causes of Failure." Journal of Development Studies 13 (July 1977).

Sidell, S.R. The Effects of International Monetary Fund Supported Adjustment Programs on the Political Instability of Developing Countries. New York: St. Martin's Press, 1986.

Sierra Leone National News Bulletin, 25 December 1984.

Sklar, Richard. Nigerian Political Parties. Princeton: Princeton University Press, 1963.

Soleye, Onaolapo. "Nigeria-IMF Negotiation," West Africa. 20 February 1984.

_____. Nigeria Daily Times. 19 February 1984.

_____. "Nigeria/IMF: The Prudence and the Fear, Managing Austerity with the IMF." Nigeria Daily Times. 1 October 1984.

Solomon, Robert. The International Monetary System, 1945-1981. New York: Harper and Row, 1982.

Sonaki, Olyinka. "Economic Dependence: The Problem of Definition." Journal of Asian and African Studies XIV (1979).

Southard, Frank A. The Evolution of the IMF. Princeton, New Jersey: Princeton University Press, 1979.

Special Correspondent. "Nigeria: The Second Tier Foreign Exchange Market Economy and the Limbs of Development." West Africa January 1985.

_____. "Putting SFEM Together." West Africa July 1986.

Spero, Joan E. The Politics of International Economic Relations. New York: St. Martin's Press, 1980.

Statesman. 1 April 1986.

Sunday Triumph, 14 October 1984.

Sweezy, Paul M. and Baran, Monopoly Capital, New York: Monthly Review Press, 1968.

Tew, Brian. The Evolution of the International Monetary System, 1945-1977. New York: Wiley, 1977.

"The Bank, the Fund and the People of Africa." West Africa (September 1987).

The Guardian, Lagos, 11 December 1983.

The Guardian, Lagos, 21, 27, 30 August 1984.

The Guardian, Lagos, 17, 18, 19 and 25 October 1984.

The Guardian, Lagos, 14 April 1985.

The Guardian, Lagos, 18 August 1985.

The Guardian, Lagos, 16 Janaury 1986.

The Guardian, Lagos, 13 July 1986.

The Guardian, Lagos, 2 August 1986.

The IMF. "Ten Common Misconceptions About the IMF." Washington, D.C.: External Department, 1987.

"The IMF, The World Bank and Monetary Reform." Issues Before the 37th General Assembly of the United Nations, 1982-1983.

The New York Times, 9 September 1980.

The New York Times, 22 November 1986.

The New York Times, 25 February 1987.

The Nigerian Enterprises Promotion Decree Amendment, No. 2, (1977).

Todaro, Michael. Economic Development in the Third World. New York: Longman Inc., 1977.

Tomori, S. and Fajana, F.O. Development Planning in F.A. Olaluki, et al., Structure of the Nigerian Economy. New York: St. Martin's Press, 1979.

Trifflin, Rovert. Gold and the Dollar Crisis: The Future Convertibility. New Haven, Connecticut: Yale University Press, 1960.

Turner, T. "Multinational Corporations and the Instability of The Nigerian State," Review of African Political Economy. Vol. 5 (January 1976).

Uchem, Dianne. "The Question and Nature of Development." Newswatch 11 March 1982.

Ugochukwu, Onyema. "Structural Adjustment Budget Aiming for Self - Reliance," West Africa 14 May 1984.

_____. "Charting A New Cause," West Africa January 1987.

Ugochukwu, Onyema. "World Bank/IMF Moving Towards Greater Conditoinality." West Africa Weekly October 1984.

_____. "IMF/World Bank: Through Tinted Glasses." West Africa October 1984.

_____. "Nigeria Debt Rescheduling Brightens the Outlook." New Nigeria 21 February 1987.

_____. "The Trouble with the IMF." New Nigeria October 1984.

_____. "Nigeria: The IMF Bogery." West Africa October 1985.

_____. "Nigeria: The Banks Agree to a Moratorium." West Africa March 1986.

_____. "The Political Economy of IMF" Newswatch, February, 1987.

_____. "And Now for the IMF" West Africa April 1984.

Ukwu, Peter. "The Evolution and Destruction: Program For Reconstruction and Development." Nigerian Daily Times, 2 November 1988.

Umesi, Godfrey. "Goodbye To Import Levy.," Business Concord, Lagos, 8 July 1986.

U.S. Department of commerce "Foreign Economic Trade and Their Implications for the U.S.-Nigeria," International Trade Administration, Washington, D.C., January 1985.

U.S., Government Finance Statistics Yearbook. Washington,D.C.: IMF, 1977.

Wai, Tun U. and Acquah, Paul A. "Experience With Exchange Rate Adjustment in African Countries," Newswatch, May 20, 1985.

Wall Street Journal. 21 February 1984.

Walter, James. The Political Economy of Nigeria: Problem of Technology Dependency. New York: Praeger, 1980.

Washington, D.C. Joint Library of the IMF and the IBRD. The Developing Assistance: A Closed Bibliography of the Joint Bank-Fund Library. Washington, D.C./Boston: G.K. Halls, 1977.

Washington Post. 9 March 1984.

Waziri, Sidney. "Stabilization: the Political Economy of Over Kill" Statesman 16 June 1984.

West Africa, 14 March 1981.

West Africa, 20 February 1984.

West Africa, 23 April 1984.

West Africa, 24 April 1984.

West Africa, 14 May 1984.

West Africa, 23 May 1984.

West Africa, 9 July 1984.

West Africa, 1 October 1984.

West Africa, 15 October 1984.

West Africa, 22 October 1984.

West Africa, 25 October 1984.

West Africa, 14 January 1985.

West Africa, 4 March 1985.

West Africa, 6 May 1985.

West Africa, 20 May 1985.

West Africa, 2 July 1986.

West Africa, 4 August 1986.

West Africa, 5 January 1987.

West Africa, 12 January 1987.

Whitaker, C.S. Politics of Tradition: Continuity and Change in Northern Nigeria, Princeton: Princeton University Press, 1970.

Whitehead, John. "The African Economic Crisis," Current Policy U.S. Department of State Bureau of Public Affairs, No. 157, (October 1985).

Wilber, Charles K. The Political Economy of Development and Underdevelopment. New York: University of Notre Dame, 1988.

Willett, Thomas. Floating Exchange Rates and International Monetary Reform. Washington, D.C.: American Enterprise Institute for Public Policy Research, 1977.

William, Dale. "Financing and Adjustment of Payments in Balances" The Guardian 14 May 1984.

Wiliamson, John. The Lending Policies of the IMF. Washington, D.C.: Institute for International Economic, 1982.

_____. The Failure of World Monetary Reform, 1971-1974. Nelson, Sunbury on Thomas, Inc., 1977.

Witcher, K. "World Bank Approve Loan To Nigeria to Aid Nation's Bid to Liberalize Trade," The Wall Street Journal, October 1986.

World Bank. "Accelerated Development in Sub-Saharan Africa: An Agenda For Action" African Review 16 May 1982.

World Bank. World Tables, Washington, D.C., 1976.

World Bank. World Tables, 2nd Edition, Washington, D.C., 1980.

World Bank. World Development Report, New York: Oxford University Press, 1983.

World Bank. "World Development Report 1981: Accelerated Development in Sub-Sahara Africa," African Red Family 16 May 1982.

World Bank. World Tables, 3rd ed., Vol. 2. Baltimore: John Hopkins University Press, 1983.

Yansan, Y. Decolonialization and Dependency: Problems of Development in African Society, Greenwood Press, 1980.

"Zambia: Another IMF Colony Explodes." EASA 1 January 1987.

Zambian Economic Report 6 March 1985.

Zartman, William I. The Political Economy of Nigeria. New York: Praeger, 1983.

Zulu, Justin and Nsouli, Saleh M. Adjustment Programs in Africa: The Recent Experience, Occasional Paper, No. 34, Washington, D.C.: IMF, 1985.

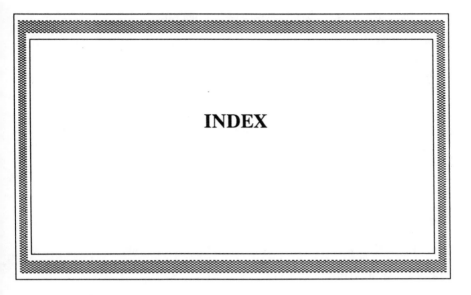

INDEX